JM

THE PERSONAL INJURY LIBRARY FROM WILEY LAW PUBLICATIONS

ARBITRATING PERSONAL INJURY CLAIMS
John Farrell Fay

AUTOMOTIVE ENGINEERING AND LITIGATION (VOLUMES 1–5)
George A. Peters and Barbara J. Peters

AUTOMOTIVE ENGINEERING AND LITIGATION (VOLUME 6): THE INTERNATIONAL
DIRECTORY OF EXPERTS AND CONSULTANTS IN AUTOMOTIVE ENGINEERING 1993
George A. Peters and Barbara J. Peters

DIRECT AND CROSS-EXAMINATION OF ORTHOPEDIC SURGEONS
Thomas J. Murray and Jeffrey D. Robertson

EMERGENCY DEPARTMENT STANDARDS OF CARE (SECOND EDITION)
Mikel A. Rothenberg

EMERGENCY MEDICINE MALPRACTICE
Scott M. Lewis

EVALUATING AND SETTLING PERSONAL INJURY CLAIMS
George M. Gold, Editor

EVALUATING TMJ INJURIES
Reda A. Abdel-Fattah

FIRE LITIGATION SOURCEBOOK: TECHNICAL, MEDICAL, AND LEGAL ASPECTS
Alexander J. Patton

HANDLING BIRTH TRAUMA CASES
Stanley S. Schwartz and Norman D. Tucker

LITIGATING HEAD TRAUMA CASES
Arthur C. Roberts

LITIGATING TMJ CASES
A. Clark Cone

ORTHOPEDIC DISABILITY AND EXPERT TESTIMONY (FOURTH EDITION)
Harold F. Goodman

MODERN TORT LIABILITY: RECOVERY IN THE '90S
Terrence F. Kiely

OB/GYN MALPRACTICE
Scott M. Lewis

PERSONAL INJURY DAMAGES LAW AND PRACTICE
Edward C. Martin

ORTHOPEDIC DISABILITY AND EXPERT TESTIMONY
FOURTH EDITION

SUBSCRIPTION NOTICE

This Wiley product is updated on a periodic basis with supplements to reflect important changes in the subject matter. If you purchased this product directly from John Wiley & Sons, Inc., we have already recorded your subscription for this update service.

If, however, you purchased this product from a bookstore and wish to receive (1) the current update at no additional charge, and (2) future updates and revised or related volumes billed separately with a 30-day examination review, please send your name, company name (if applicable), address and the title of the product to:

Supplement Department
John Wiley & Sons, Inc.
One Wiley Drive
Somerset, NJ 08875
1-800-225-5945

ORTHOPEDIC DISABILITY AND EXPERT TESTIMONY
FOURTH EDITION

HAROLD F. GOODMAN, M.D., F.A.C.S.

Editor

Wiley Law Publications

JOHN WILEY & SONS, INC.

New York · Chichester · Brisbane · Toronto · Singapore

Library of Congress Cataloging-in-Publication Data

ISBN 0-471-59231-5

Printed in the United States of America

10 9 8 7 6 5 4 3 2 1

PREFACE

Understanding the terms and processes used and the conclusions reached by physicians in the legal determination of orthopedic disability is critical for the personal injury litigator. At the same time it is critical to understand the use of the experts in the litigation of such an injury.

Gathered herein are the most commonly used techniques of practicing physicians for determining orthopedic impairment. By using the provided text and illustrations by Donald W. Robertson, Ph.D., attorneys facing orthopedic disability issues can familiarize themselves with the processes and terminology used in orthopedic impairment determinations and be able to recognize a clear, well-reasoned medical conclusion. They also will recognize a conclusion presented without adequate testing, examination, or analysis.

Many of the physical impairment levels listed within are presented in whole-body percentages. These percentages reflect impairment values contained in *Guides to the Evaluation of Permanent Impairment*, 3rd edition, a publication of the American Medical Association. The *Guides* provide clinically reliable and reproducible standards for rating permanent impairment. However, the permanent impairment ratings within the *Guides* and this volume are not ratings of disability; they are ratings of impairment which should be used as starting points for determining the consequences of the impairment. Permanent physical impairment is judged by the medical status of the individual. Disability is judged by personal, social, occupational, and legal effects of the impairment.

The third edition of the *Guides* provides a reference framework within which attorneys, physicians, and judges may evaluate and report medical impairment. Because the workers' compensation system regards the AMA *Guides* as the standard reference, this volume, available from the American Medical Association in Chicago, Illinois, is a valuable reference for the physicians involved in disability problems. The *Guides* are an attempt to unify reports from different observers regarding the same injured individual to create comparable content and completeness for the purposes of analysis and comparison.

The first step in using the *Guides* is to do a clinical evaluation supported by appropriate tests and diagnostic procedures. This documents the clinical status of the allegedly injured individual. If the current findings are consistent with the results of previous clinical examinations performed by other observers, then one can conclude with a reasonable degree of confidence that standard reference tables can be used to determine a percentage rating of impairment. The physician analyzes the history and the clinical and laboratory findings to determine the nature and extent of the loss of use of affected body parts. The physician then compares the results of this analysis with the criteria specified in the *Guides* for the particular body part, system, or function.

I would emphasize that this process is definitely distinct from the clinical evaluation of the treating physician and need not be performed by the same physician doing that evaluation. It is not unusual for insurance companies, for example, to pay an "independent examiner" to review records and/or examine a patient to determine degree of impairment. Hopefully any knowledgeable physician or any other knowledgeable person can compare the clinical findings on a particular patient with the criteria in the *Guides*.

For essentially medical-legal reasons, the reference tables determine impairment of a specific body part. It is then necessary to relate this impairment to a "whole person" impairment rating. The final impairment value, whether the result of one or more impairments, is then expressed in terms of the nearest five percent. It should be emphasized that the AMA *Guides* are literally that— guidelines rather than absolute numbers. Take, for example, a back injury to a 25-year-old laborer which causes substantially greater "whole person" impairment than the same back injury to a 69-year-old bedridden nursing home patient.

Furthermore, impairment should not be considered "permanent" until repeated clinical findings over time support the conclusion that the medical condition is stabilized or static. Obviously a condition can become worse as a result of an aggravation or clinical progression.

Finally, it should be emphasized that the percentages of impairment in the *Guides* are often misleading. A patient with only subjective back complaints which may legitimately be disabling from gainful employment might only have a zero percent impairment if one follows the guidelines in the *Guides* strictly. It is often more accurate to describe a patient's pain and the activities which a patient cannot do in terms of recreation as well as employment rather than use the absolute numbers found in the *Guides*. For example, a patient with two separate back operations and a moderate restriction of motion of the lumbosacral spine might be 100 percent disabled from the patient's usual gainful employment but would only have approximately a 25 percent permanent physical impairment and loss of physical function if one relied on the AMA *Guides*. For this reason, many physicians tend not to refer to the *Guides* when making statements about physical impairment and loss of function.

Therefore, though only a physician can measure a person's physical impairment, it is the legal system, guided by well-informed attorneys, which determines disability. It is the well-informed attorney who bridges the gap between the doctor and the court and serves the best interests of the client.

The last four chapters of this book discuss the relationship of the orthopedic expert to litigation. **Chapter 8,** by Steven Friedland, outlines the guidelines for selecting, preparing, and using experts in orthopedic litigation. **Chapter 9,** by Stacey D. Mullins, applies the voir dire process to an orthopedic case. **Chapters**

10 and **11** provide a wealth of practical techniques and procedures to use in the examination of the orthopedic expert. **Chapter 10,** by Samuel D. Hodge and J. Craig Currie, focuses on the direct examination, while **Chapter 11,** by Mark R. Kosieradzki, presents guidelines and strategies for cross examinations of the orthopedic experts.

Quincy, Massachusetts   HAROLD F. GOODMAN
February 1993

ABOUT THE EDITOR

Dr. Harold F. Goodman is a board-certified orthopedic surgeon practicing in Quincy, Massachusetts. He has more than 17 years of experience evaluating disability claims for attorneys. He is an orthopedic consultant for the cities of Boston and Quincy, Braintree Rehabilitation Hospital, and numerous towns, corporations, and insurance companies. Dr. Goodman graduated from Harvard University *cum laude* and received his M.D. from New York University Medical School in 1968. He had his internship and residency in general surgery at New York City's Bellevue Hospital and his residency in orthopedic surgery at the New York University Medical Center. Dr. Goodman has published five medical papers.

ABOUT THE CONTRIBUTORS

J. Craig Currie is a graduate of Williams College and received his J.D. in 1971 from the University of Pennsylvania. He has been a law clerk to Alexander F. Barbieri of the Pennsylvania Supreme Court as well as Clifford Scott Green, U.S. District Court, Eastern District of Pennsylvania. He is currently the Senior Partner in the law firm of J. Craig Currie & Associates in Philadelphia.

Steven I. Friedland is a professor at Nova University in Fort Lauderdale, Florida, teaching trial advocacy, constitutional and criminal law, evidence, and law and psychiatry. He received his B.A. from Southern University New York and his J.D. from Harvard University in Cambridge, Massachusetts. Professor Friedland clerked for the Honorable James L. King of the Southern District of Florida in Miami, and worked in the U.S. Attorney's Office from 1983 to 1985.

Samuel D. Hodge, Jr., is a partner of the firm Cohen & Huntington in Philadelphia. Formerly an Associate Professor and Chairperson of the Department of Legal and Real Estate Studies at Temple University, he received his J.D. from Temple University School of Law in 1974. He is the author of *Thermography and Personal Injury Litigation* (John Wiley & Sons, Inc. 1987).

Mark R. Kosieradzki is a partner in the Minneapolis law firm of Sieben, Grose, Von Holtum, McCoy & Carey, Ltd. He received his B.S. from Iowa State University and his J.D. from Drake University. He is a member of the Panel of Arbitrators, American Arbitration Association and served as a member of the Board of Governors of the Minnesota Trial Lawyers Association from 1987 to 1990. He is certified as a Civil Trial Advocate by the National Board of Trial Advocacy and Civil Trial Specialist by the Civil Litigation Section, Minnesota State Bar Association. He is also a member of the Association of Trial Lawyers of America and Academy of Certified Trial Lawyers of Minnesota.

Donald W. Robertson, Ph.D., is an associate professor at the University of Minnesota School of Medicine. He has a joint appointment in the Department of Cell Biology and Neuroanatomy and the Department of Otolaryngology. Dr. Robertson also teaches anatomy in the University of Minnesota School of Dentistry. He teaches human gross anatomy, ENT anatomy, and oral surgery. Dr. Robertson chairs the Medical School Admissions Committee and has served as chair of the Scholastic Standing Committee of the School of Medicine. Dr. Robertson received his B.S. in biology from the University of Minnesota-Duluth in 1956 and his Ph.D. in anatomy from the University of Minnesota-Minneapolis in 1966. He co-authored and illustrated *Understanding and Handling the Back and Neck Injury Case* (John Wiley & Sons, Inc. 1991).

Stacey D. Mullins is a member of Romano, Eriksen & Cronin in West Palm Beach and Lake Worth, Florida. She is a graduate of the University of Florida College of Law, and is admitted to the Florida Bar. While at the University of Florida, Stacey won the Association of Trial Lawyers of America's National, Regional and State Mock Trial Competitions in 1990 and 1991 as well as the Academy of Florida Trial Lawyers Intrastate Mock Trial Competition in 1990. Stacey is a member of The Association of Trial Lawyers of America as well as the Academy of Florida Trial Lawyers.

SUMMARY CONTENTS

DETAILED CONTENTS

CHAPTER 1

GENERAL PRINCIPLES OF EVALUATION OF IMPAIRMENT AND DISABILITY

§ 1.1   Introduction

Good organization makes disability evaluation more efficient and accurate.

Such organization needs to start when a disability examination is arranged. Not only the name of the patient must be recorded, but also the patient's telephone number in the event that cancellation of the appointment is necessary. The patient should be advised to bring prior medical records as well as any available X rays. The name of the party responsible for payment should be obtained, and it should be determined whether such party authorizes further tests and X rays without prior approval or if there is any limit on such further tests and their amount. If the patient is to pay for the examination, the patient should be advised to bring cash. To minimize missed appointments, the patient should be advised of the obligation to pay for the appointment if canceled with less than 12 hours' notice.

Once the patient comes to the physician's office, the medical investigation begins with a detailed and comprehensive history. The patient's identity must be established—age, sex, address, schooling, technical training, and work history (a sample history form appears at the end of this chapter). After the patient has had a chance to complete this form, a nurse or other assistant should review it; frequently, a patient may deliberately not fill in some answers or may not understand all of the questions.

The actual examination by the physician can begin with observations made while the patient is in the waiting room. Does the patient sit, or stand? Does he smoke? Is he generally relaxed, or tense with pain?

After the history form is completed, the physician should meet the patient and establish as much rapport as possible. Often at disability exams, the patient is hostile and uncooperative. Such a patient may insist that a lawyer advised him to say nothing. However, if the law did not require the patient to have a physical examination, the patient would not have been sent to the physician in the first place. No physician can realistically evaluate disability without a complete history. Any patient who refuses to cooperate should be advised, therefore, that the examination will be terminated if he does not answer relevant questions and submit willingly to a physical examination. Such a threat usually produces compliance.

The medical examination should begin by expanding relevant details shown on the medical history form, especially concerning the accident or injury. How did the patient feel immediately after the accident? How was he treated? Did such treatment follow immediately after the accident? If not, why was there a waiting period? What kind of disability does the patient now report? Has he been out of work? How long? Has he been performing any other work? What does the patient do at home?

One very important area in nearly every disability case is pain. The patient should describe the type of pain. Is it dull and steady or sharp and acute? Does pressure on a particular location cause an increase in the pain? Does the pain radiate? If so, to what locations? How severe is the pain? What kind of activity makes it worse? Related to these questions are questions of treatment for the pain. Does any medication work? Which one? When does the patient take the medication?

The disability evaluator needs to be aware that the patient may not always respond honestly to these questions. The evaluator should follow up on inconsistencies and allegations that do not appear to be medically realistic. However, the evaluator should not accuse the patient of lying. This obviously will make the patient hostile and uncooperative. The impairment evaluator probably will do a better job by just eliciting as much information as possible from the patient.

After obtaining the appropriate information, the physician should proceed with the examination of the patient. The details of various examinations are discussed later in this book.

In addition to the physical examination, the impairment evaluator may wish to conduct further tests. These are particularly helpful in obtaining objective evidence of disability or the lack of it. The evaluator should get results of all readily available previous tests. These are valuable both in determining whether the patient suffered from the disease or problem at any other time and for setting a baseline. That is, did the patient always have a disease, or was it induced by work? Moreover, lack of appropriate testing by a treating physician may lead an evaluator to think that the treating physician had doubts that the patient was truly disabled. For example, one should be suspicious of the patient alleging severe back pain for many months but who has never had a myelogram or even a CAT scan.

It should be emphasized that medical diagnosis is an art rather than an exact science. Physicians can still verify the patho-anatomic cause of back pain in only 15 percent of the patients. The other 85 percent can at best be designated soft tissue injuries or musculoskeletal dysfunction. Fortunately, most individuals recover rapidly anyway, so scientifically verifiable diagnoses are rarely made. The following information can be useful regardless of whether one is representing the plaintiff or the defendant.

Routine X rays are helpful in one out of 2,400 cases

CAT scan is scientifically shown to be positive in 35 percent of normal people

Myelogram is positive in 24 percent of normal people

EMG has an extremely low rate of reproducibility from observer to observer.

Before the general acceptance of CAT scans and magnetic resonance imaging (MRI), clinical diagnostic testing by physicians was a highly developed art. On the plaintiff's side, a common scenario is for the defense doctor to get on the stand and recite a long list of tests for which the results were negative, indicating no organic pathology. The plaintiff's lawyer needs to know whether the doctor did the appropriate tests (that is, should a negative result have been expected even if there were an organic problem?). A patient can have impairment and serious disability and still have a normal response to many of these historically interesting but not widely relied upon examinations. Clearly, the MRI and CAT scan have superseded many of the older clinical tests.

This chapter describes the diagnostic tests commonly used in orthopedic disability evaluation, which constitutes a large percentage of disability evaluations. The tests are listed and described as follows:

1. X rays
2. MRI
3. Tomography
4. CAT scan
5. Arthrography
6. Discography
7. Myelography
8. Epidural venogram
9. Arthroscopy
10. EMG
11. Video fluoroscopy
12. Bone scan
13. HLA-B27
14. Thermography.

Professional Education Systems has available videotapes that demonstrate the performance of the more commonly used diagnostic tests. Videotape is an ideal medium to show how the physician performs these tests on a patient.

COMMONLY USED DIAGNOSTIC TESTS

§ 1.2   X rays

In reviewing X rays, a number of questions need to be considered.

When and How Many Times Have X rays Been Taken?

Fractures of the navicular bone of the hand are notorious for often not being visible on X rays until two to three weeks after injury.

Have All Appropriate X-ray Views Been Taken?

X rays of the lumbosacral spine should include oblique views to reveal a spondylolysis of the pars interarticularis; X rays of the shoulder should include an axillary view to reveal possible posterior dislocation; spondylolysis of the pars interarticularis may be picked up only if oblique X rays are taken in addition to the anterior-posterior (A-P) and lateral views; patellofemoral arthritis may be seen only on a sunrise view of the knee.

Several X-ray techniques may reveal details not apparent on the usual A-P or lateral views. For example, an open mouth view is recommended to properly examine the first cervical vertebra. Oblique views of the shoulder can reveal separations or dislocations that would not appear on the A-P view. X rays of the spine in flexion or extension can locate features that remain hidden when the neck or back is in the normal position.

Who Read the X rays?

Were the X rays read by a board-certified radiologist? Perhaps, instead, they were read by a resident in the nearby teaching hospital, or a rushed and overworked emergency room moonlighter, or a general practitioner with an X-ray machine in the back room, or perhaps a chiropractor. The disability physician must make a conscientious effort to obtain results of all available previous diagnostic studies. Although obviously unnecessary radiation and expense should be avoided whenever possible, often it is necessary to obtain current X rays to make an appropriate diagnosis.

Are X rays the Appropriate Diagnostic Device?

Unfortunately, plain X rays of the spine are of relatively little value in determining the degree of back problems. Changes seen on the X rays tend to be poorly correlated with the symptoms of low back pain. They frequently are used simply as a screening device because they are readily available and relatively inexpensive. They have some value for special situations, such as for serious bacterial infection.

In plain X rays of the lumbosacral spine, the examiner looks particularly for evidence of fracture or dislocation. Narrowing of the disc spaces would suggest possible degenerative disc disease with potential protrusion of the discs posteriorly on the spinal cord. The examiner will look at the sacroiliac joints to see if there is obliteration of the joints due to severe arthritis. Loss of the normal lordotic curvature on lumbosacral spine X rays is interpreted as muscle spasm, which might be quite helpful in seeking objective evidence of subjective complaints of pain.

Other Things to Look For

X rays can be labeled in two ways: lead markers and stick-on labels. The older method is to place lead letters directly on the film cassette so that their photographic impression becomes part of the X ray. Thus, the patient's name and city and the name of the X-ray facility are permanent items on the X ray. Stick-on labels are more common today. They are typed labels affixed to the X-ray film and can be peeled off and changed.

A notch in the corner of the X ray indicates that it is a duplicate film. Most X rays brought to the examiner are duplicates, which may mean the quality is somewhat inferior to the original. If the duplicate is inferior, the examiner should consider obtaining the original film.

Artifacts—earrings, chains, necklaces, dentures—may appear on the X ray and should be closely examined because their position may hide underlying factors. For example, a necklace or dentures may cover a defect in the cervical spine.

The area to be examined on the X ray should be centered on the film and have a faint circle around it. Generally, centering of the anatomy in question demonstrates that the X-ray technician took the X ray from the most advantageous position. The faint circle, called coning, results from the X-ray beam coming to a focus. The coning should appear around the anatomy in question, and the clearer the coning the sharper the details will appear.

Preemployment Back X ray

There is considerable evidence to suggest that low back X rays are not a cost-effective control for low back injuries. Stover H. Snook, an occupational medicine consultant for Liberty Mutual Insurance Company, published a paper in the *American Journal of Occupational Medicine* in which he showed that just as many injuries were experienced by employers who used medical histories, examinations, and X rays as by employers who used no selection techniques whatsoever. Dr. Laurens Rowe of Kodak has concluded that only about 10 percent of men who become low back disability problems can be identified at the usual time of hiring by present diagnostic methods, including low back X rays.

§ 1.3 Magnetic Resonance Imaging

Magnetic resonance imaging (MRI) has been shown to be of some value in evaluating soft tissues, such as the brain or spinal cord. MRI uses the response of protons to electromagnetic forces. The force field of a powerful magnet lines up the protons into an orderly arrangement. A pulse of radial waves disrupts the alignment. MRI measures factors such as the *relaxation time*, the time it takes for the protons to return to their usual, orderly arrangement. More subtle biochemical differences may appear as well, resulting from different levels of "bound water" attached to cell membranes. The result is striking contrast between abnormal tissues, such as tumors and abscesses, and healthy tissue. The equipment generally costs more than $1 million but is rapidly becoming available at most large medical centers. Independent magnetic resonance imaging facilities are also increasing rapidly.

MRI now makes it possible to provide detailed high-contrast and high-resolution images of articular joints, supporting muscles, ligaments, cartilage, and synovium. The MRI has displaced computerized axial tomography and other diagnostic tests for giving extremely high resolution definition of soft tissue structures. MRI is capable not only of imaging bony structures as X rays do, but also of showing marrow, subchondral bone, and cartilage. The disc material itself (nucleus pulposus and annulus fibrosis) is well-visualized by MRI. Although initially used for the spine, MRI is now of value in evaluating the knee, hip, ankle, shoulder, hand, wrist, and elbow as well. Although an expensive procedure (approximately $800), MRI is a noninvasive modality that produces images without exposing the patient to ionizing radiation, unlike X rays. It should be emphasized that MRI is based on events occurring at the molecular level, thus offering the potential to provide biochemical and physiologic information as well as anatomic visualization.

MRI of the Spine

Accurate diagnosis of cervical, thoracic, and lumbar spines is essential in determining disability evaluation. As noted previously, standard X rays of the spine provide only limited interpretation of nonbony structures. X rays cannot clearly demonstrate the status of the discs, spinal cord, cerebral spinal fluid, and connecting ligaments. Computerized axial tomography (CAT) does have some value for assessing postoperative pseudarthrosis as well as fibrosis and scarring. However, it is difficult to differentiate these conditions from disc material in the absence of contrast enhancement. For this reason, MRI of the spine has value in making a diagnosis of infection, trauma, and neoplasia involving not only osseous structures but also soft tissue and the spinal cord. It is also possible to determine spinal instability.

Using MRI, early degenerative disc disease can be readily identified. It is possible to determine a decrease in disc height and bulging of the peripheral annular fibers, which can contribute to narrowing of the spinal canal (spinal stenosis). Bone spurs (osteophytes) are readily visualized if they project from the anterior and posterior vertebral body edges. Severe disc herniations may demonstrate deformity or, literally, kinking of the spinal cord.

Fractures

MRI is particularly valuable in the assessment of nontraumatic and traumatic fractures of the vertebral bodies. In burst fractures it is possible to see bony fragments impinging on the spinal cord and nerve structures. Hemorrhage and edema are also readily visualized using MRI, as are osteoporosis or nontraumatic compression fractures.

Infection

MRI is particularly useful and sensitive in the detection of vertebral osteomyelitis (bone infection). For this condition it is vastly superior to either regular X rays or CAT scans. In advanced stages of infection, such as tuberculosis, a soft tissue mass is frequently observed.

MRI of the Knee

MRI is rapidly replacing CAT scanning and arthrography for the evaluation of inflammatory and traumatic disorders of the knee joint. Arthrography is generally reserved only for conditions when it is desirable to do a joint aspiration for culture and gram staining. MRI of the knee is particularly valuable in diagnosing soft tissue structures including the articular cartilage, the menisci, and the cruciate ligaments. Tears and avulsions of the cruciate ligaments are readily imaged with minimal difficulty. In patients with juvenile chronic arthritis, as well as hemophilia or degenerative joint disease, cartilage erosions are actually visualized on the MRI scans long before joint space narrowing is observed on conventional X rays. Chrondomalacia (softening of the underside of the patella) is also readily visualized. One can even visualize the synovium (lining tissue of the joint) using the MRI technique. Early synovial reactions have been observed in patients with juvenile rheumatoid arthritis, traumatic synovitis, and hemophilia. The joint fluid itself is actually readily visualized. Even degenerative conditions such as osteonecrosis of the distal femoral condyles or the tibial plateaus are seen on MRI. It is not unusual for MRI to detect condylar and plateau compression fractures in patients with negative plain radiographs (X rays). Additionally, it is possible to differentiate tumors from inflammatory conditions.

MRI of the Hip

Acetabular and femoral cartilage, as well as the actual capsule structures, can be visualized readily with the MRI technique. One can even visualize hip-joint effusions and avascular necrosis (death of bone due to loss of blood supply). For this reason MRI is frequently used to diagnose Perthes' disease and congenital hip dislocation. One can readily document the position of the nonossified femoral head as well as interposed soft tissue, muscle or cartilage, and acetabular remodeling. The MRI technique allows the detection of traumatic injuries including acetabular (hip socket) and femoral stress fracture when bone scans are positive but regular X rays or CAT scans are negative. Arthritic change and neoplastic disease are identified in their very early stages.

MRI of the Ankle

MRI of the ankle allows visualization of the tendons about the ankle joint. One can readily diagnose abnormalities in capsular fluid, synovial inflammation, joint debris, and malignancy. MRI is ideally used in detecting ruptures of the Achilles tendon. Ligamentous and tendinous disruptions and postoperative changes after ankle reconstruction can readily be evaluated for points of ligamentous fixation and surgical complications. Cysts containing synovial fluid or mucinous material are also readily visualized.

MRI of the Shoulder

The shoulder socket (glenohumeral joint) is readily visualized using the MRI technique. The supporting muscles of the shoulder are well-visualized as are rotator cuff tendons, labrum, and bony structures of the joint. The MRI technique is unique in visualizing fluid in torn rotator cuff attachments and shows the extension of synovial fluid between the glenohumeral joint and the associated bursa.

MRI of the Hand, Wrist, and Elbow

Flexor and extensor tendons are imaged well on MRI involving the hand, wrist, and elbow. MRI is particularly valuable in diagnosing osteonecrosis of the navicular bone. One can readily see the triangular fibrocartilage complex in the wrist that is frequently associated with wrist disability. Carpal tunnel anatomy and disease can be seen readily. Lipomas, ganglions, sacromas, hemangiomas, and arteriovenous malformations can be evaluated using this technique. The complex anatomy of the elbow joint, including the relationship between the radius, ulna, and humerus, is easily demonstrated.

§ 1.4 Tomography

Tomography is a widely used and accepted technique for studying objects obscured by overlying shadows and not visible on standard X rays. The tube and film holder are in motion in opposite directions during the exposure. The effect is to blur all images above and below a singular plane so that objects in that plane are better visualized. Objects barely visible on routine X rays can be clearly visualized with tomography. The technique is especially valuable in identifying bone tumors and fractures.

§ 1.5   CAT Scan

CAT stands for computerized axial tomography. A CAT scan is a radiographic technique that allows any segment of the spine to be viewed on cross section. This results in a nondistorted picture of the spine, which is ideal for the evaluation of lesions such as a ruptured disc pushing on a nerve root. CAT scanning is not a new procedure, but its application for evaluation of ruptured discs only began in 1972. The technique basically involves taking multiple X rays that are then interpreted by a computer to reveal evidence of encroachment on the spinal canal. CAT scans have the advantage of being painless, unlike myelography, and without side effects. They often are used as a screening procedure, and in cases of clinical pathology, many orthopedic surgeons and neurosurgeons will perform a laminectomy and disc excision with an abnormal CAT scan and will simply not do a myelogram.

§ 1.6   Arthrography

An arthrogram is an X-ray study taken after radiopaque dye has been injected into a joint. It is most commonly used in the knee and has been shown to be particularly valuable in diagnosing torn menisci. It also has been used in the shoulder, hip, and wrist to demonstrate soft tissue pathology, such as partial or complete tear of the rotator cuff of the shoulder. If the patient has limitation of movement of the shoulder and this type of study has not been done, the evaluator certainly should question the competence of the treating physician. Arthrography is particularly effective in diagnosing a partial tear of the rotator cuff and a torn medial or lateral meniscus.

§ 1.7   Discography

Discography is performed by placing a very narrow spinal needle into a disc space under X-ray control. Radiopaque dye is then injected into the interspace between the discs. The amount of dye accepted into the adjacent discs is then recorded, as is the pressure necessary to inject the material, the image of the opaque material, and the extent of the patient's pain. Most orthopedic surgeons and neurosurgeons regard discography as neither essential nor particularly reliable. Also, there is enough variation that a normal discogram should not in itself be regarded as evidence that the patient is lacking in organic pathology or does not have a ruptured disc.

§ 1.8   Myelography

A myelogram is performed by injecting contrast material into the spinal canal in order to detect evidence of a ruptured disc. Neuro-contrast materials are water soluble and do not have to be removed. The agent most frequently used is metrizamide, which is absorbed by the connective tissues. The patient is placed prone on an X-ray table, then tilted to allow the radiopaque material to pass from the lower spine to the base of the skull. Various patterns of abnormalities are produced, depending on the location and size of a ruptured disc. It should be emphasized that myelography is approximately 90-percent accurate, with both false positive and false negative results. It remains an extremely helpful and essential diagnostic tool but is certainly not infallible. For example, one frequently can get abnormal patterns of the dye simply by incorrect placement of the injecting needle.

§ 1.9 Epidural Venogram

An epidural venogram is performed by inserting a large needle into the marrow of a lumbar spinous process and injecting radiopaque material that is then absorbed by the surrounding epidural veins. The procedure is based on a consistent and reliable venous pattern in close proximity to the anterior limits of the spinal canal and nerve root openings (see **Figure 1–1**). Because the easily compressible veins traverse the spinal canal near the neurostructures, abnormal venous filling is regarded as diagnostic of a ruptured disc pushing on the adjacent veins. Venography may be particularly useful in the L-S area (the lower aspect of the spinal cord). Because of the wide space in this area, a ruptured disc at this level may not be detected by a myelogram.

§ 1.10 Arthroscopy

Diagnostic arthroscopy has been used in many joints, including the knee, shoulder, and ankle. It is especially useful in examination of the knee and allows a clear view of almost the entire interior of the knee. The scope usually is introduced through an anterolateral incision near the inferior pole of the patella. A probe often is introduced from an anteromedial incision to allow palpating intraarticular structures while viewing through the arthroscope. Potential complications include infection and damage to articular surfaces.

§ 1.11 EMG (Electromyography)

Electromyography is a method of studying the activity of a muscle by recording action potentials from the contracting fibers. This is done by applying surface electrodes (hollow needles) to the overlying skin. An insulated wire core is passed through the needle into the soft tissues. This electrode then records potentials from muscle fibers in its vicinity. These potentials are amplified and

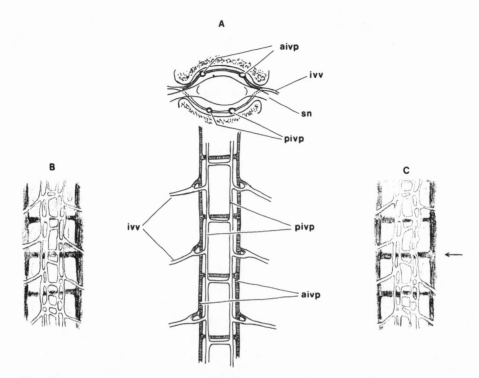

Figure 1–1. Epidural venogram. A depicts, in diagrammatic fashion, longitudinal and cross-sectional views of the internal vertebral venous plexuses. The anterior internal vertebral plexus (aivp) and the posterior internal vertebral plexus (pivp) unite laterally to form the intervertebral veins (ivy), which then exit through the intervertebral foraminae, in company with corresponding spinal nerves. View B shows this pattern in simulated X ray. This should be compared with view C, which indicates a deficiency in this pattern.

can be displayed on a cathode ray tube or, more commonly, printed. Electromyography is used normally for the diagnosis and prognostic assessment of peripheral nerve lesions and to differentiate peripheral nerve problems from diseases affecting voluntary muscle. Electromyography has been used relatively infrequently in more recent years.

§ 1.12 Video Fluoroscopy

Video fluoroscopy is a technique of recording the patient's movements under a continuous X ray. Unfortunately, this involves substantial radiation to both the patient and the operator and has only limited applications. Video fluoroscopy might be used to determine whether a shoulder joint is actually slipping out of place—subluxing as opposed to dislocating. Obviously, there is some benefit from watching joints in motion that cannot be observed from static films, but because of the hazardous radiation this is a technique used only under very special circumstances, such as determining the instability of a hip joint or shoulder joint.

§ 1.13   Radionuclide Bone Scans

In many cases, X rays will be negative even though the patient may have an occult fracture or malignancy. An alternative, bone scanning, actually has been in use for about 15 years, although interest in it has increased rapidly with the improvement in the isotope material available for the test. Prior to the mid-1970s, bone scanning was used specifically for the detection and localization of bone metastasis in cancer patients. Today, special phosphorus compounds are available that can be injected intravenously into a patient, and excellent images are obtained about two to three hours later. The radioactive material appears as a dark area (hot spot) in regions of acute bone destruction. In these areas, demineralization is rapidly occurring so that labeled phosphorus compound is rapidly absorbed into the bone.

The crucial advantage of bone scanning is that before a lesion will appear on regular X rays about 30- to 50-percent demineralization takes place. For a lesion to appear on a bone scan, as little as 10-percent demineralization is necessary. A number of displaced fractures may be missed on regular X rays. However, the site of a fracture will show increased accumulation of the radionuclides within a few hours after injury.

The procedure is brief and painless. It normally takes no more than a half hour, and the patient experiences no significant discomfort or side effects. The only major drawback is that the technique is highly sensitive. The isotope can localize in any region of increased bone activity, so it is important to correlate the bone scan with the patient's history, physical examination, X rays, and other clinical tests.

§ 1.14   HLA-B27

Ankylosing spondylitis (Marie-Strumpell's disease) is a chronic inflammatory condition that characteristically affects the sacroiliac and spinal joints. Onset usually is in the third decade, and etiology is unknown. The incidence of ankylosing spondylitis in the general population has been variously estimated at one to three per thousand. Approximately 95 percent of ankylosing spondylitis patients have the antigen HLA-B27, although it is found in only 7 percent of the healthy male population. HLA-B27 positive patients, therefore, will include almost all ankylosing spondylitis patients.

A diagnosis of ankylosing spondylitis must be considered in patients complaining of pain and stiffness in the lumbar spine. Tenderness of the paraspinal muscles and spinous processes, pain on motion, and limited motion are common findings. Obviously, detection of the HLA-B27 antigen strongly supports the diagnosis of ankylosing spondylitis. Unfortunately, as yet the test is expensive and not generally available. Unless the test has been done, however, one must be cautious in evaluating disability in individuals in the third or fourth decade who complain of stiffness and decreased range of motion of the spine. Therefore, whenever possible the disability evaluator should determine whether the test has been done and, if so, what the results are.

§ 1.15   Thermography

Thermography is heat photography. There are two main techniques available: infrared thermography uses a camera, a television monitor, and a keyboard; liquid crystal thermography involves applying a flexible rubber sheet containing heat-sensitive liquid crystals to the affected area. Using either technique, it is now possible to accurately measure the human body surface temperature. Alteration of body temperatures has been shown to correlate with nerve fiber irritation on soft tissue injury.[1] Thermography creates a color picture that can provide objective evidence of subjective pain. Asymmetric temperature differences between opposite sides of the body indicate pathology. Symmetry between both sides of the body is consistent with absence of pathology.

Abnormal temperature differences result from vasoconstriction of blood vessels supplying sympathetic nerve fibers. Injury to sympathetic nerves supplying the fine vessels in the superficial portions of the skin cause them to constrict, causing a cooling in the involved area.

Although thermography initially enjoyed considerable interest because of its ability to provide a "picture of pain," the results of thermography are often not reproducible. Thermography is no longer widely used and is included in this edition more for historical interest than for practical application. It is not generally accepted as a diagnostic tool for disability evaluation.

It should be emphasized that the thermographic technique has been used in medicine for many years in detecting breast cancer, although it has been replaced for breast cancer diagnosis by newer techniques. It is generally felt that thermography is useful in detecting sympathetic dystrophy, but in spinal thermography it is still unclear how asymmetry correlates with underlying pathophysiology. One of the leaders in thermography, Dr. Charles E. Wexler of California, has been quoted as stating that thermography is 100-percent sensitive but only 60-percent specific—there are too many false positives.

Thermography versus X rays.   X rays simply show bony anatomic structures, not soft tissue pathology. Proponents of thermography claim that it is a test

---

[1] K. Nakano, *Liquid Crystal Contact Thermography in the Clinical Evaluation of Traumatic Low Back Pain*, 5 J. Neurological & Orthopedic Med. & Surgery (Oct. 1984).

of function and physiology that can demonstrate injuries not demonstrated by X ray.

Technique.   The patient undresses and equilibrates for 30 minutes in a draft-free room with the temperature close to 68 degrees Fahrenheit, which permits neither chilling nor sweating. The area to be examined is cleaned with room temperature tap water and dried with a hair dryer. To constitute a positive abnormal temperature difference, the examination must show an asymmetry of at least 2 degrees Celsius three times.

Advantages.   Thermography is totally safe, risk-free, and painless. It is totally noninvasive and does not require radiation or injections. It measures the invisible infrared rays emitted from the body and has been compared to a picture taken by a camera. It can be used even on pregnant women or children. It also can be used on extremely obese patients who are too big for CAT scanning or myelography. The equipment is readily available, and costs range from approximately $6,000 for liquid crystals (Flexitherm, Westbury, NY) to about $40,000 for infrared equipment. There is some evidence that thermography may be more accurate than other available tests. Dr. Rubin Pochaczevsky, M.D., noted a 92-percent accuracy rate from liquid crystal thermography as opposed to an 82-percent accuracy rate for myelography.[2]

TREATMENT

§ 1.16   Treatment History

When determining a percentage of physical impairment and loss of physical function, it is first necessary to determine whether all appropriate tests have been done and, obviously, whether the patient has reached an end point. Has everything appropriate been done? For example, take the case of a patient who has been seen only three or four times by a physician prescribing mild analgesics (parafon forte, norgesic forte, or darvon) and who has been told to rest and take hot baths. If the above regimen fails, the patient may be told to simply "live with it." The physician examining to determine possible disability must ask whether all treatment options have been exhausted. Have appropriate drugs in therapeutic doses been prescribed? Has the patient had the benefit of physical therapy? Has appropriate surgery been considered or performed? Has the patient been to a pain center or back school? Have psychological or psychiatric evaluation and intervention been considered? Has vocational counseling or retraining been attempted? Has the patient made a serious attempt to stop smoking?

---

[2] 247 JAMA 3296–3302 (June 25, 1982).

§ 1.17 Drug Therapy

If the patient has been treated solely by a chiropractor, who is, of course, not licensed to prescribe controlled substances, the patient will have received no effective chemical analgesics. Some chiropractors will "prescribe" zinc, vitamins, or pain formulas in which the only effective agent is aspirin. Surely it is reasonable for the disability physician to consider whether appropriate analgesics might permit the patient to resume useful work.

There are also patients who "hate pills" or refuse to take any drugs because drugs might mask their condition or cause a reaction. Such patients often do not want to get better.

Has the patient had a trial of appropriate analgesics in effective doses? This includes not only darvon or parafon forte, but also codeine or percodan. Or has the patient had a course of hospitalization that included demeral or morphine?

Anti-inflammatory Drugs

Anti-inflammatory drug therapy has shown to be effective, not only for chronic synovitis of joints, but also for low back pain. The treating physician may have overlooked the fact that most back disorders are associated with some degree of inflammation. Obviously, the well-known rheumatologic disorders, such as ankylosing spondylitis or juvenile rheumatoid arthritis, will respond to indomethacin, phenylbutazone, or sulindac (as the drugs of choice). It should be stressed that these same drugs often are effective for the low back strain and perhaps should be tried before the patient with "low back syndrome" is determined to have reached an end point.

Aspirin.   In an age of extensive advertising and drug-oriented people, aspirin is often forgotten. Clearly, it is the least expensive and, milligram for milligram, the most potent of the salicylates. At dosages of less than 3.5 grams per day, aspirin has primarily an analgesic effect. At 3.5 grams per day or more, a distinct anti-inflammatory effect can be demonstrated.

Phenylalkanoic Acids.   Drugs in this category interfere with prostaglandin synthesis and may be even more effective than aspirin. These drugs include Motrin (ibuprofen), Nalfon (fenoprofen), and Naprosyn (naproxen).

Pyrules.   Tolectin (tolmetin) and Indocin (indomethacin) also are potent inhibitors of prostaglandin synthesis and are quite effective anti-inflammatory drugs.

Pyrazoles.   Butazolidin (phenylbutazon) is an effective anti-inflammatory drug, although it is used with caution because of adverse side effects, including occasional bone marrow depression.

Sulindac.   Clinoril (sulindac) was introduced after a massive public relations campaign in 1979 and has proven its value since that time. It is particularly effective as an anti-inflammatory drug for osteoarthritis.

Fenamates.   Meclomen (meclofenamate) also is an effective anti-inflammatory drug, although it has a higher incidence of gastrointestinal side effects than the above-noted drugs.

Chymopapain

Chymopapain is derived from papaya enzymes and has been proven effective in reducing the size of swollen boggy intervertebral discs. It usually is injected under X-ray control into the affected disc by an orthopedic surgeon or neurosurgeon in the operating room. While not effective for a protruding disc fragment, it has been shown to be an effective modality in selective cases of degenerative disc disease.

§ 1.18   Physical Therapy

Cryotherapy.   Application of ice or cold works best for superficial rather than deep pain. The usual treatment plan is several short sessions of applying ice or cold spray to the tender area or over the paravertebral musculature. Most advocates suggest a broad sweeping motion of ice cubes or vasocoolant spray. This should be followed by gentle passive or active muscle stretching.

Heat.   Heat application has been used extensively and has proven to be useful, especially for back pain. The mechanism of action is thought to be increasing the blood supply to the muscle, leading to increased oxygenation and reduction of metabolic products from sustained muscle contraction. Various forms of heat are used, including hot packs, diathermy, and ultrasound. Ultrasound is prescribed for deep heat. Hot baths are especially effective in providing conduction and convection of heat through the deeper tissues.

Massage.   Massage is an ancient remedy for pain and sore muscles and has been shown to increase blood flow, stretch tissues, and provide counterirritation. It may also improve lymphatic drainage.

Exercise therapy.   Exercises may be prescribed to restore normal flexibility and to promote muscle strength and endurance. William's exercises, essentially modified sit-ups, are widely used to strengthen the abdominal wall, tending to increase intra-abdominal pressure and consequently to reduce intradiskal pressure. Knee-chest exercises are prescribed to elongate the erector spinae muscles. Pelvic tilting exercises are prescribed to decrease lumbar lordosis.

Epidural steroid injections. Epidural steroid injections are indicated for treatment of nerve root entrapment and irritation secondary to disc disease. Discogenic disease usually presents with radicular pain over dermatome distribution and increased pain on coughing, sneezing, or straining at stool. Because nerve root compression is extradural, the steroid is given epidurally, whether at the site of compression or one level above that of emergence of the affected roots. The procedure itself is quite simple. The epidural space is identified by loss of resistance on hanging drop techniques. Eighty ml of Depo-Medrol (methylprednisolone acetate) or 50 ml of Aristocort (triamcinolone diacetate) is slowly injected into the epidural space (see **Figure 1–2**). After the injection, the patient remains in the lateral position for 15 minutes to maintain the drug-affected side.

Facet joint injections. Injection of facet joints is done ideally by injecting lidocaine into the facet joint area under an X-ray image intensifier. With the patient lying prone, two to four facets are injected on either side. Most doctors report a 60-percent or more sustained improvement following this treatment. Facet injection may be especially useful after failed disc surgery, which may produce subluxation of the facet joints. Facet injection is less useful for soft tissue involvement, vascular pain, or nerve damage.

Transcutaneous nerve stimulation. Transcutaneous nerve stimulation became very popular in the 1970s. It is based on the counterirritation principle. The patient wears a small battery-powered stimulator that emits constant or intermittent low-grade electrical shocks. Under the gate theory, it is thought that such constant low-grade stimuli might keep greater pain stimuli from reaching higher centers. The stimulator costs about $500, is about the size of a pack of cigarettes, and is worn constantly by the patient.

§ 1.19   Surgery

Surgery generally is regarded as a last resort used after failure of conservative treatment, and many problems respond well to surgical intervention. However, surgery should be performed to relieve leg pain, not back pain. Generally, surgery has the best results when performed within three months of the onset of sciatica. Obviously, disc herniation is a self-limited disease; if the pain can be controlled reasonably well with conservative measures, and if the patient can be returned to modified work duty, the end result in three or four years will be the same with or without an operation. The pendulum has swung from a large exploration of the disc using a long surgical incision to microsurgery, a limited diskectomy through a tiny incision. The alternative, chemonucleolysis, was popular several years ago, but the results are not as good as with surgery in cases of clear sciatica. Furthermore, chemonucleolysis is fraught with many serious complications.

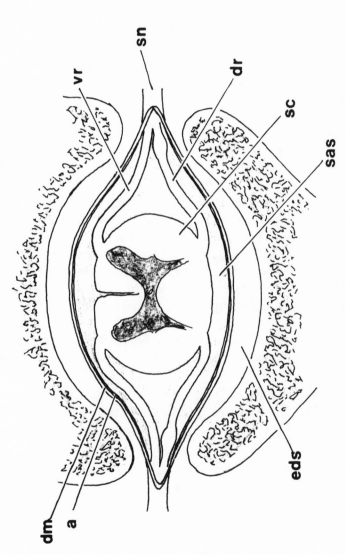

Figure 1–2. Cross section of the spinal cord and vertebral column. Indicated are the spinal cord (sc), with its ventral or motor root (vr), and the dorsal or sensory root (dr), which are combining to form the definitive spinal nerve (sn) for that level. Surrounding the cord are the fibrous dura mater (dm) and the thinner anachnoid layer (a). The area internal to the arachnoid is the subarachnoid space (sas), which is filled with cerebrospinal fluid. Peripheral to the dura mater is the epidural space (eds).

Spinal fusions are no longer generally used except for very unstable spines. Unless there is definite radiological demonstration of instability, spinal fusion is generally not indicated. This is defined as in excess of 3 millimeters of translational or 10 degrees of angular motion. The results of repeat surgery are notoriously poor. The second operation can expect a 30-percent success rate, the third only 15-percent, and the fourth is bound to make the patient worse. Spondylolysis/spondylolisthesis can usually be managed conservatively with job modification. However, in selected cases a combination of decompression and postero-lateral fusion can be quite successful.

Because of the dimension of the back problem, much experimental work is ongoing. Although still in the research stage, techniques such as argon lasers to dissolve disc material and bone spurs and disc implants using fiber-reinforced polymer sacs filled with a fluid certainly hold some potential, but they are not currently used in general clinical practice.

Has the patient been seen by an appropriate, qualified surgeon? This is especially necessary with patients who may have a preconceived aversion to surgery. Highly anxious individuals often will suffer rather than take treatment. For example, a musician suffering from carpal tunnel syndrome may prefer to "eat right" to cure the illness when surgical release of the transverse carpal ligament with neurolysis of the median nerve will solve the problem, if performed properly. A patient with a trigger finger may believe, on poor advice, that suffering is inevitable, when minor outpatient surgery can provide dramatic relief. Details of surgical procedures are beyond the scope of this book. A few examples of common cases when surgery is indicated follow:

Cervical or lumbar laminectomy should be considered if persistent pain has not responded to conservative therapy and appropriate testing (myelogram or CAT scan) is positive.

Recurrent dislocation of the shoulder is correctable with surgery. It is advised in the younger individual with three documented occurrences of dislocation.

Persistent tennis elbow can be corrected by partial surgical resection of the annular ligament.

Ligamentous instability of the knee can be surgically repaired.

Multiple recurrent ankle sprains are indicative of a need for ligamentous reconstruction of the ankle.

§ 1.20   Pain Centers

Pain centers usually are in-patient treatment centers that stress a supportive psychological approach designed to reduce drug dependence and to encourage the patient's acceptance of living with some pain. Such centers usually are indicated for patients with the following criteria:

1. Pain of six months' duration or more
2. No psychoses
3. No other severe illnesses
4. Disabled, inactive, and on medication
5. Some type of family support
6. Not living alone
7. No other personal problems.[3]

HISTORY FORM

Patient

Name: _____

Address: _____

Age: _____   Date of Birth: _____

Marital status: _____

Number of children and ages: _____

Highest grade completed: _____ Date

Vocational training: _____ Date

                                      _____ Date

Most recent place of employment: _____

                                 Date started

Job description: _____

Description of duties: _____

Prior employment: _____ Date

Job description: _____

Military service, if any: _____

Medical History

Nature of present problem: _____

Health providers: _____

Treatments/medications:

_____ Date

_____ Date

Dates of hospitalizations, if any: _____

Prior Medical History

Any known diseases: _____

Dates acquired: _____

Prior injuries, if any, and dates: _____

---

[3] A.L. Magliozzi & P. LeClair, *Pain Centers, Transcutaneous Electrical Nerve Stimulation, Vocational Rehabilitation—A Panacea?*, Lecture at the Liberty Mutual Back Pain Symposium, Boston, Mass. (Mar. 22–24, 1981).

CHAPTER 2

EVALUATION OF LOW BACK PAIN

§ 2.1   Dimensions of the Problem

Back complaints are by far the largest and most challenging category physicians are asked to evaluate in determining medical impairment. The total annual cost of back pain in the United States was almost $16 billion in 1984. More recent figures suggest $38 billion spent on low back care in 1988. There are approximately two million back injuries per year in the United States, and approximately seven million adults seek treatment for back pain each year. Eighty percent of people will have back pain at some time in their lives, but something like 98 percent of low back injuries will get well or at least be asymptomatic in a short time.

Because orthopedic injuries, and particularly back injuries, make up the bulk of workers' compensation cases, the workers' compensation system in the United States is becoming extremely painful to all parties concerned. Business owners are complaining about increasing workers' compensation insurance costs. Parties ranging from business organizations to organized labor are pushing to sharply modify the workers' compensation system. A California assemblyman, Burt Margolin, recently described the current workers' compensation system as "a disgrace." He recently introduced a reform bill into the state legislature that would increase certain workers' compensation benefits while restricting the types of injuries that would be eligible for payments. In the past decade, workers' compensation rates have risen more than twice as fast as the general inflation rate, according to Richard Victor, executive director of the Workers' Compensation Research Institute in Cambridge, Massachusetts. In 1986 compensation-related payouts were an estimated $25 billion, more than three times the level a decade earlier.

In California insurance companies' lawyers and doctors all deny that they are responsible. Workers' compensation insurance premiums, however, have approximately tripled in the past 10 years. Litigation costs have risen as much as sixfold, while medical bills for examining workers have increased as much as eightfold in the same period. In California a business owner, Steven Kalen, has become something of a one-man crusade for reform. The 69-year-old Mr. Kalen has lobbied to get law enforcement officials to start undercover investigations of local medical practitioners whose methods he considers suspect. Mr. Kalen says that he never thought about workers' compensation until several years ago when an employee filed what he regarded as a false claim. Over his objections, his company's insurer settled the case. Mr. Kalen found that insurance companies almost always settle. According to the California Workers' Compensation Institute, a San Francisco group funded by the insurance industry, nearly 75 percent of all disputed cases are settled before going to trial.

Physicians affect these statistics whenever they determine whether a patient alleging disability due to back problems can resume limited work, may return to full duty, or cannot work at all. This chapter outlines the fundamental tools to generate an accurate, fair, and impartial evaluation. Beginning with a brief review of the anatomy of the spine, the chapter then looks in more detail at the etiology of back problems and delves into history taking before proceeding to the physical examination. The specific orthopedic problems discussed include chronic sprains, compression fractures, spondylolisthesis, and disc injuries.

A detailed history often is far more helpful than the physical examination in evaluating back problems. This chapter also presents a comprehensive series of questions that help physicians evaluate back patients and distinguish between pain due to organic and nonorganic pathology—and ferret out malingering. After this important section, details of the orthopedic physical examination are described and guidelines to clinical impairment are offered. The chapter concludes with a discussion of prognosis and the "back loser," the person who is permanently disabled by low back pain.

ANATOMY

§ 2.2 Spine

The anatomy of the spine is too complex to not include a brief review here. Detailed knowledge of the structure of the spine is essential for adequate diagnosis and management of back problems.

The spine consists of 33 vertebrae: 7 cervical, 12 thoracic, 5 lumbar, 5 sacral (fused into one), and 4 coccygeal (fused into one) (see **Figure 2–1**). Because the sacrum and coccyx usually are regarded as one unit, humans effectively have 26 vertebrae. The vertebrae are connected by a system of ligaments, interposed cartilage, and muscles that act to keep the entire complex chain from collapsing. The primary ligaments are the anterior and posterior longitudinal ligaments, situated along the anterior and posterior surfaces of the vertebral bodies, and the ligamenta flava, which connect the laminae and extend laterally to the articular facets. The supraspinous ligaments join the tips of the spinous processes. The interspinous ligaments connect the adjoining spinous processes from their tips to their roots and aid the supraspinous ligaments in strengthening the spine.

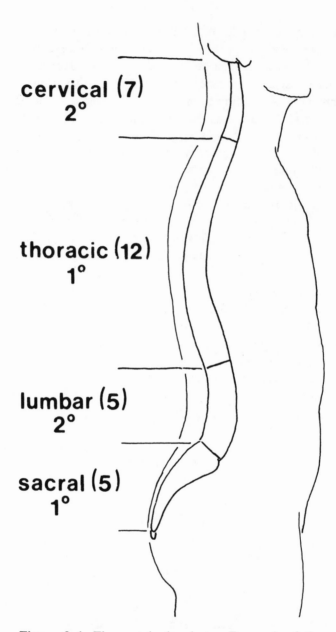

Figure 2–1. The vertebral column. For each of the four primary regions of the column the number of associated vertebrae is given in parentheses, and the nature of the curve is indicated. Primary curves are those present at birth; secondary curves develop as a consequence of maturation and the assumption of erect posture.

§ 2.3 Lumbar Vertebrae

In the lumbar area, where most back pain occurs, the vertebrae are large because of their primary weight-bearing function (see **Figure 2–2**). Short, strong pedicles arise from each side of the vertebral body. In the central portion of each vertebra is a foramen through which pass the spinal nerves. The spinal nerve roots exit through holes just behind each vertebral body. These nerve roots are particularly vulnerable in the lumbar area to space-occupying tumors, as well as to the consequences of some degenerative conditions.

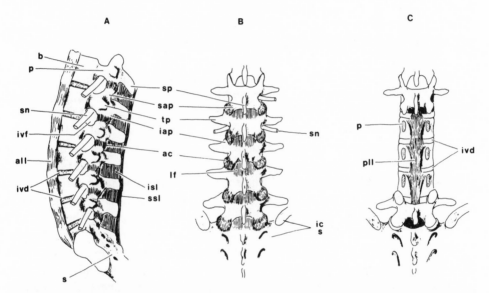

Figure 2–2. The lumbar spine. A and B are lateral and posterior views, respectively. View C is a posterior view in which the vertebral arches have been removed. Osseous structures depicted are the body (b), pedicle (p), superior articular process (sap), inferior articular process (iap), and the transverse process (tp). Ligaments and other structures uniting the bony elements are the anterior longitudinal ligament (all), ligamentum flavum (lf), articular capsule (ac), interspinous ligament (isl), supraspinous ligament (ssl), the posterior longitudinal ligament (pll), and the intervertebral disc (ivd). The upper portion of the sacrum (s) and the crest of the ilium (ic) are also depicted.

§ 2.4 Disc

The disc is the coupling mechanism and pad between the vertebral bodies. Each disc has an outer casing of semielastic fibers attached to the edges of the vertebral bodies above and below. Inside this outer casing is a gelatinous packing under positive pressure.

The disc allows one vertebral body to bend against the next while preventing any front, back, or lateral slippage. Slippage of one vertebral body in relation to another can impinge on the vulnerable spinal nerve roots.

Despite its clever design, the disc has limitations. Although it tolerates straight compression well, the disc does not tolerate sheer stress. Sheer stress occurs at the L_1 and L_5 interspaces because of the forward slope of the lumbar vertebrae (see **Figure 2–3**). This forward slope is essential to allow two-legged vertical body function and is associated with the normal lumbar lordotic curve.

The disc also is vulnerable because it has no blood supply and, therefore, cannot repair itself when it has been damaged. The disc is nourished by tissue fluids that circulate through it as a result of osmotic forces, gravitational pressure, and the pumping effect of movement. Therefore, its nourishment improves with activity and is adversely affected by immobilization through bed rest or a spinal fusion. Smoking has also been found to have a negative influence on its metabolism. Without a proper balance of water, solutes, protein, and collagen, the disc will gradually deteriorate, and fissures will develop in the surrounding annulus. There can then be herniation of the disc with penetration of the nuclear material into peripheral areas, which are highly sensitive to both mechanical and chemical stimulation. Irritation of the longitudinal ligaments is generally perceived as referred pain involving the low back, buttocks, and thighs. However, when an inflamed nerve root is compressed, the resulting radiculopathy is perceived as pain along with a neurological deficit involving the distribution of the particular nerve root involved. It should be noted that pain related to osteoarthritis, rheumatic disease, spondylolisthesis, and various nonmechanical medical problems is usually gradual in onset and unrelated to any particular traumatic event. However, an acute back strain obviously can be superimposed on those medical conditions.

For a long time it was felt that discs did not have sensory innervation. Recent evidence suggests that, in fact, discs do have some sensory innervation so that traumatic or degenerative changes to the disc material itself can cause discogenic pain.

Degenerative disc disease.   Degenerative disc disease usually begins in the patient's 20s and is due to repeated microtrauma to the fibers in the surrounding casing. Body weight is the prime culprit. It tends to be concentrated over the posterior third of the two lower lumbar discs. This pressure, on a relatively small area, can result in small tears in the disc casing fibers. Clinically, these tears may present as relatively mild back pain. Even if the pain is severe, it tends to last only a few days.

Disc damage.   Unlike degenerative disease damage, gross damage to the disc casing is irreparable. The gelatinous content of the disc escapes slowly through the hole in the casing, reducing pressure inside the disc. As a result, simple, unguarded movements can cause considerable back pain. If further leakage occurs, one vertebra may slip against the other, pinching the nerve root.

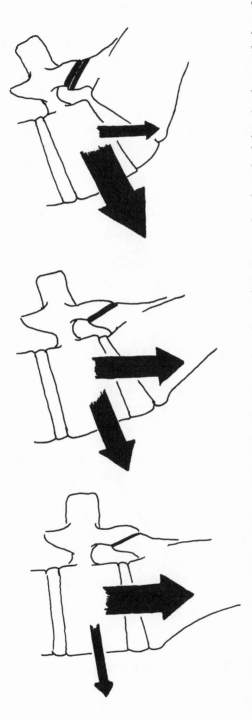

Figure 2–3. Diagrammatic depiction of the effect of the lumbosacral angle on the stresses placed on the joint. As the angulation of the sacrum relative to the lumbar column increases, the shear force acting upon the joint increases, while the compressive force decreases. This also increases the strain put upon the articular processes of the vertebra and the sacrum.

§ 2.5   Nerve Root Damage

A pinched nerve root becomes inflamed and painful. Pain may radiate into a buttock, thigh, or even all the way down the leg into the toes. If the pressure is prolonged, weakness may present in the muscles of the leg or foot, perhaps also depression of the knee-jerk and ankle-jerk reflexes. This clinical picture often develops in the patient's 30s or 40s.

Sufficient escape of disc content can place direct mechanical pressure on the nerve root. This produces the classical picture of the ruptured or herniated disc. Surgical removal of the herniated material is necessary, but the decision must wait at least three to six weeks to allow the symptoms to subside. By that time, pain due to secondary inflammation of a pinched nerve root usually will have abated, but pain from mechanical pressure on a nerve root will persist. Only if the symptoms do not decrease after prolonged bed rest should surgical decompression be considered. Even surgical decompression of the nerve root may relieve symptoms only temporarily.

Normal slipping and sliding between the vertebrae eventually subject the joints between the posterior aspects of the vertebral bodies to ever greater mechanical stress. As a result, arthritic changes often develop beginning in the late 40s.

§ 2.6   Facet Alignment

The articular facets of the spine normally overlap like the shingles on a roof. Malalignment may increase rotational stresses on the facet joints. This condition is known as *facet tropism*.

When one facet is completely disconnected from the next facet, it is referred to as *dislocation*. This is usually an unstable condition associated with paralysis and can be a surgical emergency. If the articular cartilage of one facet joint is only partially in contact with the articular cartilage of the adjacent facet joint, it is described as *subluxated*. Most orthopedic surgeons would regard this as a relatively rare condition that is very difficult to scientifically document. Chiropractors, on the other hand, regard this as a very common condition requiring manipulation or "adjustment," which chiropractors suggest eliminates the subluxation and reduces pain. Most orthopedic surgeons would suggest that it is impossible to apply enough external pressure to a human spine to move the vertebra significantly (see **Figure 2–4**).

§ 2.7   Dermatomes

This discussion concentrates on the lumbar dermatomes—the areas of skin innervated by specific nerve roots (see **Figure 2–5**). For example, the L_5 dermatome includes a strip of skin extending anteriorly, roughly from the outside of the knee

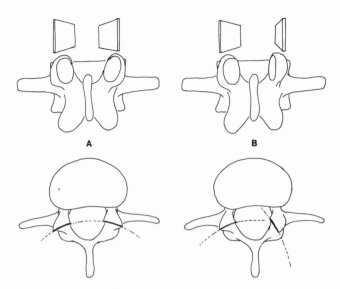

Figure 2–4. Facet tropism. A depicts, above and below, a symmetrical disposition of articular facets and the arc of movement allowed by this symmetry. In B, the facets are not symmetrical, resulting in two different arcs of movement. This creates considerable strain on the joints.

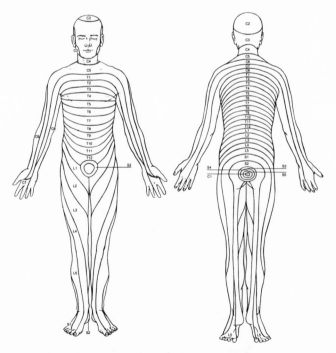

Figure 2–5. Dermatome map of the body showing which nerve roots innervate areas of the skin (front view, back view).

to the top of the foot, involving approximately the first, second, third, and fourth toes, and also the middle of the sole of the foot. **Table 2–1** summarizes the clinical findings characteristic of lumbar nerve root compression.

Table 2–1

Clinical Findings Characteristic of Lumbar Nerve Root Compression

Nerve root	Dermatome	Typical symptoms
L_5 L_4	L_5 L_3–L_4	Pain in low back, posterior lateral thigh, anterior leg; numbness in knee and anterior medial thigh; quadriceps weakness and atrophy; diminished knee-jerk reflex
	L_4–L_5	Pain over sacroiliac joint, hip, lateral thigh, calf; numbness of lateral leg and web of great toe; weakness on dorsiflexion of foot and great toe; possible foot drop, quadriceps atrophy; normal knee and ankle reflexes
	L_5–S_1	Pain over sacroiliac joint, hip, posterior lateral thigh, leg to heel; numbness and muscular atrophy over back of calf, lateral heel, foot, toes; weakness on plantar flexion of foot and great toe; difficulty walking on toes; diminished or absent ankle-jerk reflex

ETIOLOGY OF LOW BACK PAIN

§ 2.8   Trauma

By far the most frequent cause of back pain is trauma. If the patient has a reasonable history of injudicious lifting or a fall, with an otherwise negative medical history, trauma is the most likely cause of persistent back pain.

To be fair to the patient, a physician should bear in mind the many possible causes of back pain, other than trauma, that may have brought the patient to the office.

§ 2.9   Organic Causes

Congenital disorders.   Common congenital structural abnormalities of the spine include the presence of five lumbar vertebrae, transitional terminal lumbar vertebrae, increased lumbosacral angle, spina bifida, spina occulta, leg length discrepancy, asymmetrical facet joints, spondylolysis, and spondylolisthesis. In the past, preemployment X rays were used to look for abnormalities in the low back. There is increasing agreement that most structural anomalies produce very little low back pain or disability. However, it is easy to understand how a history of trauma combined with spondylolisthesis (a crack in the vertebral body) can combine to produce back pain.

Benign tumors.   Benign tumors involving the nerve roots or meninges include neurinomas, hemangiomas, and meningiomas. Benign tumors involving the vertebrae include osteoid osteomas, Paget's disease, and osteoblastomas.

Malignant tumors.   The malignant spinal tumors include primary bone tumors, such as multiple myeloma, and secondary tumors, such as metastases from the kidney, breast, prostate, thyroid, or lung.

Metabolic disorders.   The most common metabolic cause of low back pain is osteoporosis, a decrease in bone density. Osteoporosis may be associated with inadequate intake of protein, hormonal changes such as those of Cushing's syndrome or menopause, or vascular abnormalities such as inflammation or Sudeck's atrophy.

Inflammatory diseases.   The most common inflammatory diseases causing back pain include rheumatoid arthritis and Marie-Strumpell disease. Usually attacking women between ages 25 and 45, rheumatoid arthritis primarily affects the hip and hand joints and also may cause severe low back pain. Marie-Strumpell disease often presents initially with low back pain. It usually is progressive and can lead to bony union between the vertebral bodies.

Degenerative disorders.   Degenerative disorders include spondylosis, osteo-arthritis, ruptured disc, and spinal stenosis (see **Figure 2–6**).

Infections.   Acute infections include pyogenic disc-space infections. Chronic infections involving the spine are tuberculosis, chronic osteomyelitis, and fungal diseases.

Circulatory diseases.   The primary circulatory disorder causing back pain is abdominal aortic aneurysm. This usually occurs in men over age 50 who complain of deep, growing pain in the lumbar region or pelvic region. Prompt, accurate diagnosis is extremely important to avoid a fatal rupture of the aneurysm.

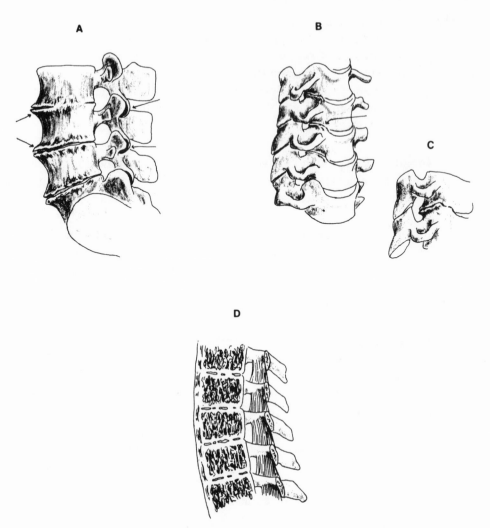

Figure 2–6. Degenerative disorders of the vertebral column. View A depicts degeneration of the lumbar intervertebral discs, with the formation of osteophytes and subluxation of articular joints (due to narrowing of the space between the adjacent vertebrae). B shows the formation of ostephytes in the cervical column. These are most common along the lateral aspect of the bodies, where they may impinge upon the intervertebral foraminae, as shown in C. View D shows thickening and ossification of the anterior longitudinal ligament, with ossification of the intervertebral discs (ankylosing spondylitis, or Marie-Strumpell disease).

Musculoskeletal problems. Musculoskeletal problems usually are divided into intrinsic and extrinsic mechanical causes. Intrinsic causes include poor muscle tone, chronic postural strain, unstable vertebrae, and myofascial pain. Extrinsic mechanical causes include pelvic tumors or infections, uterine fibroids, hip diseases, prostate disease, sacroiliac joint infections and sprains, and untreated lumbar scoliosis. It is important to differentiate the course of treatment between patients who present with back pain—musculoskeletal problems—and those who present with sciatica or other radicular patterns. Of the former, approximately 5 percent go to surgery, compared to 17 percent of the latter.

§ 2.10 Nonorganic Causes

Hysteria, malingering, compensation neurosis, and the like are less easy to identify as causes of low back pain. The following sections offer techniques of history taking and physical examination that help distinguish between pain of organic and nonorganic origin.

HISTORY

§ 2.11 Purpose

The basic medical school course in physical diagnosis emphasizes that the vast majority of correct diagnoses are made from the patient's history rather than from the physical examination. This is particularly true in disability evaluation of the back. A physician does not always have to be a medical Sherlock Holmes, however, to decide whether a patient is truly disabled for any occupation, grossly malingering, or, as is most often the case, somewhere in between.

A list of routine questions is helpful. Their purpose is to detect inconsistencies in the history that will tell physicians whether the patient is exaggerating the medical condition. These questions must be asked by the examining physician, not delegated to a nurse or receptionist, because the manner in which they are answered often is more important than the content of the answers. Needless to say, a friendly, relaxed manner will do much to calm the patient and generate the desired information. Following is a simplified series of questions important to ask of patients claiming to have disabling low back pain.

§ 2.12 Patient

Q: How old are you?

People are unlikely to develop nontraumatic back problems until the late 20s, 30s, or 40s, when degenerative changes in the disc become significant. Physicians should be very suspicious of an 18-year-old person with back pain of six to eight months' duration that does not radiate to either lower leg. On the other hand, a 60-year-old with obvious degenerative changes on X ray may never be able to return to heavy labor after a legitimate back injury.

Q: How much education have you had?

Individuals with less than average education tend not to be motivated to return to work because of their limited vocational potential.

Q: How much do you weigh?
How tall are you?

Obese individuals are known to be at greater risk for back problems.

Q: Have you hurt your back before?

Repetitive trauma to the back is thought to cause tears in the annulus fibrosus and herniation of disc material in older people. Thus, a history of two or three prior serious back injuries treated with hospitalization is consistent with legitimate impairment. Physicians should suspect malingering or psychoneurotic problems in a younger patient with frequent absenteeism from work for apparently insignificant or minor trauma.

§ 2.13   Patient's Job

Q: What is your job?

A longshoreman or construction laborer legitimately may take longer to return to work after injury than a clerk or secretary. Special occupational hazards must also be considered; caisson workers, for example, are liable to develop aseptic necrosis of the hips.

Q: Is your job still available?

The patient may be staying away from work not for medical reasons but because of an imminent or ongoing strike, bankruptcy of an employer, or elimination of a job by mechanization.

Q: Have you tried going back to work, perhaps to light duty?

Physicians should tend to believe the individual who has tried to work for a day or two but could not manage it. In contrast, many individuals do not go back to work because nobody has told them to, and besides, they still are getting weekly checks. Physicians also may hear answers like, "My attorney said not to go back until the case is settled," or, "The compensation payments would stop," or, "I am fine now, but I might injure myself again and have trouble getting back on compensation."

Q: How do you feel about your employer and your employer's insurance company?

Physicians may find that a patient has stayed away from work because of anger at an employer or the employer's insurance company. This may be a result of initial delay in receiving workers' compensation benefits or some other grievance. The patient may admit to the intention of never returning to the same job and may be in school or seeking other work.

§ 2.14 Patient's Accident

Q: When was the accident?

Most simple back strains resolve in six to eight weeks. If the injury occurred only two to three weeks before, the patient may be entitled to the benefit of the doubt when claiming disabling pain. Physicians should tend to be suspicious if months or years have elapsed and all objective tests have been negative.

Q: How did the accident happen?

While back injuries certainly can be caused by trivial trauma, physicians should tend to believe the patient who says that the injury occurred while moving a refrigerator and the other guy slipped and let go, and tend to be suspicious of a patient who alleges frequent nonspecific injuries to the back in an apparently nonstrenuous job.

Q: How much damage to the car?

Obviously, a dented fender would be expected to result in less personal injury than a totally demolished car that turned over three times.

Q: Where were you sitting?
   Were you wearing a seat belt?

A patient who was sitting in the front passenger seat without a seat belt might be expected to have greater injury than a back seat passenger wearing a seat belt. Physicians also should ask how fast the car was going.

Q: When did you report the accident?
To whom? In writing or orally?

Physicians should tend to believe an account of an accident that was reported immediately and treated in the company medical department or a nearby hospital emergency room. They should be suspicious of a patient who refers to a vague untreated injury, say, two years previously.

Q: Were there any witnesses?
What are their names?

Obviously, corroborative evidence tends to support the patient's claim of injury. The manner in which the patient describes the degree of involvement of co-workers can be revealing: the more specific the story, the more credible it is likely to be.

Q: When did you stop work?

Physicians should tend to believe a patient who has not worked since incurring a documented injury, as opposed to an individual who stopped work four weeks after the accident on the advice of co-workers or perhaps a lawyer.

§ 2.15   Patient's Medical Problem

Q: Where is the pain?

Physicians should tend to believe an individual who claims localized low back pain radiating down one leg and to be very suspicious of a patient who says everything hurts (arms, legs, neck, upper and lower back). There is a high correlation between complaints of multifocal pain (back, arms, shoulders, neck) and nonorganic pathology. Glove-and-stocking sensory loss also points to a nonorganic source.

A typical leg pain—pain that does not follow dermatomes—also suggests nonorganic pathology. Physicians should suspect a patient who complains of groin pain but claims no hip joint pathology, for example.

Q: What is the pain like?
Do you take any medication for it?

Physicians should be suspicious if a patient claims severe pain requiring constant narcotics yet is carrying no pain pills. They should ask to see the patient's pill bottles. They also should be suspicious if a patient claims to have agonizing pain yet takes only an over-the-counter product, or "dislikes pills" and takes nothing at all.

Q: Is the pain any better?

Physicians should be suspicious of a patient who says she is absolutely no better months after the injury, despite appropriate treatment. Rest always should relieve mechanical back pain. Even a patient with a grossly ruptured disc eventually requiring surgery usually will get some relief from time, bed rest, physical therapy, and medication.

Q: Do you have any bladder or bowel problems?

Incontinence or poor control suggests serious disc protrusion requiring urgent surgical intervention. I have seen a patient with urinary frequency and incontinence treated unsuccessfully for months by a chiropractor with manipulation and diathermy. Eventual laminectomy and disc excision gave poor results because of the delay of getting proper treatment.

Q: Are you working under the table or doing any heavy work at home, such as gardening or car maintenance?

Having gotten the usual negative answer, physicians should examine the patient's hands. They should be very suspicious if the hands are covered with paint, grime, or calluses.

Q: Are you able to drive a car?

The malingerer will say, "Never." Physicians then should ask how the patient got to the office. The malingerer will say she was driven by a friend. They should make it a point to observe how the patient actually leaves their office. It is a revelation to see the patient who "cannot drive" get into a car alone and drive away. I have even seen a young man with crutches put them on the back of his motorcycle and drive off.

Q: Do you have a lawyer? Who?

Obviously, the involvement of an attorney may suggest nothing more than an employer or insurance company that has failed to meet its legal obligations to the worker. However, the patient may mention the name of a well-known attorney who consistently advises clients not to return to work until a lump-sum settlement is awarded, even if the patient is medically cured.

§ 2.16   Patient's Treatment

Q: What medical treatment have you received?

Physicians should be suspicious of a patient who was seen by the company nurse right after the accident but failed to seek medical care in the subsequent six months. They should ask what the treating physician said or did. A patient who was seen initially by a family physician, referred to a neurologist, orthopedic surgeon, or neurosurgeon, hospitalized, and had a positive CAT scan, myelogram, or other test is more believable than a patient who has had two or more negative myelograms or CAT scans and has seen several orthopedic surgeons and neurosurgeons who could find nothing objectively wrong.

Q: Have X rays been taken? How many times?

Were X rays read by a local chiropractor, by a first-year radiology resident at a nearby teaching hospital, or by a board-certified independent radiologist?

In general, radiologic changes are poorly correlated with symptoms of low back pain. For example, X rays occasionally reveal spondylolisthesis, staphylococcal discitis, chondrosarcoma, or marked disc-space narrowing in asymptomatic individuals.

Q: Have you had a bone scan?

A positive bone scan might suggest a fracture or malignancy, metastatic or primary.

Q: Have you had a CAT scan?

CAT scans are painless and even less traumatic than myelograms. Physicians should be suspicious when a patient has been disabled for months but has never had a CAT scan. This may cast doubt on the reality of the complaints, the quality of the patient's medical care, or both.

Q: Have you had a myelogram?

Injection of contrast medium provides a highly accurate way to evaluate disc protrusion. Physicians should be suspicious of the patient who claims agonizing, disabling pain yet refuses to consider myelography and possible surgical disc excision.

Q: Have you had a chymopapain injection or laminectomy?

A patient with a positive myelogram or CAT scan who has not improved on the usual regimen of bed rest and analgesics, yet refuses chymopapain or laminectomy, either may have legitimate anxiety or may not want to get better.

Q: Do you have any other medical problems?

There are many potential causes of low back pain besides trauma, as reviewed earlier. It is essential to keep them in mind. For example, a patient being treated for leukemia may have back pain due to malignancy rather than to an alleged minor fall.

CLINICAL FINDINGS

§ 2.17   Coordination

The clinical examination can be performed efficiently by any physician. Of course, it must be coordinated with the history in order to test subjective complaints such as stiffness, pain, and weakness and correlate them with the extent and nature of the injury. The neurologic examination should include reflexes, and the findings correlated with functional consequences. Finally, surgical scars and contractures, if any, should be measured for size and described in detail. It is essential that scars be related to involvement of the underlying structures.

§ 2.18   Before and After the Examination

The patient should be carefully observed in the waiting room, either by the physician or by her medical assistants. How the patient sits, gets up from the waiting room chair, and leaves the office must be noted. A patient may claim to barely be able to walk in the examining room but may exhibit no difficulty walking down the hall for X rays or out to the street to the car.

While observing the patient, the physician should determine whether the patient's gait is appropriate for back disease. For example, shuffling or stooping over is consistent with back pain. In contrast, an antalgic gait (limp) is due usually to leg pain.

"Histrionics," such as grimacing, exaggeration of complaints, clutching body parts, or leaning on the wall for support, are inconsistent with organic back pain, as are grunts and groans. Abnormal dress, such as wearing a back brace outside the clothing to draw attention to the problem, also suggests nonorganic pathology or malingering.

Finally, it is important to observe how the patient undresses and dresses with regard to limitation of movement. The physician should make it a point to observe the patient through a crack in the examining room door, without the patient's knowledge, at the conclusion of the examination. The physician may notice that a patient who could barely bend at the waist in her presence now has no difficulty bending over to pick up shoes and put them on. Such observations, of course, suggest that the patient may be exaggerating the symptoms, if not faking them outright.

§ 2.19   Observations During the Examination

Before the patient even sits on the examination table, the physician should notice her general body type. The physician should observe the patient's posture and note any obvious deformities, such as leg length discrepancy, pelvic obliquity, lordosis, kyphosis, or scoliosis. Obesity, as noted, also predisposes to back problems.

While the patient is still standing, the physician should ask her to walk on her heels and then on her toes. Discrepant weakness (marked weakness of the extensor halluces against resistance in a patient who is able to walk on tiptoe) suggests nonorganic pathology.

The physician should have the patient go through flexion, extension, side bending, and rotation of the back. While putting the patient through this range of motion, the physician should observe her movements for indications as to the site of pain and direction of radiation. I frequently ask patients to repeat these movements several times in the course of the examination to determine whether they reveal any significant discrepancy.

Next, the physician should ask the patient to lie on the examination table. First, all hip movements should be tested, and both legs from the anterior superior iliac spine to the medial malleolus should be measured. The abdomen should be palpated for masses such as hernia or abdominal aortic aneurysm. I always check for peripheral pulses and listen for a bruit.

With the patient prone on the examination table, the physician should palpate the renal area for tenderness, test extension of the hips and spine, and test extension of the femur to determine femoral nerve stretch.

Neurologic examination.   The physician should perform a complete neurologic examination, using a safety pin, reflex hammer, and tape measure. I always keep these instruments in my pocket for easy access. The physician should make it a point to check all reflexes for sensation and motor power and measure the calves and thighs for symmetry.

Rectal examination.   When indicated in patients of either sex, the physician should include a digital rectal examination—in men, looking particularly for prostatic masses suggestive of carcinoma of the prostate with possible metastases to the spine.

Pelvic examination.   When indicated, the physician should perform a pelvic examination in women.

Laboratory and other tests. Frequently, patients will bring old hospital charts and records with them. The physician should review all available data, including serum phosphorus, calcium, alkaline phosphatase concentrations, blood counts, sedimentation rate, and urinalysis. In men, the serum acid phosphatase level should be determined to rule out carcinoma of the prostate. Several objective tests are available to assist in evaluating the back: CAT scan, X rays, thermography, myelography, ultrasound, and electromyography (EMG). **Table 2–2** lists some simple nonquantitative tests that can be performed as part of the physical examination.

Table 2–2.

Main and Waddell Low Back Pain Assessment Scales[1]

	Yes	No
I. Inappropriate Symptoms		
1. Pain at the tip of tailbone	1	0
2. Whole leg sometimes painful	1	0
3. Whole leg sometimes numb	1	0
4. Whole leg sometimes gives way	1	0
5. Spells in the past year with very little pain	0	1
6. Intolerance of or reactions to treatment	1	0
7. Emergency admissions to hospital with back trouble	1	0

(Each symptom is scored 1 if present and 0 if absent; a "no" answer to question five is scored 1. A higher score creates a higher index of suspicion. Total scores range from 0 to 7.)

II. Inappropriate Signs

Tenderness. Examiner looks for sensitivity to superficial touch, especially in areas not corresponding to anatomical pattern.

Simulation. Examiner gives impression a test will cause pain when it should not—e.g., pressing down on patient's head (axial loading), having patient rotate entire body (versus rotating at waist), and pressing flexor tendons at sides of knee (versus pressing on sciatic nerve).

Distraction. Examiner looks for discrepancies between abilities to perform the same test in different positions—e.g., having patient try to touch toes while standing, then while sitting; having patient raise leg while sitting, then while supine.

Regional Disturbances. Examiner looks for reports of weakness or sensory disturbances that do not correspond to anatomical patterns.

Over-reaction to Examination. Examiner watches for groaning, grimacing, clutching body parts, etc.

(Signs are scored 1 if present and 0 if absent.)

---

[1] C.J. Main & G. Waddell, *The Detection of Psychological Abnormality in Chronic Low Back Pain Using Four Simple Scales*, 2 Current Concepts in Pain 10–15 (1984).

Psychological examination.   Occasionally, if the history, observations, clinical examination, and laboratory and radiologic tests are inconclusive or inconsistent, it may be necessary to refer a patient for psychological testing to determine whether pain has an organic or nonorganic source. The *Handler Questionnaire* and the *Minnesota Multiphasic Personality Inventory* (MMPI) are considered useful for this purpose.

EVALUATING IMPAIRMENT

§ 2.20   Chronic Subjective Complaints

Trauma to the ligaments between the vertebrae and the paravertebral muscula-ture, by definition, implies no specific involvement of the intervertebral discs. Ligament and muscle injury is relatively rare in healthy people below the age of 30. It is much more common in people over age 30 who gain weight and exercise only occasionally, if at all. It is very common in women who have had several pregnancies with marked weight gain.

   If there is no involuntary muscle spasm and only subjective symptoms, and if the pain is not substantiated by demonstrable structural pathology, the patient should be regarded as having no (zero percent) whole-body permanent physical impairment (loss of physical function).

§ 2.21   Chronic Pain: Objective Findings

Pain lasting more than six to eight weeks is considered chronic. If the patient has had a severe contusion or strain of the low back, combined with persistent muscle spasm and rigidity, and if pain is substantiated by demonstrable degenerative pathology, such as arthritic changes on X ray, the patient is entitled to 10-percent whole-body permanent physical impairment (loss of physical function). The percentage of impairment simply is a rough guideline to be tempered by the physician's overall impression of the patient, the patient's job, treatment to date, and all the other factors already discussed.

§ 2.22   Fractures

A compression fracture usually results from a fall and is most common in the lower thoracic and upper lumbar vertebrae. It can be readily diagnosed on X ray by the wedge-shaped appearance of the vertebrae. If the patient has marked osteoporosis, the trauma needed to cause a compression fracture of the vertebra often is quite minimal—a minor slip or fall or even sudden lifting of a relatively light object.

Most compression fractures are treated conservatively with bed rest and analgesics. A very small percentage may be associated with initial medical complications, such as secondary paralytic ileus or retroperitoneal hematoma. Occasionally, there may be venous thrombosis with pulmonary embolism.

Compression fracture 25 percent of the vertical height of the vertebral body.
A compression fracture of 25 percent involving one or two vertebral bodies, with no fragmentation and no neurologic manifestations, entitles the patient to approximately 10-percent whole-body permanent physical impairment (loss of physical function).

Compression fracture 50 percent of the vertical height of the vertebral body.
A compression fracture of 50 percent, with involvement of posterior elements but no neurologic manifestations and persistent pain, would entitle the patient to approximately 20-percent whole-body permanent physical impairment (loss of physical function).

Total paraplegia (total paralysis of the lower extremities).   In the rare case of vertebral fracture resulting in total paraplegia, the patient would be entitled to 100-percent whole-body permanent physical impairment (loss of physical function).

§ 2.23   Spondylolysis and Spondylolisthesis

Spondylolysis and spondylolisthesis are caused by stress on the pars inter-articularis of the vertebral body. *Spondylolysis* is strictly defined as a unilateral or bilateral defect in the isthmus with no definite vertebral slippage. *Spondylolis-thesis* is a bilateral defect in which the affected vertebral body and transverse processes slip forward in relation to the vertebral body immediately below. The posterior elements of the affected vertebral body (spinous process and lamina) remain in their normal positions.

Spondylolisthesis is classified from grade I (0 to 25-percent slippage) to grade IV (complete forward displacement). Most commonly, the fifth lumbar vertebra is involved; next in order is the fourth lumbar vertebra.

Spondylolysis and spondylolisthesis can be seen readily on oblique X ray view. A normal vertebra gives the appearance of a Scotty dog. If the dog seems to have a collar, there is a defect in the isthmus, and the patient has spondylolysis. If the dog appears decapitated, the condition is spondylolisthesis (see **Figure 2–7**). Progressive spondylolisthesis may require spinal fusion.

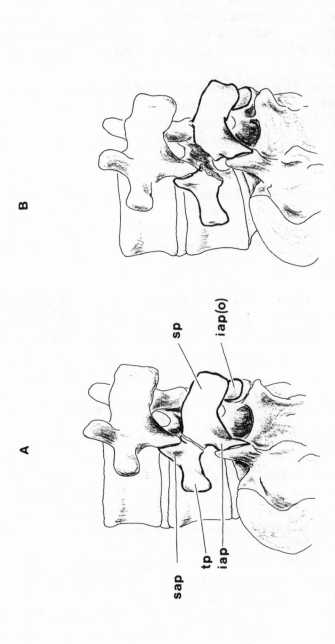

Figure 2–7. Spondylolysis and spondylolisthesis. Both views are posterior oblique views. A indicates spondylolysis; B shows spondylolisthesis. In use of the "Scotty dog" analogy, the transverse process (tp) is the nose, the superior articular process (sap) the ear, the inferior articular process (iap) the front leg, the spinous process (sp) the body, and the inferior articular process of the opposite side (iap(o)) the hind leg. Presence of a "collar" indicates spondylolytic condition; decapitation indicates spondylolisthesis.

In general, grade I or II spondylolisthesis proven on X ray, but treated without surgery, entitles the patient to 20-percent permanent physical impairment (loss of physical function). If the patient has grade III or IV spondylolisthesis, with persistent pain but no surgery, she is entitled to 35-percent permanent physical impairment (loss of physical function). A patient who has any degree of spondylolisthesis, but only moderate pain after spinal fusion, is entitled to 25-percent permanent physical impairment (loss of physical function).

§ 2.24   Disc Injury

Acute disc herniation.   Acute disc herniation (rupture of the nucleus pulposus through the annulus fibrosus, see **Figure 2–8**) often will respond to conservative treatment: total bed rest, pain medication, heat, and sedatives. Most patients will respond to this regimen at home, but some require total bed rest in a hospital, often with traction. Prolonged bed rest usually decreases the pain and irritation of the affected nerve roots. Although the disc does not retreat into the disc space, it tends to shrink somewhat with clinical improvement. After pain has sufficiently decreased, the patient usually is started on spinal exercises to strengthen the back and prevent recurrences. A back brace or corset may give some relief during this phase. In general, however, the patient should be encouraged to strengthen her back with regular exercises, especially sit-ups, rather than depend on a brace, which may eventually cause atrophy of the paravertebral musculature.

Periodic acute episodes.   A patient with periodic acute episodes of back pain with positive sciatic tests and temporary recovery after five to eight weeks is entitled to 5-percent permanent physical impairment (loss of physical function).

Disc problems after laminectomy.   A small percentage of patients with ruptured disc documented by myleogram and/or CAT scan will not respond to bed rest and conservative care. Such patients may benefit from surgical intervention (see **Figure 2–9**). Unfortunately, surgery, even in the best of hands and under the best of circumstances, gives unpredictable results. A patient who has had surgical excision of the disc and laminectomy but no fusion, with good results and no persistent sciatic pain, is entitled to approximately 10-percent permanent physical impairment (loss of physical function). If, however, moderate pain and stiffness aggravated by heavy lifting persist after surgery and require modification of activities, the patient is entitled to 20-percent whole-body permanent physical impairment (loss of physical function).

Laminectomy and fusion.   In the past, most laminectomies were accompanied by spinal-fusion—bone taken from the patient's pelvis applied to one or more vertebral bodies to fuse them to the pelvis. Fusion now is thought to yield no

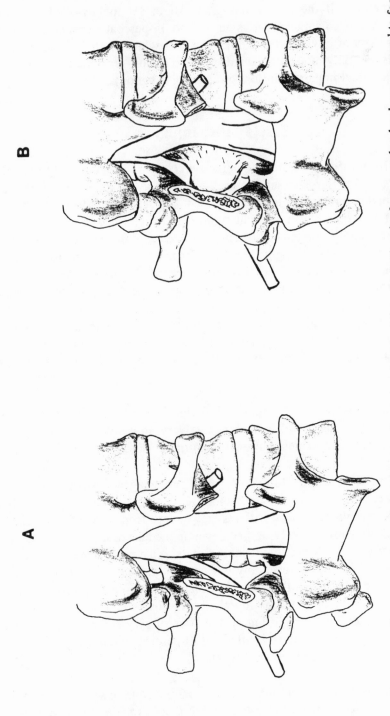

Figure 2–8. The herniated disc. View A depicts normal anatomy. Much of the vertebral arch of one vertebra has been removed to facilitate visualization. View B shows the protrusion (herniation) of an intervertebral disc, with impingement on the spinal nerve as it exits from the column through the intervertebral foramen.

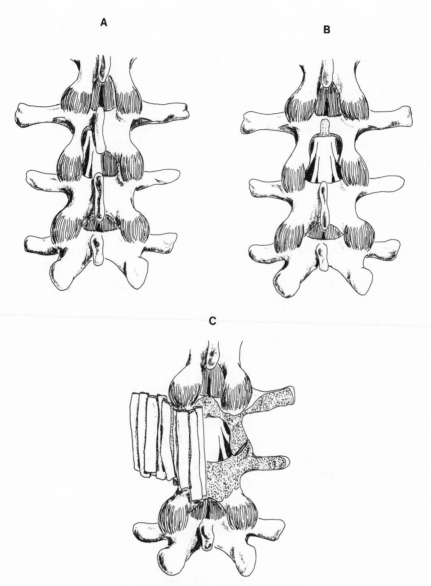

Figure 2–9. Laminectomy, spinal fusion. View A shows the removal of a portion of the vertebral lamina to expose the spinal cord and spinal nerves. View B is a bilateral laminectomy, indicating the extent of the defect produced. View C shows removal of the outer layer of bone from the posterior surfaces of the vertebral arches of two adjacent vertebrae, with positioning of bony grafts (shown on one side only) to attain fusion of the vertebrae and thereby increase stability.

sufficiently better results than laminectomy alone that would justify the additional morbidity and pain. However, if a patient does heavy work and has proven spinal instability, spinal fusion may be justified. A patient who has had surgical excision of a disc with fusion, requiring moderate modification of activities involving lifting, is entitled to 15-percent whole-body permanent physical impairment (loss of physical function). If pain persists after surgical excision of a disc with fusion and is aggravated by heavy lifting that necessitates modification of all activities requiring heavy lifting, the patient is entitled to 25-percent whole-body permanent physical impairment (loss of physical function).

§ 2.25   Who Pays

Frequently, a patient may sustain injury on different jobs covered by different workers' compensation insurers. Take the case of Joe Jones, who strains his back in December 1985 digging ditches for Alpha Construction Company (protected by Great Eastern Insurance Company). He recovers completely after several weeks and gets a job with Beta Construction Company (protected by Great Western Insurance Company). Joe strains his back again in September 1986 and seeks benefits. Great Western may claim this is an exacerbation of the previous injury of December 1985 and refuse to pay, saying Great Eastern is responsible. Great Eastern may claim the second injury is new and totally unrelated and suggest that Great Western must pay. The physician may be asked to solve the problem. The answer is that if more than six months have elapsed between episodes of back strain (with no objective evidence of disc herniation) the second episode is new and unrelated to the first. Great Western must, therefore, pay for Joe's September-1986 injury.

PROGNOSIS

§ 2.26   Factors in Recovery

Before determining whether physical impairment and loss of physical function are permanent, the physician must determine whether all potentially beneficial treatments have been exhausted.

The time interval between injury and examination is critical. If only two or three weeks have elapsed and the patient is relatively young, the chance of complete recovery is quite good. If more than 18 months have elapsed since the injury and the patient is in her 40s or 50s, the prognosis must be guarded. Even after back surgery, a full year must be allowed before maximal improvement can be expected.

§ 2.27   The Back Loser: Failed Back Syndrome

It is somewhat deceiving to think that evaluation of low back pain is merely a matter of knowing spinal anatomy and physiology and the potential biochemical or structural causes of back problems. Some patients with back complaints never recover, despite appropriate treatment. Novack has defined the *low back loser* as a "person who physically, psychiatrically, vocationally, and socially is totally and permanently disabled due to low back pain and its treatment."[2]

Novack differentiates the low back loser from the manipulator: "Manipulators are patients who are believed to have back pain, but are able to change or use social structures and supporting systems to their advantage." Manipulators are very different from malingerers, who consciously exaggerate or fake symptoms to avoid responsibility.

Table 2–3 summarizes the characteristics Novack found most often in a series of 220 patients referred to him who failed to respond to conservative and surgical treatment after 18 months. If a patient had seven of these characteristics, that patient became a back loser.

Table 2–3.

Ten Most Common Characteristics of the Low Back Loser[3]

Characteristic	Number of patients
Had work- or accident-related pain	217
Was mismanaged	187
Received excessive conservative management	145
Received excessive medication without relief	140
Showed psychosocial problems	90
Was treated surgically	69
Was obese	67
Reported more pain and neurologic deficit after treatment than originally after the accident	62
Showed drug dependence or addiction	45
Had less than average education	36

Consider the case of John Jones, a 48-year-old male driver of a car involved in a collision in which his vehicle sustained $3,000 in damage. He continued to work but developed back pain for the first time six weeks after the accident and only then took time off from work. He did not see a physician until six weeks after the accident because he tried to "live with the discomfort." A CAT scan done six

---

[2] J. Novak, *The Back Loser*, Lecture given at the Liberty Mutual Back Pain Symposium, Boston, Mass. (Mar. 22–24, 1981).

[3] *Id.*

weeks after the injury was interpreted as "negative," although the patient alleged
that he could not do his usual heavy and strenuous work.

Some useful observations:

1. The force of the collision clearly was substantial, judging by the dollar
   estimate of damage to the car.

2. Any blow of this magnitude can cause both immediate and delayed
   complications.

3. It is a reasonable medical certainty that the tissue which holds an intervertebral disc in place could be so weakened by the accident that a subsequent
   minimal twist could rupture the disc.

4. Although a "ruptured disc" was not demonstrated on the one CAT scan, a
   CAT scan has at least a 10-percent chance of giving either a false positive
   or a false negative result unless a dye-contrast material is used. Dye contrast
   is used in a very small percentage of CAT scans because of the potential
   reaction to the dye material itself.

5. One should remember that the cervical, thoracic, and lumbar vertebrae are
   all connected by a network of ligaments and muscles. If one area sustains a
   trauma, the other areas to some extent can compensate for the immediate
   injury and pain so that complaints may not be noted for some time.

6. As in cutting diamonds, a small blow or strain at exactly the crucial point
   can cause an already weakened disc to rupture.

CHAPTER 3

EVALUATION OF CERVICAL IMPAIRMENT

§ 3.1   Cervical Spine: Functional Anatomy

The cervical spine includes seven vertebrae (see **Figure 3–1**). Each two adjacent vertebrae and their interposed vertebral disc form a functional unit surrounding and protecting the spinal cord and associated nerve roots. The disc consists of the inner colloidal gel (nucleous pulposus) surrounded by the fibrous covering (annulus fibrous). The disc is a hydraulic shock absorber that permits movement of the functional unit. Each vertebral body is joined by ligaments that limit neck motion. Limitation in extremes of neck motion prevents damage to the intervertebral discs. The normal cervical spine has a lordotic curve, with its convexity anteriorly. This lordotic curve normally is maintained by two major functional muscle groups—flexors and extensors. Chronic spasm of these muscles will produce an X ray that shows a perfectly straight spine or even one with reversal of the normal lordotic curve. Such an X-ray finding is strongly suggestive of chronic cervical spasm and pain.

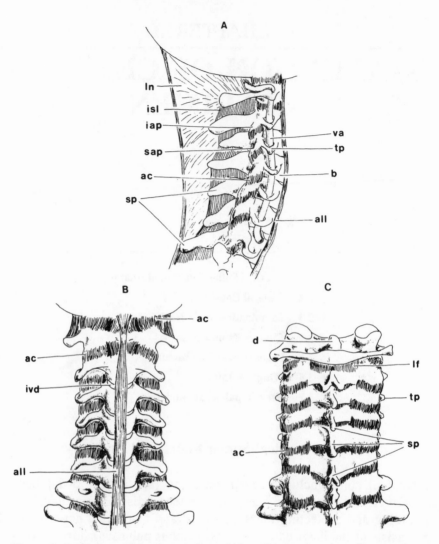

Figure 3–1. The cervical spine. A, lateral view; B, anterior view; C, posterior view of the cervical spine. Osseous elements depicted are the body (b), transverse process (tp), superior and inferior articular processes (sap, iap), spinous process (sp), and the dens (d) of the second cervical vertebra, or axis. Ligaments and other structures contributing to the union of the osseous components are the anterior longitudinal ligament (all), the interspinous ligaments (isl), the ligamentum flava (lf), the articular capsules (ac), the ligamentum nuchae (ln), and the intervertebral disc (ivd). Also depicted in the lateral view is the vertebral artery as it passes through the foraminae within the transverse processes on its way to the central nervous system within the skull.

§ 3.2   General Considerations

Steindler[1] has stated that the two most frequent causes of neck pain are arthritis and trauma. Both are related in that they cause encroachment of space and impairment of motion. Trauma in the cervical spine usually causes pain by creating inflammation of the soft tissues. Arthritis usually is a reparative condition after stress or injury.

Rene Cailliet[2] properly emphasizes that pain can be understood by reproducing the pain by a movement or position. It is, therefore, essential to understand the normal range of movement of the cervical spine to evaluate abnormal deviations and the mechanism of pain production.

§ 3.3   Examination of the Neck

Maximal movement of the spine occurs in the cervical area. The physician's exam must include flexion, extension, right and left lateral bending, and rotation (see **Figure 3–2**).

The physician should ask the patient to actually go through the range of movement up to the point of pain on several different occasions during the course of the examination and note carefully any discrepancies. Does the patient wear a cervical collar or brace? The patient should be observed leaving the office. It is not unusual to see the brace removed after the patient gets into his car, suggesting the collar was for the disability examiner's benefit, not the patient's.

In addition to testing range of motion, the examiner must do a complete neurologic examination, including sensory testing and motor strength in the arms and hands.

§ 3.4   Clinical Examination

Clinical examination must be used to localize the root level affected.

Paresthesia.   Forearm pain usually suggests C_6 or C_7 root involvement. Paresthesia in the thumb indicates compression of the C_6 nerve root. Paresthesia of the thumb and index finger suggests involvement of the C_7 nerve root. Paresthesias of the ring and little finger indicates C_8 root involvement (see **Figure 2–5**).

---

[1] A. Steindler, *The Cervical Spine Syndrome*, 14 Instructional Course Lectures, The American Academy of Orthopedic Surgeons (1975).

[2] *Neck Pain Originating in the Soft Tissues*, in Neck and Arm Pain 42–48 (2d ed. 1981).

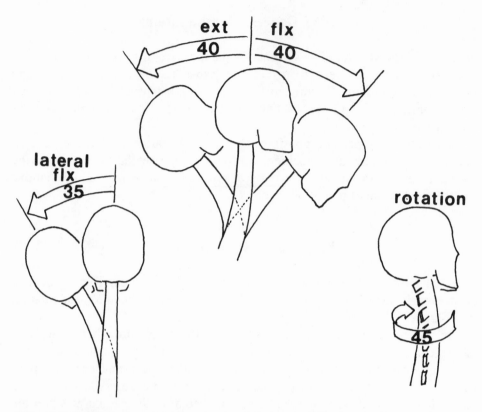

Figure 3–2. The range of motion (average) for each of the four basic movements of the cervical vertebral column.

Muscle testing.　Muscle testing is especially useful for localizing root lesions. C_5 weakness is revealed on arm abduction (deltoid) or external arm rotation (supraspinous, infraspinous). C_6 weakness is demonstrated by forearm suppination (biceps) and elbow flexion (brachialis). C_7 root involvement is demonstrated by elbow extension (triceps).

Tendon reflex testing.　Tendon reflex testing also is of value. Abnormality of the triceps reflex suggests C_7 root involvement. Brachioradialis reflex is diminished in C_6 root involvement.

X rays.　The physician should note in the X ray any obvious fractures or dislocations. Holdsworth[3] has made the important observation that if a vertebral body has dislocated less than half the width of the vertebrae below (A-P width), only one facet has dislocated (see **Figure 3–3**). This suggests a relatively stable

---

[3] F.W. Holdsworth, *Fractures, Dislocations, and Fracture Dislocation of the Spine,* 45D J. Bone & Joint Surgery 6–20 (1963).

A   B

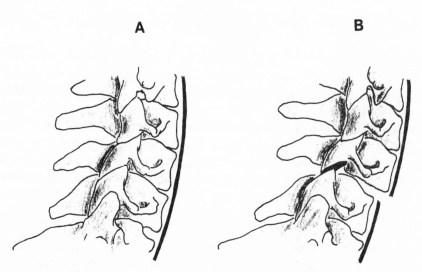

Figure 3–3. Subluxation in the cervical vertebral column. A indicates the normal configuration. In B, there has been forward movement of the superior elements of the column, disrupting the smooth contour of the cervical curvature and reducing the area of articulation between the facets of the involved vertebrae.

dislocation. Dislocation of both facets is represented by forward dislocation of *more than half* the A-P width of the vertebral body below. The physician should note any evidence of disc-space narrowing, suggesting degenerative changes in the affected disc, and any diffuse osteoarthritic changes, which might include osteophyte formation, deformity of the vertebral bodies, calcification in the anterior or posterior longitudinal ligaments, and other degenerative changes (see **Figure 2–6**).

§ 3.5 Degenerative Disc Disease

Degenerative disc disease is most common in C_5-C_6 and C_6-C_7 discs, the area of maximal movement of the cervical spine. Degenerative changes in the disc ultimately occur in all intervertebral discs and play a much greater role in pain production and disability than does acute disc herniation. Degeneration is the normal consequence of wear and tear, aging, injuries, and emotional stresses. Degenerative changes in the disc can alter local biomechanics, and eventual rubbing of one vertebral body on another can cause localized pain and be associated with limitation of neck motion. Pain radiating to the upper back, shoulder, and arms implicates the intervertebral foramen and all its contiguous tissues. Appropriate treatment may consist of analgesics, muscle relaxants, anti-inflammatory drugs, cervical traction, collar immobilization, or even cervical laminectomy.

§ 3.6 Whiplash Injury

Whiplash injury refers to ligamentous strain, most commonly seen when the patient is injured in a rear-end collision. The cervical spine undergoes rapid acute hyperextension reaction to a deceleration injury. The impact propels the body forward. Inertia leaves the head and neck in their initial position followed by abrupt movement in the opposite direction. See **Figure 3–4**. As a result, the neck musculature is suddenly stretched beyond normal physiological limits. This rapidly leads to edema, hemorrhage, spasm, and pain. The disability examiner should obtain a detailed history to determine the direction of impact and severity of the blow. The dollar damage to the car can suggest the severity of the impact. Most hyperflexion-hyperextension injuries resolve fully in six to eight weeks, but persistent symptoms documented by clinical objective findings and X-ray changes (loss of lordotic curvature) entitle the patient to about 10-percent permanent physical impairment and loss of physical function to the cervical spine.

The term "whiplash" is deeply entrenched medically and legally, although it is really quite vague and somewhat misleading. When a patient is injured in a rear-end collision, the terms *deceleration* or *acceleration* would more accurately describe the mechanics of the force, as would *hyperflexion* or *hyperextension*, terms which describe the reaction to the force by the head and neck. The degree of injury can further be defined as *sprain* (injury to a joint with possible rupture of some of the ligaments and tendons but without dislocation or fracture) or *strain* (torn muscles). One must further specify whether there is *subluxation* (partial malalignment of the articular cartilage of one vertebra with the adjacent

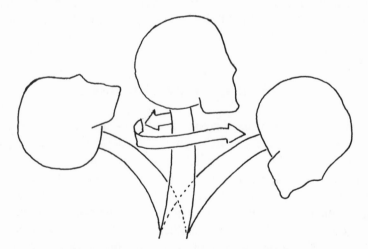

Figure 3–4. Diagrammatic representation of the hyperexten-sion/ hyperflexion sequence in whiplash injury. The relative degree of each of the movements should be compared with the normal extension/flexion movements (**Figure 3–2**).

vertebra), *dislocation* (complete lack of contact between the articular cartilage of adjacent vertebra) or *fracture* (broken bone).

Thus, an individual seated in a stopped car that is violently struck from behind is suddenly moved forward and his head "snapped" back—an acute cervical sprain due to an acute hyperextension reaction to an acceleration injury. The impact abruptly moves the lower portion of the body forward. The head obviously remains momentarily in place but then arcs backward through the path of extension. The backward movement is quick and catches the protective muscle reflex unprepared, causing abnormal force on the ligaments that would normally be protected by muscle contraction. As the extensor phase proceeds, the protective flexor muscles contract and cause a rebound motion as well as a compressive effect. Cervical pain results from cervical sprain in a deceleration injury, and irritation of contiguous tissues within the region of the neck can cause referred pain down either arm. The patient can also have symptoms affecting the sympathetic nervous system—deafness, dizziness, blurred vision, and pain behind the eyeballs. Professional Education Systems has prepared a videotape with computer simulation that graphically describes a whiplash accident. This tape can be very useful in demonstrating the mechanism of injury to a judge and jury.

§ 3.7   Neck Impairment Guidelines

Vertebral compression fractures of about 25 percent of one or two adjacent vertebral bodies, with no root involvement but moderate neck rigidity and persistent soreness, will entitle the patient to 20-percent impairment. Severe cervical dislocation with surgical fusion entitles the patient to 25-percent impairment if the results include no residual motor or sensory changes and to about 35-percent impairment if the end result includes partial paralysis, persistent radicular pain, and motor involvement.

Patients who have had surgical removal of a ruptured cervical intervertebral disc are entitled to about 10-percent impairment, even if there has been relief of pain and no neurologic residua. However, if the patient has neurological manifestations, such as persistent pain, numbness, and weakness of the fingers, even after cervical laminectomy, then a 20-percent impairment rating is appropriate.

CHAPTER 4

EVALUATION OF UPPER EXTREMITY IMPAIRMENT

SHOULDER AND HUMERUS

§ 4.1   Applied Anatomy

The shoulder joint consists of a rather shallow socket (glenoid fossa) in the scapula, which articulates with the humeral head (see **Figure 4–1**). The shallowness of the glenoid fossa allows for tremendous mobility of the humerus but also for considerable instability. The shoulder joint is capable of a considerable range of abduction and adduction, flexion, extension, internal and external rotation, and circumduction. About one-sixth of the articular surface of the head of the humerus is in contact with the glenoid surface. The shoulder, thus, is the joint most commonly dislocated, usually anteriorly. The scapula also articulates with the clavicle at the acromioclavicular joint. This joint is stabilized by the acromioclavicular, coracoacromial, and coracoclavicular ligaments. Damage to these ligaments results in the commonly seen acromioclavicular separation. The *axilla* is the pyramidal space formed between the arm and the thoracic wall. It contains the axillary vessels, the lymph nodes, and the brachial plexus, which includes nerve fibers from C_5 to T_1.

The shoulder itself is covered with the usual synovium, capsule, and multiple ligaments. This, in turn, is covered by the muscles acting on the shoulder, including the deltoid, which is responsible for the roundness of the shoulder.

Scapulothoracic rhythm.   Scapulothoracic rhythm describes the elevation of the normal arm (see **Figure 4–2**). In the first stage of abduction, movement occurs mainly at the glenohumeral joint. In the second stage, movement occurs mostly between the scapula and the thoracic cage. It is important to distinguish between glenohumeral movement and scapulothoracic movement. For example, in a frozen shoulder, the patient still is able to move the arm by rotary movement between the scapula and thorax. The examiner must fix the scapula by holding it firmly against the thoracic wall before asking the patient to abduct the arm.

Rotator cuff.   The *rotator cuff* is a musculotendinous structure that covers the upper half of the humeral head before insertion into the anatomical neck of the humerus (see **Figure 4–1**). It is formed by the fusion of the tendons of three muscles: supraspinatus, infraspinatus, and teres minor. Partial or complete tear of the rotator cuff will result in limitation of abduction.

Subdeltoid bursa.   The *subdeltoid bursa* is a fluid-containing sac that separates the rotator cuff from the acromial arch (see **Figure 4–1**). An effusion of the bursa will, therefore, be accompanied by pain when shoulder movement occurs due to distension of the bursa—subdeltoid bursitis.

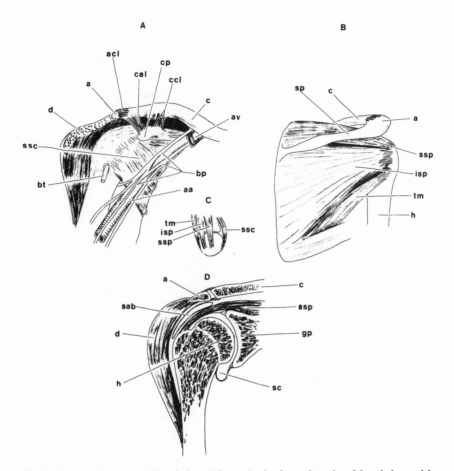

Figure 4–1. The shoulder joint. View A depicts the shoulder joint with the anterior element of the rotator cuff, ligamentous structures lending to stability of the shoulder, and the relationship to the axillary neurovascular elements. Structures indicated are the clavicle (c), acromion (ac), and coracoid process (cp). Uniting these bony elements are the acromioclavicular ligament (acl), the coracoacromial ligament (cal), and the coracoclavicular ligament (ccl). Muscles depicted are the deltoid (d), the subscapularis (ssc), and the tendon of the biceps muscle (bt). The axillary artery and vein (aa, av) and the brachial plexus of nerves are indicated. View B shows the posterior elements of the rotator cuffs. They are the supraspinatus (ssp), infraspinatus (isp), and teres minor (tm) muscles. Bony structures are the clavicle (c), acromion (ac), spine of the scapula (sp), and humerus. View C is a coronal section through the joint to show the relative shallowness of the glenohumeral joint and associated joint structures. The glenoid process (gp), synovial cavity (sc), and the subacromial bursa (sab) are depicted.

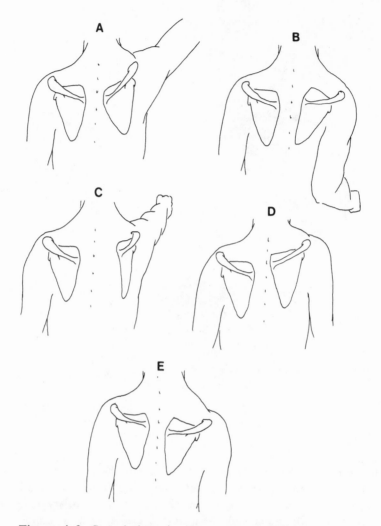

Figure 4–2. Scapulothoracic movements. A indicates upward (medial) rotation; B is downward (lateral) rotation; C is protraction; D is elevation; and E is depression. Scapular position in all movements should be compared with the neutral position of the opposite (left) side.

§ 4.2 Examination of the Shoulder

The patient is examined with the shoulders uncovered and the arms free. The examiner should carefully observe any muscle wasting of the deltoid muscle or rotator cuff. Careful palpation may reveal bursitis or rotator cuff tears.

Shoulder Movement Guidelines (see **Figure 4–3**)

forward flexion	160°
horizontal flexion	135°
backward extension	53°
abduction	170°
adduction	50°
rotation—arm at side	
internal rotation	70°
external rotation	70°
arm in abduction	
internal rotation	70°
external rotation	90°

§ 4.3 X rays

Dislocation. The examiner should observe carefully for any evidence of anterior or posterior dislocation (see **Figure 4–4**). It is not unusual for a posterior dislocation to have been missed on ordinary A-P and lateral X rays. The examiner should suspect posterior dislocation in cases of decreased ability to supinate the forearms. The suspicious examiner may need to obtain an axillary view or transthoracic lateral X ray.

Calcification. The examiner should observe for any evidence of calcification in the long head of the bicep tendon—calcific tendonitis.

Separation. The examiner should look for acromioclavicular separation (see **Figure 4–4**). If there is any tenderness over the acromioclavicular joint, it often is a good idea to take an A-P X ray with 15 pounds of weight held in the patient's hand to distinguish between first-, second-, and third-degree separation of the acromioclavicular joint.

Arthritic changes. The examiner should note arthritic change in the acromioclavicular joint as well as in the glenohumeral joint. This will manifest itself by narrowing, soft tissue calcification, and osteophyte formation.

Fractures. Fractures of the humeral head must be evaluated in terms of damage to the articular surface. The examiner also should check for the relatively rare case of osteomyelitis or malignancy.

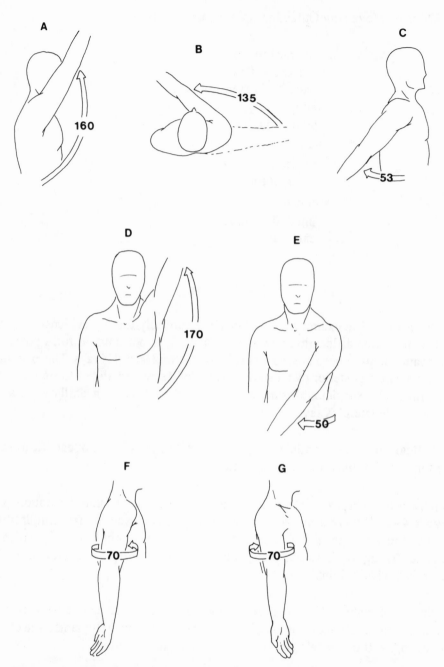

Figure 4–3. Types and normal range of basic arm movements. Depicted are forward flexion, A; horizontal flexion, B; backward extension, C; abduction, D; adduction (beyond anatomical position), E; internal rotation, F; and external rotation, G.

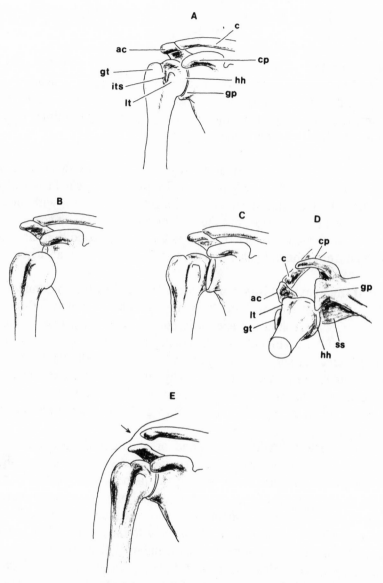

Figure 4–4. Shoulder dislocations and acromioclavicular joint separation. A depicts normal osseous anatomy. Shown is the clavicle (c), acromion (ac), coracoid process (cp), greater tubercle of the humerus (gt), lesser tubercle of the humerus (lt), the intertubercular sulcus (its), the head of the humerus (hh), and the glenoid process of the scapula (gp). B depicts an anterior dislocation; C and D posterior dislocation. C is the anterior-posterior projection; D is an axillary view (ss is the spine of the scapule). View E depicts separation of the acromioclavicular joint.

§ 4.4   Common Conditions Affecting the Shoulder Joint

Chronic tendonitis.   Chronic tendonitis is characterized by a dull ache caused by degeneration in the suprasinatus tendon near its insertion. It usually occurs in middle age and may persist for several months. The condition usually responds to heat, anti-inflammatory medication, steroid injections, and time. It seldom is responsible for significant permanent impairment.

Frozen shoulder.   Frozen shoulder usually occurs in individuals over 40 years of age and frequently has prolonged course. Initially, there is pain and stiffness in the shoulder. The pain may become severe, often interfering with sleep. Over several months it may subside, but the patient may be left with some permanent restriction of movement and disability. It is a traumatic condition that should be distinguished from tuberculosis, premature arthritis, and osteoarthritis.

Fracture of the proximal humerus.   Most fractures of the anatomical and surgical neck of the humerus heal well with application of a sling for three months, followed by Codman shoulder exercises (see **Figure 4–5**). Unless there is an associated tear of the rotator cuff, usually no major loss of function occurs. Fractures involving the articular surface of the humeral neck, especially three-part and four-part comminuted fractures, must be treated by open reduction and internal fixation or a replacement arthroplasty-Neer prosthesis. Unfortunately, the results usually are less than optimal and are associated with significant restriction of movement.

Shoulder dislocation.   A single episode of shoulder dislocation usually responds well to a sling applied for about a week and usually has no significant residua. The prognosis, however, for a repeat dislocation depends on the age of the patient and the degree of trauma. Younger individuals are more likely to have a recurrence, especially if the initial trauma was relatively minimal. Alternatively, the older individual who sustains a major blow to the shoulder has considerably less likelihood of recurrence. After three documented dislocations, surgical repair is indicated. Recurrent dislocation, as frequently as every four to six months, entitles the patient to a 35-percent loss of function to the arm.

Acromioclavicular joint separation.   Separation of the acromioclavicular joint may result in arthritic changes in this joint. Most orthopedic surgeons will wait a full year for a surgical resection of the joint because many patients may be asymptomatic except for a bump in the area of the joint. Resection of the distal end of the clavicle for this condition, when necessary, entitles the patient to about a 5-percent impairment to the extremity.

Fractured clavicle.   Clavicle fractures usually heal with conservative treatment, leaving no significant impairment. At worst, the patient usually has only

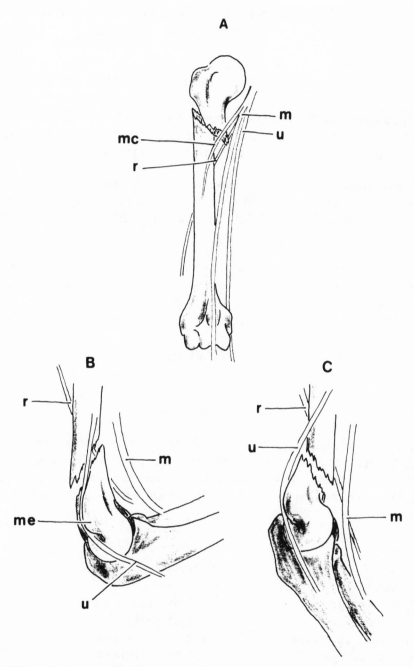

Figure 4–5. Humeral fractures. A indicates a fracture through the "surgical neck" of the humerus and the proximity of the four primary branches of the brachial plexus: the musculocutaneous (mc), radial (r), median (n), and ulnar (u) nerves. B and C indicate supracondylar fractures of the flexion and extension types, respectively, and the relationships to primary nerves.

minor cosmetic disfigurement from the healing callus. The occasional case of nonunion, however, may result in some limitation of motion.

§ 4.5 Shoulder Limitation Guidelines

Mild limitation.   Mild limitation of motion with no abduction beyond 90 degrees, but full flexion and extension, entitles the patient to about a 5-percent permanent physical impairment and loss of function to the arm.

Moderate limitation.   Moderate limitation of motion means no abduction beyond 60 degrees with flexion and extension limited to 30 degrees. Moderate limitation of motion would entitle the patient to about a 20-percent impairment to the arm.

Severe limitation.   Severe limitation of motion means no abduction beyond 25 degrees with flexion and extension limited to 20 degrees. This would entitle the patient to 50-percent impairment and loss of physical function to the arm.

ELBOW AND FOREARM

§ 4.6 Applied Anatomy

The trochlea of the humerus articulates with the semilunar notch of the ulna and the capitulum of the humerus with the fovea of the radial head (see **Figure 4–6**). The joint is surrounded by an articular capsule and radial and ulnar collateral ligaments, as well as a very extensive synovial membrane. Muscles acting on the joint are as follows:

Flexion	Extension
biceps	triceps
brachialis	anconeus
brachioradialis	extensor carpi radialis
pronator teres	longus and brevis
flexor carpi radialis and ulnaris	extensor digitorum communis
palmaris longus	extensor digiti minimi
flexor digitorum	extensor digiti carpi ulnaris supinator

All of these muscles combine to produce a humeroulnar joint which permits flexion and extension.

Pronation and supination (rotation) of the forearm is provided by the radioulnar joint, which is a trochoid or pivot joint. It is made up of the head of the radius

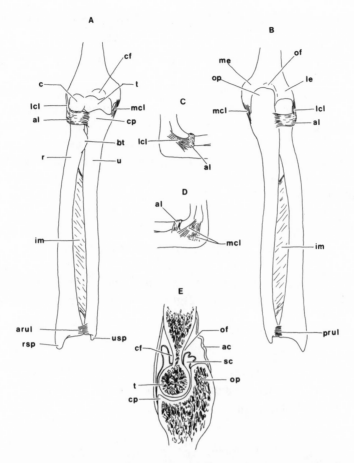

Figure 4–6. Normal osseous and ligamentous anatomy of the elbow and forearm. Views A and B depict anterior and posterior views, respectively. The indicated features of the humerus include the capitulum (c), trochlea (t), coronoid fossa (cf), the medial and lateral epicondyles (me and le), and the olecranon fossa (of). Features of the ulna (u) are the coronoid process (cp), the olecranon process (op), and the ulnar styloid process (usp). Features of the radius (r) are the bicipital tuberosity (bt), and the radial styloid process (rsp). The ligamentous elements of elbow, depicted in A, B, C, and D, include the lateral collateral ligament (lcl), the medial collateral ligament (mcl), the annular ligament (al) surrounding the head of the radius, the anterior and posterior radioulnar ligaments (arul and prul), and the interosseous membrane (im). View E is a sagittal section through the elbow, indicating the hinge nature of the joint, and depicting, in addition to the previously identified features, the extent of the synovial cavity (sc), and the attachments of the articular capsule (ac).

and the radial notch of the ulna. Muscles acting on the proximal radioulnar joint include:

Supination	Pronation
biceps and supinator	pronator teres
extensor of the thumb	pronator quadratus

As has been pointed out, the elbow really is a complex of three joints, all interrelated. Understanding of the anatomy is essential in evaluating impairment because structural damage often leads to decreased range of motion and measurable functional impairment.

§ 4.7   Examination of the Elbow

The patient is asked to actively move from full flexion to full extension and from full pronation to full extension (see **Figure 4–7**). Some rough guidelines are as follows:

Elbow	
flexion	145°
hyperextension	0°
Forearm	
pronation	70°
supination	85°

§ 4.8   X rays

The examiner should check carefully for any osteocartilaginous loose bodies in the joint that might limit movement. Calcification in the area of the lateral epicondyle sometimes is associated with tennis elbow. The presence or absence of fractures or other disruptions of the articular surface should also be noted. Periarticular heterotopic ossification is most commonly seen in the elbow after head trauma in the adult, even though the elbow was not initially injured in the direct trauma.

§ 4.9   Special Disability Conditions

Supracondylar fracture.   Supracondylar fractures usually are very comminuted and frequently are seen in high-speed vehicular injuries, as well as falls from heights. Whether treated surgically or closed, they result in substantial adhesions and secondary loss of motion.

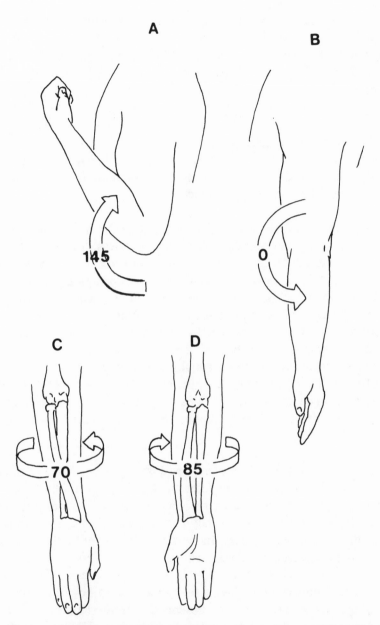

Figure 4–7. The four basic movements of the elbow and forearm and the degrees of average range of motion for each. A indicates flexion; B is extension (zero degrees indicates the extension does not go beyond normal position); C is pronation of the forearm, in which the radius crosses the ulna; D is supination. The range of movement for pronation is from anatomical position, while the range given for supination is from the pronated position (i.e., supination from the anatomical position would be approximately 15 degrees).

Olecranon fractures (see **Figure 4–8**).　The patient must be allowed a full year before an end point is reached in olecranon fractures. Slow or gradual improvement is noted with use, time, and physical therapy. Noncomminuted, nondisplaced fractures of the olecranon can be treated by splint or cast immobilization. Most olecranon fractures must be treated by open reduction with internal fixation, using either a long screw or tension band wiring.

Elbow dislocation (see **Figure 4–8**).　Relatively common, elbow dislocations usually do well after two to three weeks of immobilization. Formal physical therapy stressing active rather than passive range of motion exercises is essential to restore strength and prevent recurrence.

Radial head fractures (see **Figure 4–8**).　Most radial head fractures respond well to closed rather than surgical treatment, regardless of the extent of depression or comminution of fragments. Many orthopedic surgeons feel that the only indication for operative intervention is a loose fragment in the joint. Depending on its size, this either can be removed or internally fixed. Preservation of the radial head is important because complete removal of the radial head has been shown to be associated with about 15-percent permanent physical impairment and loss of physical function to the arm. In every case of radial-head fracture, the examiner should check carefully for a tear or complete avulsion of the triceps tendon. This may be manifested clinically as swelling, tenderness, ecchymosis, and a palpable gap in the tendon continuity. The gap is often best demonstrated by having the patient extend the elbow against gravity.

Fractures of the radial and ulnar shaft (see **Figure 4–8**).　Fractures of the radial and ulnar shaft (both bones of the forearm) are notoriously disabling injuries, ideally treated in major centers by surgeons with considerable experience. Open reduction with internal fixation, usually compression plates, is the treatment of choice. In the best of hands under the best of circumstances, the usual result is significant loss of pronation and supination.

Tennis elbow.　Tennis elbow often is seen in workers who use the wrist strenuously and repetitively. Tennis elbow presents clinically as marked tenderness on deep palpation over the lateral epicondyle of the humerus. It also presents as pain in the elbow when the patient is asked to forceably extend the index finger against resistance. Pathology is microscopic rupture of the tendon of the extensor carpi radialis brevis. Microscopically, there is invasion of fibroblasts and vascular granulation. Most of the time, the condition will respond to rest, heat, steroid injections, and a tennis-elbow band worn two inches distal to the elbow. Although surgery is occasionally necessary, tennis elbow usually is a self-limiting condition not associated with significant impairment.

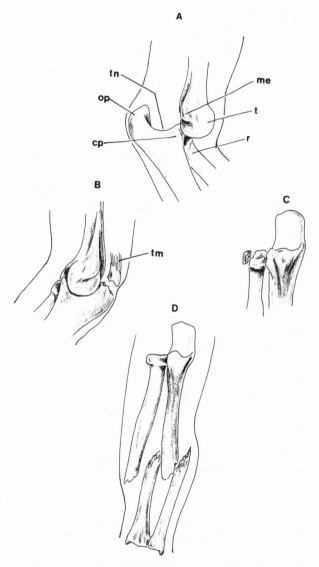

Figure 4–8. Dislocation and fractures of the elbow and the forearm. View A shows posterior dislocation of the elbow. Indicated is the medial epicondyle of the humerus (me), the trochlea of the humerus (t), the trochlear notch (tn), olecranon process (op), and coronoid process (cp) of the humerus, and the radius (r). View B is of a fractured olecranon process, with the proximal fragment being displayed by the pull of the triceps muscle (tm). In C one of many different forms of radial head fracture is depicted. View D shows fracture and displacement of the shafts of both the radius and ulna.

Compartment syndrome. The devastating condition known as compartment syndrome can develop rapidly or insidiously. It is associated with neurovascular compromise and measurable intracompartmental pressures exceeding 40 mm of mercury. Failure to make the diagnosis early and to perform a fasciotomy can lead to partial or full paralysis of the hand and the forearm. The most sensitive early diagnostic test is pain produced by passive motion of the fingers.

§ 4.10   Elbow Limitation Guidelines

Mild limitation of motion. Motion limited from 10-degrees flexion to 100-degrees further flexion entitles the patient to about 10-percent impairment of the arm.

Moderate limitation of motion. Motion limited from 30-degrees flexion to 75-degrees further flexion entitles the patient to about 20-percent impairment of the arm.

Severe limitation of motion. Motion limited from 45-degrees flexion to 90-degrees further flexion entitles the patient to about 35-percent impairment of the arm.

Total ankylosis. With the elbow in optimal position at a 45-degree angle, the patient is entitled to about 50-percent impairment of the arm.

WRIST AND HAND

§ 4.11   Applied Anatomy
(see Figures 4–9, 4–10, 4–11)

The distal radius and ulna articulate with the four proximal carpal bones: scaphoid, lunate, triquetrum, and pisiform. The navicular is the most frequently fractured and dislocated of all the carpal bones. Its blood supply is provided by branches of the dorsal and volar carpal arteries via the dorsal and volar ligaments from the radius. Although the bone can survive if only one ligament is torn and early reduction is effected, tear of both ligaments invariably results in asceptic necrosis. Distal to the four proximal carpal bones are the distal carpal bones: trapezium, trapezoid, capitate, and hamate. Moving distally, the next bones are the five metacarpals and five phalanges. The palmar carpal ligament is a transverse band of fascia extending between the radial and ulnar styloid process. Entrapment of the medial nerve beneath this ligament is the cause of the quite common carpal tunnel syndrome, which is best treated by surgical incision of this ligament.

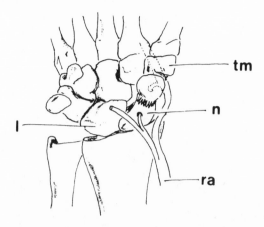

Figure 4–9. The osseous wrist, palmar aspect. Indicated are the navicular (n), trapezium (tm), and lunate (l) bones. The most frequent site of the fracture of the navicular is indicated by the chevroned line. The blood supply to the navicular is commonly from both palmar and dorsal branches of the radial artery (ra).

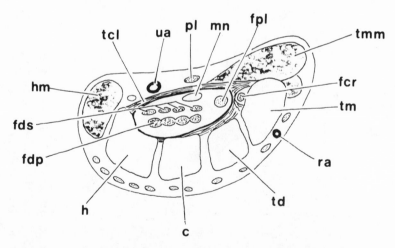

Figure 4–10. A cross section through the wrist, indicating carpal tunnel, its contents, and other related structures. The carpal tunnel is formed by the transverse carpal ligament (tcl), and the distal row of carpal bones: the hamate (h), cuboid (c), trapezoid (td), and trapezium (tm). Passing through the tunnel are the median nerve (mn), tendons of the flexor pollicis longus (fpl), flexor digitorum superficialis (fds), and flexor digitorum profundus (fdp). More superficially related to the tunnel are the hypothenar, or little finger muscles (hm), the thenar or thumb muscles (tmm), the ulnar artery (ua), and the tendon of palmaris longus (pl). Also indicated are the radial artery (ra) and the tendon of flexor carpi radialis (fcr).

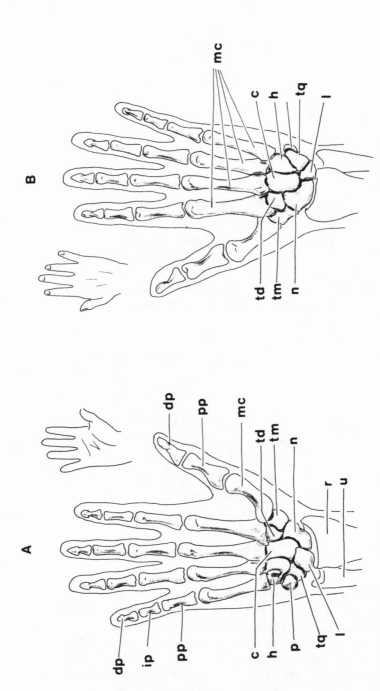

Figure 4–11. The osseous hand, palmar (A), and dorsal (B) views. Within the proximal row of carpals are the navicular (n), lunate (l), triquetral (tq), and pisiform (p) bones. The distal row consists of the trapezium (tm), trapezoid (tz), capitate (c), and hamate (h) bones. Each digit has a single metacarpal bone (mc). The thumb has two phalangeal bones, the proximal (pp) and distal phalanx (dp), while each of the medial four digits has a proximal, intermediate, distal phalanx (pp, ip, and dp, respectively). Also indicated are the distal radius (r) and

The superficial position of the vessels, nerves, and tendons at the wrist makes them very vulnerable to injury (see **Figure 4–10**).

Radial artery.   The radial artery is quite superficial, with the flexor carpi radialis tendon just medial to it.

Ulnar artery.   The ulnar artery is covered only by a carpal ligament and skin. Substantial collateral circulation is present so that laceration of either artery above the wrist usually is not associated with impairment.

Tendon of palmaris longus.   The tendon of palmaris longus is very superficial, crossing the wrist near its middle. It usually is absent in 10 percent of the population and is frequently surgically excised for tendon grafting without functional loss.

Tendons of flexor digitorum sublimus.   The flexor digitorum sublimus tendons are arranged so that the middle and ring fingers are superficial to those of the index and little finger.

Tendons of the flexor digitorum profundus.   The flexor digitorum profundus tendons are arranged in order, deep to the sublimus tendon. Complete laceration of a sublimus tendon without damage to the profundus tendon to the same finger is not associated with significant impairment.

§ 4.12   Nerve Damage

Nerve damage may present itself as (1) loss of sensation in the area of cutaneous distribution or (2) paralysis of voluntary muscle supplied (see **Figure 4–12**). The latter is demonstrated by an inability to perform certain functions and by the atrophy of the muscles supplied.

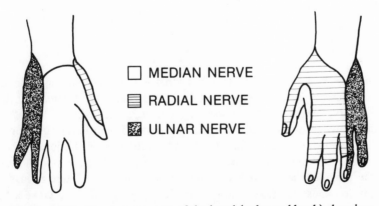

Figure 4–12. Dermatome map of the hand (palm and back) showing which nerves innervate skin areas.

Ulnar nerve damage.   Ulnar nerve damage presents as loss of sensation on the medial side of the palm and the little finger, as well as wasting of the hypothenar eminence and the interosseous muscles (see **Figure 4–13**). The result is an inability to abduct or adduct the fingers and an inability to adduct the thumb.

Radial nerve damage.   Radial nerve damage presents as loss of sensation on the dorsum of the hand and wrist drop (see **Figure 4–13**).

Median nerve damage.   Median nerve damage presents as loss of sensation on the palmar surface of the index and middle fingers, wasting of the thenar eminence, and inability to oppose the thumb (see **Figure 4–13**).

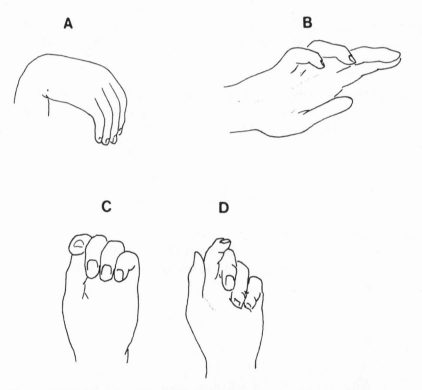

Figure 4–13. Functional loss in the wrist and hand following primary nerve injury. A indicates the "wrist drop" characteristic of damage to the radial nerve. Extension of the wrist and the fingers is lost. B indicates the "ulnar claw" resulting from damage to that nerve. The little and ring fingers are in hyperextension at the m-p joints and are flexed at the i-p joints. There is wasting of the intrinsic muscles of the hand, with the exception of those of the thumb. C and D indicate median nerve damage. There is loss of ability to oppose the fingers to the thumb (C) and inability to make a fist (D).

§ 4.13 General Considerations

Lee Milford stresses the importance of the function of the hand, not just of anatomic restoration. As Milford points out,

> The hand is an organ of exquisite sensation, able, for example, to recognize and distinguish by fingertip touch, the various qualities of cloth textures, of knife blade sharpness, of paper thickness—qualities not always obvious to the eye. It also performs the mechanical functions of hook, grasp, and pinch; hook, as in tilting a book from a shelf; grasp, as in picking it up; pinch, as in turning its pages. The loss or diminution of any of these functions is a serious disability.[1]

Anthropologists have attributed the rise of civilization to the human hand, especially the placement of the thumb that allows the use of tools. The ape has a very proximal thumb, which does not allow significant pulp-to-pulp opposition or the ability to hold and use tools. Preservation of maximal thumb length is essential for effective care of the hand. Although the thumb is only one of five digits, its complete loss entitles the patient to at least a 50-percent impairment of the hand.

§ 4.14 Examination of the Hand

The patient is asked to go through a complete active and passive range of motion of the wrist and fingers. Deep palpation of the navicular may reveal an acute navicular fracture that may not appear on X rays for two to three weeks.

Wrist Movement Guidelines (see **Figure 4–14**)

Wrist	
extension	70°
flexion	75°
ulnar deviation	35°
radial deviation	20°

Thumb and Fingers Movement Guidelines (see **Figure 4–15**)

Thumb	
abduction	60°
flexion	
I-P joint	80°
M-P joint	55°
M-C joint	15°

---

[1] Campbell's Operative Orthopedics 111 (1980).

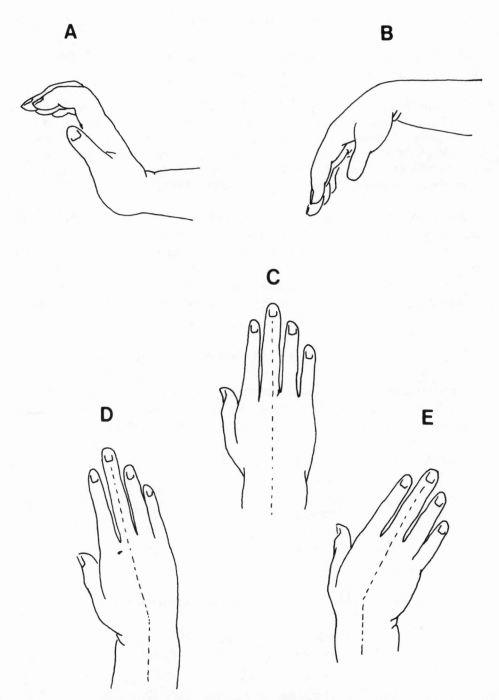

Figure 4–14. The basic movements at the wrist. A is extension; B is flexion. C indicates the neutral position and the fact that the axis of the hand passes through the middle finger. D is radial deviation at the wrist; E is ulnar deviation.

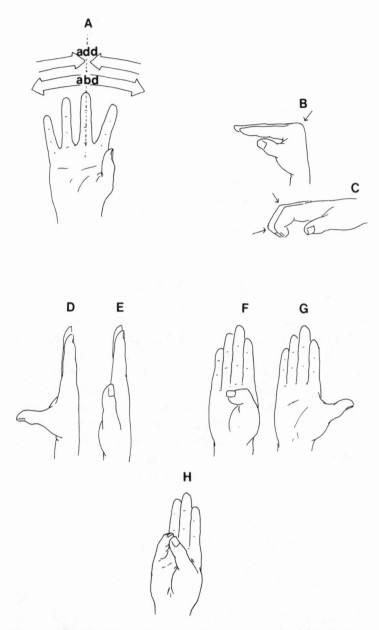

Figure 4-15. Basic movements of the fingers and thumb. View A illustrates abduction and adduction. Note that the middle finger is the axis of the hand. In view B, metacarpophalangeal flexion is displayed; view C shows flexion of the proximal and distal interphalangeal joints. Views D–H show the basic movements of the thumb. They are abduction, D; adduction, E; flexion, F; extension, G; and opposition, H.

extension	
distal joint	15°
M-P joint	10°
M-C joint	20°
Fingers	
flexion	
distal joint	80°
middle joint	100°
proximal joint	90°
extension	
distal joint	0°
middle joint	0°
proximal joint	45°

§ 4.15   X rays

The examiner should always look at the lateral view of the wrist for a lunate dislocation that may have been missed. A fracture of the navicular (see **Figure 4–9**) may not appear on the X rays for two to three weeks, so most orthopedic surgeons suggest that a "sprained wrist" and marked tenderness over the navicular be treated with a cast followed by repeat X rays and repeat examination after two weeks. Arthritic degeneration will manifest itself by joint-space narrowing and diffuse osteophyte formation. The presence of foreign bodies should always be noted. Metallic fragments are readily visible, and glass fragments are identifiable if the glass contains lead. Angulation of up to 40 degrees of the fifth metacarpal (Boxer's fracture) normally is not associated with any functional impairment.

§ 4.16   Some Common Conditions

Painful amputation stump.   Pain in an amputation stump is usually due to a neuroma located in an unpadded area near the end of the stump. Diagnosis is made by pressing the stump with the blunt end of a pencil and identifying a well-localized area of tenderness one or two millimeters in diameter, usually in line with a digital nerve. The treatment of choice is division of the nerve at a more proximal level where its end will be padded by sufficient soft tissue. Pain in an amputation stump also may be caused by inadequate distal skin coverage, requiring a limited advancement flap.

Dupuytren's contracture.   Dupuytren's contracture is caused by proliferated fibroplasia of the palmar fascia, resulting in nodules and cords (see **Figure 4–16**).

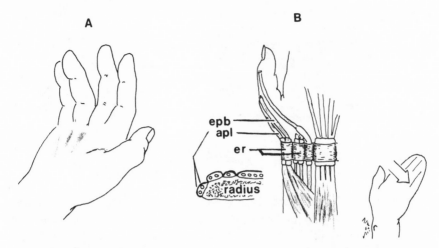

Figure 4–16. Dupuytren's contracture and stenosing tenosynovitis. A indicates the formation of fibrous cords in the palmar aponeurosis of the hand, pulling the fingers into flexion at the m-p joints. B depicts basic anatomy of the radial aspect of the dorsum of the wrist, showing the two tendons involved in stenosing tenosynovitis. They are the extensor pollicis brevis (epb) and abductor pollicis longus (apl). Also shown is the extensor retinaculum, which holds the tendons and their associated tendon sheaths next to the lateral margin of the radius. Ulnar deviation of the hand produces pressure of these structures against the radius, producing pain.

Pitting or dimpling of the skin is also usually seen. Etiology is unknown. It is seen more commonly in males than in females (10:1), typically after age 40. It usually involves the ring and little fingers, often bilaterally (45 percent). The treatment of choice is partial fasciectomy. Impairment depends on the amount of associated flexion, contracture of the fingers.

Carpal tunnel syndrome. Carpal tunnel syndrome occurs most commonly in females (5:1), usually between the ages of 30 and 60. It can be caused by any condition that reduces the capacity of the carpal tunnel (see **Figure 4–10**), such as a malaligned Colles' fracture (see **Figure 4–17**), infection, tumor, diabetes, thyroid disfunction, and trauma. It is quite common in women who use their wrists repetitively, as in cooking, typing, or knitting. Clinically, it presents as paresthesia over the sensory distribution of the median nerve (volar surface of the thumb, index, and long fingers). Thenar eminence atrophy is seen to some degree in about 50 percent of cases. Strenuous use of the hand or acute flexion of the wrist for 60 seconds increases the paresthesia. Persistent symptoms usually respond well to early surgical removal of the deep transverse carpal ligament.

DeQuervain's stenosing tenosynovitis. DeQuervain's disease is often seen in carpenters, elevator operators, and waitresses, usually in ages 30 to 50. These

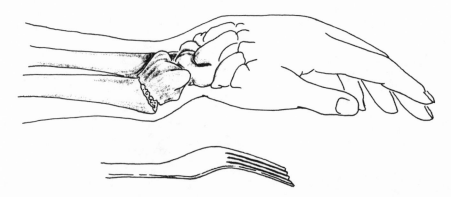

Figure 4–17. Colles' fracture of the wrist. The distal portion of the radius has been displaced subsequent to fracture, imparting to the wrist and hand the "silver fork" deformity.

individuals experience recurrent mild trauma to the wrist. The condition consists of inflammation of the abductor pollicis longus and extensor pollicis brevis tendons on the radial side of the wrist (see **Figure 4–16**). Finklestein's test is usually positive: "[O]n gripping the patient's thumb and quickly abducting the hand ulnaward. . . . [p]ain over the styloid tip is excruciating."[2] DeQuervain's disease usually responds to splinting and injection of cortisone but occasionally requires surgical release of the first dorsal compartment on its ulnar side.

Osteoarthritis.   Osteoarthritis in the hand presents as tenderness by palpation, stiffness, pain, and occasional joint swelling. It is frequently associated with osteophyte formation on the distal and proximal interphalangeal joints— Heberden's and Barchand's nodes, respectively. Relief can be obtained by rest, intra-articular steroid injections, and anti-inflammatory medication. Sometimes surgical joint fusion or resection arthroplasty is beneficial.

Bennett's fractures of the thumb.   Fractures at the base of the thumb, not including the joint, do well with closed reduction and casting. A Bennett's fracture occurs through the base of the thumb metacarpal, separating a triangular fragment of the metacarpal. Early surgical pinning is essential to prevent lateral and upward metacarpal displacement with subsequent severe degenerative arthritis.

Raynaud's phenomena.   Raynaud's phenomena is arterial spasm that may be triggered by emotional stress or exposure to cold. It usually occurs bilaterally in women around age 40. An acute episode may consist of sudden pallor or blanching of the fingers followed by cyanosis. Treatment consists of avoidance of exposure to cold, therapeutic drugs, and a surgical sympathectomy.

---

[2] H. Finklestein, 30 J. Bone & Joint Surgery 509 (1930).

§ 4.17   Wrist Limitation Guidelines

Mild limitation of motion.   Mild limitation of motion of the wrist—15-degrees palmar flexion to 20-degrees dorsiflexion—entitles the patient to a 10-percent impairment.

Moderate limitation of motion.   Moderate limitation of motion of the wrist—10-degrees palmar flexion to 10-degrees dorsiflexion—entitles the patient to a 20-percent impairment.

Severe limitation of motion.   Severe limitation of motion of the wrist—5-degrees palmar flexion to 10-degrees dorsiflexion—entitles the patient to a 25-percent impairment.

Surgical resection of ulna.   Surgical resection of the distal end of the ulna after malunited Colles' fracture entitles the patient to a 10-percent loss of function.

§ 4.18   Fingers and Thumb Limitation Guidelines

Mild limitation of motion.   Mild limitation—the patient can flex to touch palm and thumb—involves 15-percent impairment and loss of physical function to the finger.

Moderate limitation of motion.   Moderate limitation—the patient lacks one-half inch of touching palm—involves 50-percent loss of physical function to the individual finger.

Severe limitation of motion.   Severe limitation of motion—total closing lacks one inch of touching palm—involves 75-percent loss of physical function to the finger.

Soft tissue loss.   Isolated soft tissue loss of the end of the digit should have a value of up to 25 percent of the digit.

Amputation of digit excluding the thumb.   Up to half of distal phalanx—25 percent of the digit; from half to all of the distal phalanx—50 percent of the digit; any of the finger proximal to distal interphalangeal joint—100 percent.

Amputation of the thumb.   One-half of the distal phalanx—25 percent of the digit; at interphalangeal joint—25 percent of the digit; proximal and interphalangeal joint—100 percent.

CHAPTER 5

EVALUATION OF LOWER EXTREMITY IMPAIRMENT

PELVIS AND HIP

§ 5.1 Applied Anatomy

The pelvis is really a ring composed of three fused bones: the ilium, ischium, and pubis (see **Figure 5–1**). The anatomic functions of the pelvis include protection for abdominal viscera as well as support for the spine and legs. It also serves as a place of attachment for muscles to the trunk and lower extremities. On each side of the pelvic ring, the acetabulum or hip socket articulates with the head of the femur to form the hip joint. The femoral head points upward and forward in the acetabulum to allow the anterior portion of the head not to be engaged in the socket in the neutral leg position. This lack of coverage of the femoral head explains hip dislocation.

The joint is surrounded by a fibrous capsule, ligaments, synovial lining, and surrounding musculature. Trauma to any of these structures has been shown to elicit pain.

The articular cartilage itself is insensitive because it is avascular and lacks sensory pain fibers. However, the integrity of the articular cartilage is essential for lubrication and normal pain-free motion. Osteoarthritis (degenerative joint disease) can be painful and debilitating. It is characterized by degeneration of articular cartilage and eventual subchondral sclerosis. Blood supply is provided by the medial femoral circumflex, lateral femoral circumflex, obturator arteries, and branches from the gluteal artery. Damage to the circulation from trauma, fractures, or exposure to decreased oxygen tension (caisson disease) can produce aseptic necrosis of the femoral head, requiring eventual total hip replacement.

§ 5.2 Pathophysiology and General Considerations

Most fractures of the pelvis can be treated with bed rest. They may be associated with mild post-traumatic osteoarthritis but no significant functional impairment. For example, a simple fall may cause a stable impacted ramus fracture. With substantial impact—a motor vehicle accident or fall from great heights—serious disruptions of the pelvis may result. Such injuries may be associated with substantial blood loss and damage to intra-abdominal viscera. They are best treated with external fixation frames (Wagner apparatus). Extensive pelvis displacement may be associated with approximately 15- to 20-percent permanent impairment and loss of physical function. Acetabulum fractures require anatomic restoration of the articular surface, often obtainable by longitudinal traction with an open reduction and internal fixation. A step-off in the superior weight-bearing portion of the acetabulum of greater than 1 mm to 2 mm is associated with a particularly poor prognosis.

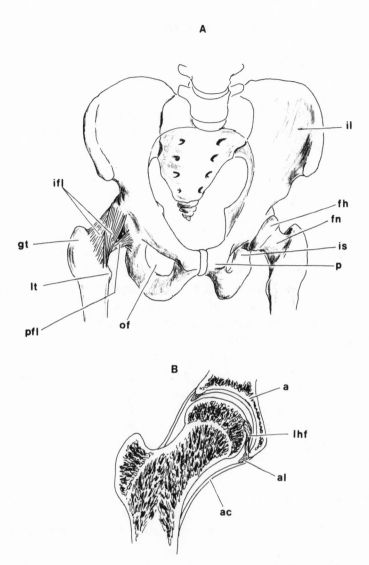

Figure 5–1. The bony pelvis and the hip joint. View A illustrates the basic bony components of the pelvis, and features of the proximal femur, and ligaments of the hip joint. Indicated pelvic features are the ilium (il), the ischium (is), the pubis (p), and the obturator foramen (of). Features of the femur are the head (fh), neck (fn), and the greater and lesser trochanters (gt; lt). Ligaments depicted are the iliofemoral (ifl) and the pubofemoral (pfl). B is a coronal section of the hip joint showing the relatively deep acetabulum (a), the acetabular labrum (al), the ligament of the head of the femur (lhr), and the attachments of the articular capsule (ac).

§ 5.3   Hip Dislocation

Hip dislocation is relatively rare and requires substantial force, such as high-speed vehicular accidents. Anterior dislocation accounts for about 15 percent of all traumatic dislocations of the hip. Posterior dislocation is associated with a very high incidence of post-traumatic osteoarthritis. Osteonecrosis may occur in about 10 percent of cases. Disability is directly related to severity of the injury as well as to the time elapsed between occurrence and reduction.

§ 5.4   Radiologic Considerations

X rays should be used to check the amount of displacement of pelvic fractures. Special attention should be given to the integrity of the hip socket (acetabulum) for loss of congruity. The physician should check the femoral heads for evidence of aseptic necrosis (associated with caisson disease), alcoholism, and chronic steroid use. Narrowing of the joint space and osteophyte formation on the edge of the acetabulum is pathognomonic for degenerative arthritis—either infectious, post-traumatic, or rheumatoid. Physicians should note the presence and position of internal fixation devices, such as plates and screws, commonly used in fractures. They should note whether such devices have migrated out of the femoral head into the joint space or pelvis and if there has been any breakage or loosening of metallic implants in the soft tissues. If a total hip arthroplasty is present, it should be observed carefully for a "windshield wiper sign" suggesting loosening of the bone cement or of cement prosthesis interface.

Push-pull films.   Push-pull films can be useful to reveal loosening and migration of a Moore, Thompson, or Bateman arthroplasty. They should be checked for possible dislocation of the prosthesis in relation to the acetabulum or femoral shafts.

Postreduction X rays.   Postreduction X rays should be checked carefully after hip dislocation to be sure there is a perfectly concentric relationship of the femoral head to the acetabulum. Lack of concentric relationship implies presence of trapped capsule or osteochondral fragments. A CAT scan is especially useful in such cases.

§ 5.5   Measuring Movement of the Hip

Movement at the hip's "ball and socket" joint is considerably less than at the shoulder's joint. Motions usually are measured with the patient lying supine (see **Figure 5–2**). Approximate average normal ranges of motion are:

flexion	115°
extension	30°
abduction	50°
adduction	30°
internal rotation in flexion	45°
external rotation in flexion	45°
internal rotation in extension	35°
external rotation in extension	50°
abduction in 90° of flexion	45° to 60° depending on age

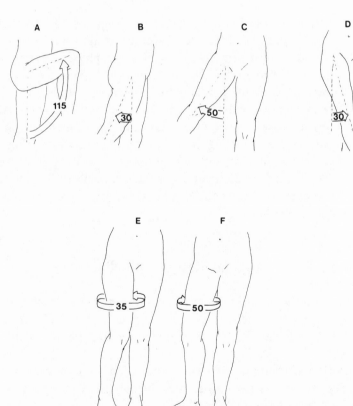

Figure 5–2. Types and range of normal hip movements. Depicted are flexion, A; extension (beyond anatomical position), B; abduction, C; adduction (beyond anatomical position), D; internal rotation in extension, E; external rotation in extension, F.

§ 5.6   Common Disability Conditions

Hip fractures.   Hip fractures, 80 percent of which occur in females, account for 30 percent of all patients hospitalized for the treatment of fractures (see **Figure 5–3**). They are notoriously disabling, often being associated with cardiac disease, osteoporosis, and senility. Mortality rates of 20 percent within six months of hip fracture have been reported. Usually, the treatment of choice is open reduction with internal fixation using sliding nails, plates, and screws.

—Displaced subcapital fractures.   Displaced subcapital fractures usually are treated with replacement arthroplasty (Moore's prosthesis) because of the high incidence of aseptic necrosis.

—Infratrochanteric fractures.   Infratrochanteric fractures usually are treated with intramedullary fixation (Ender's rods, Sampson rods, Zickel rods) because of the high incidence of instability and nonunion.

Degenerative arthritis.   Degenerative arthritis leading to pain and decreased range of motion is quite common in the later age group. After trial of conservative therapy—heat, rest, cane, anti-inflammatory medication, physical therapy—total hip replacement is the treatment of choice. Although there have been major advancements in recent years, the procedure still is fraught with early and late complications. Even when relatively successful in 90 percent of cases, it still will be associated with decreased range of motion and impairment of about 30 percent. Significantly more disabling complications include loosening of the bone-cement or cement-prosthesis interface, superficial or deep infection, and stem fracture. Less frequent complications include thromboembolism, sciatic and femoral nerve palsies, vascular accidents during surgery, and dislocation and nonunion of the greater trochanter.

§ 5.7   Hip Limitation Guidelines

Mild limitation of motion.   Mild limitation of motion (0- to 120-degrees flexion) with about 50-percent reduction in rotation, abduction, and adduction entitles the patient to a 10-percent loss of physical function to the entire body.

Moderate limitation of motion.   Moderate limitation of motion (15-degrees flexion to 110-degrees further flexion) entitles the patient to a 15-percent physical impairment and loss of physical function.

Severe limitation of motion.   Severe limitation of motion (30-degrees flexion to 90-degrees further flexion) or total ankylosis entitles the patient to a 25-percent permanent physical impairment and loss of physical function.

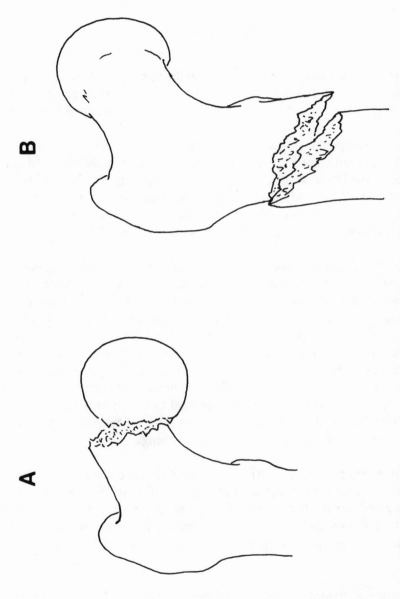

Figure 5–3. Fractures of the proximal femur. A depicts a subcapital fracture with displacement of the head; B depicts an infratrochanteric fracture through the shaft of the femur.

Nonunion of a fracture without reconstruction entitles the patient to a 40-percent whole-body permanent loss of physical function.

KNEE

§ 5.8 Anatomy

The knee joint is the most complicated joint in the human body and the one most prone to occupational injuries. Adequate impairment evaluation requires an understanding of the role of the osseous structures, menisci, and ligamentous structures.

The osseous component of the knee joint consists of the distal end of the femur and the proximal tibia (see **Figure 5–4**). Interposed between the tibia and femur are the medial and lateral menisci, which contribute significantly to load bearing and joint stability. The menisci do this by distributing the pressure between the tibia and femur and assisting in lubrication. Ligaments and muscles that surround the joint guide movement and stabilize joint motion.

Menisci.   The medial meniscus is a 10 mm-wide strip of cartilage firmly connected to the joint capsule and the medial collateral ligament. The lateral meniscus has a width of 12–13 mm and provides much greater mobility than does the medial meniscus because of little or no capsular connection. The greater mobility of the lateral meniscus explains the far greater incidence of tears of the medial meniscus as compared to the lateral meniscus—a ratio of 8:1. Recent research suggests that menisci do have some healing potential. The peripheral 10 to 30 percent of the medial meniscus and the peripheral 33 percent of the lateral meniscus are vascularized and have the potential to heal if repaired. Therefore, whenever possible, menisci should be repaired rather than excised in order to prevent instability and progressive degenerative change.

Medial lateral collateral ligament.   The medial lateral collateral ligament is a selective thickening of the fibrous joint capsule. It attaches superiorly to the medial epicondyle of the femur and inferiorly to the tibia just below the medial meniscus (see **Figure 5–4**). The medial collateral ligament provides rotatory stability and protects against valgus (away from the midline) stress (see **Figure 5–5**).

Lateral collateral ligament.   The lateral collateral ligament attaches superiorly to the lateral epicondyle of the femur and inferiorly to the head of the fibula (see **Figure 5–4**). It also provides rotatory stability and protects against varus (toward the midline) strains (see **Figure 5–5**).

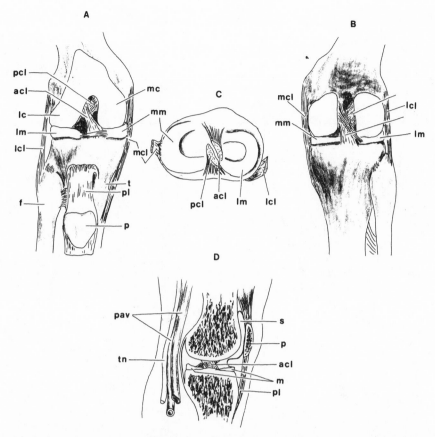

Figure 5–4. The knee. A and B represent anterior and posterior views, respectively. Depicted are the medial and lateral femoral condyles (mc and lc), the medial and lateral menisci (mm and lm), the anterior and posterior cruciate ligaments (acl and pcl), the medial and lateral collateral ligaments (mcl and lcl), the proximal tibia (t), the fibula (f), the patella (p), and the patellar ligament (pl). C is a superior view of the tibia, with the menisci in place. The attachment of the medial meniscus to the medial collateral ligament should be noted. View D is a sagittal section through the knee, indicating the close relationship of the popliteal artery and vein (pav), and the tibial nerve (tn) to the posterior aspect of the joint. The space of the knee joint (s) is shown extending superiorly beneath the patellar ligament.

Anterior and posterior cruciate ligaments. The anterior cruciate ligament runs from its anterior tibial attachment to the medial aspect of the lateral femoral condyle. The posterior cruciate ligament runs from the posterior aspect of the tibia to the medial femoral condyle. The cruciate ligaments act to prevent sheer motion of the knee joint and to assist in flexion and rotation. The anterior cruciate ligaments prevent hyperextension. The posterior cruciate aids normal knee flexion (see **Figure 5–4**).

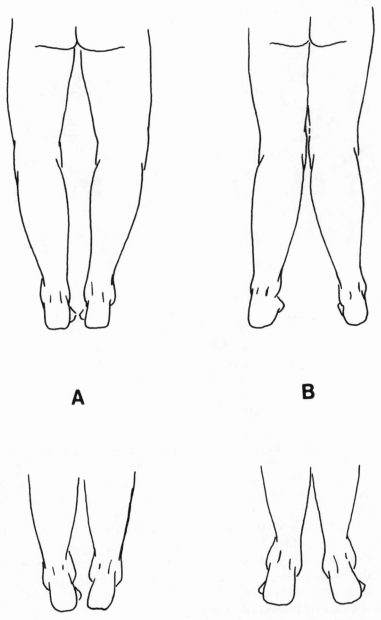

Figure 5–5. Varus and valgus deformities of the knee and ankle. A indicates, above and below, genu valgus (bow legs) and pes valgus. B indicates genu varus (knock-knees) and pes varus.

Extensor group muscles. The extensor group consists mainly of the quadriceps femoris: rectus femoris, vastus medialis, vastus lateralis, and vastus intermedius. These all converge to form the patella tendon after crossing the knee joint.

Flexor group muscles.   The flexor group can be subdivided into medial and lateral flexors. The medial group includes the semimembranosus and semitendinosus muscles. The main lateral flexor of the knee is the biceps femoris, which serves to flex and externally rotate the knee.

§ 5.9   Function

When all of these structures are functioning properly, the result is a joint capable of full extension at approximately 110 degrees of full flexion. Slight abduction and adduction also are possible, even with the tibia fully extended on the femur. Several definitions are essential to avoid confusion when describing the function of the knee.

Laxity.   Laxity should refer to physiologic motion of a joint in the absence of prior injury. The laxity commonly is observed in loose-jointed individuals, according to the *Orthopaedic Knowledge Update*.[1]

Instability.   Instability refers to a joint with abnormal increase in motion, usually as a result of damage to a ligament. Functional instability occurs if the patient's symptoms include giving-way.

§ 5.10   Diagnostic Tests

The patient should be observed walking. Is a cane or crutch necessary? The patient should be asked to walk without such devices even if they are used. Does the patient use any external device such as a knee brace or Ace bandage? The physician should observe the patient's gait in the examining room as well as in the waiting room and, if possible, on the street, noting carefully any differences. The physician should be suspicious of the patient who limped in the examining room yet had a normal, rapid gait when leaving the office. The patient should be asked to squat fully. Inability to do so suggests cartilage tear. A loud click while squatting also suggests meniscal damage. Clicking, however, can also be caused simply by grating (associated with osteoarthritis), patella movement over the femoral condyle, or even a tendon slipping over a bony exostosis.

A simple tape measure should be used to measure the thigh bilaterally six inches above the superior pole of the patella. There is a high correlation between quadriceps strength and quadriceps muscle mass with impairment. The patient with a strong bilaterally symmetrical quadriceps mechanism is unlikely to have

---

[1] American Academy of Orthopaedic Surgeons, *Knee and Leg Trauma (Soft Tissue)*, in Orthopaedic Knowledge Update: Home Study Syllabus 319 (1984).

significant functional impairment. The patient should be asked to straighten both knees completely and bend them completely. The normal side, obviously, is used for comparison.

Checking the medial meniscus.   The McMurray test is used to determine whether there is a torn medial meniscus. It is performed by placing the patient supine on the examining table. The physician's fingers of one hand should be placed on the joint line to rotate the tibia forcibly in one direction then another while the patient's knee flexes fully. A click detected by the fingers on the joint line suggests a meniscal tear. The click is caused by a mobile strip of meniscus being caught between the articular surfaces on rotation.

Checking the collateral ligaments.   Medial and lateral collateral ligaments are checked by passive movement (see **Figure 5–6**). With the knee flexed 15 degrees, to relax the posterior capsule, varus and valgus stress is applied. To check the medial collateral ligament, the physician should place one hand on the lateral aspect of the lower femur and the other hand on the proximal tibia and apply valgus (away from the midline) pressure. The lateral collateral ligament is similarly checked by applying varus (toward the midline) pressure. Comparison with the normal side will reveal any pathologic instability.

Checking the cruciates.   The cruciate ligaments are tested by the drawer sign (see **Figure 5–7**). The patient lies on the examining table with the knee flexed to a right angle. Both of the examiner's hands grasp the tibial head just below the joint. A forward pull will reveal the presence or absence of normal mobility to indicate torn anterior cruciate. Comparison to the opposite side is, of course, essential. A backward pull similarly will test the integrity of the posterior cruciate ligament.

Pivot shift phenomena.   A newer and very important concept describing reduction or subluxation of the tibia over the femur under low flexion (at approximately 25 degrees) is pivot shift phenomena. The patient describes a situation in which there is excess anterior rotatory motion of the lateral tibial plateau in relation to the femur, producing a phenomenon of giving-way. With the patient supine, the knee is flexed 25 degrees and held in external rotation. The examiner then gradually extends the knee to determine if there is a jerk or shift present on reaching full extension.

Arthroscopy and arthrography.   The examiner should inquire whether arthroscopy or arthrography have been performed, and if so, what the results were. An arthrogram is done by injecting Renograffin mixed with saline into the knee. An Esmarch bandage is then wrapped around the knee for compression, and the knee is flexed to express intra-articular fluid through any tears in the menisci, synovium, or capsule. Multiple X-ray views are then taken. Arthrograms generally

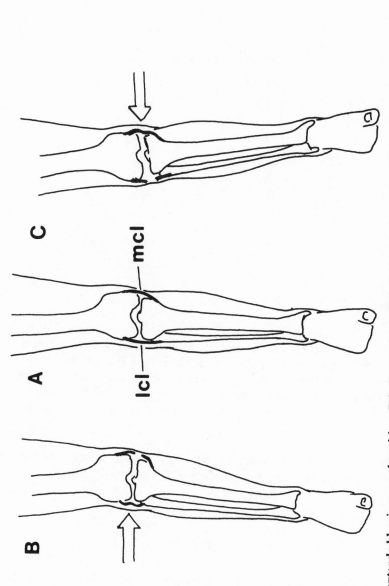

Figure 5–6. A is the extended leg in normal position. B indicates the application of force to the lateral aspect of the knee, resulting in rupture of the medial collateral ligament (mcl). C shows rupture of the lateral collateral ligament (lcl) with application of force to the medial aspect of the knee.

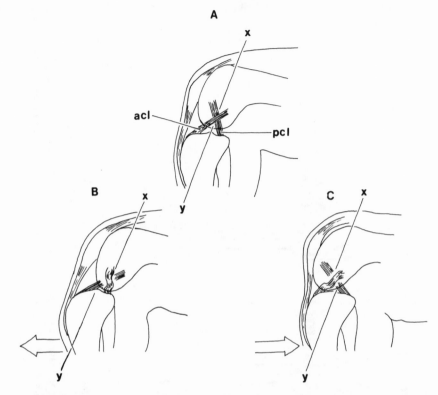

Figure 5–7. The cruciate ligaments. View A depicts normal anatomy of the flexed knee, showing the anterior cruciate ligament (acl), and the posterior cruciate ligament (pcl). Line XY is a reference line. View B shows the anterior displacement of the tibia which is allowed by rupture of the anterior cruciate ligament (anterior drawer sign). View C shows the posterior displacement of the tibia which is allowed by rupture of the posterior cruciate ligament (posterior drawer sign).

are most valuable for detecting medial meniscus tears. Lateral meniscus tears are best determined by arthroscopy, examination of the knee under direct vision in the operating room using an arthroscope.

§ 5.11   X rays

X rays are of relatively little help in determining knee impairment. Regular X rays will not reveal torn menisci or ligaments. Stress X rays, usually done under anesthesia, may give some guidance in determining medial or lateral collateral ligament tears. X rays, however, always should be taken in case of fracture to determine the degree of destruction of the articular bony surface. Degenerative arthritic change will be revealed best on A-P views by demonstrating narrowing of the medial and lateral compartments as well as osteophyte formation. A special sunrise view is indicated to reveal patellofemoral arthritis in severe cases of chondromalacia. X rays can reveal the rare case of osteomyelitis, malignancy, or loose bodies in the joint.

§ 5.12   Determination of Impairment

Menisci.   Torn menisci usually cause pain by being trapped between the femur and the tibia during activity. Partial or complete removal of the torn meniscus usually relieves the symptoms. However, even if the patient has an excellent result immediately after meniscectomy, the patient can anticipate substantial degenerative osteoarthritis 5 to 10 years later. Therefore, surgical removal of medial or lateral meniscus, even without complications, entitles the patient to at least a 5-percent permanent physical impairment and loss of physical function to the lower extremity. Complications such as infection, degenerative changes, or sympathetic dystrophy may double or triple the 5-percent figure. Surgical removal of both cartilages with intact ligaments is considerably more disabling in terms of subsequent degenerative changes and quadriceps atrophy. Such a patient may be entitled to at least a 20-percent impairment.

Cruciate tears.   Torn cruciate and medial collateral ligaments are associated with marked instability. Just by surgical repair, the patient generally will be entitled to a 20- to 30-percent impairment, depending on the amount of laxity. The patella has shown to be a crucial fulcrum for the effective functioning of the quadriceps mechanism.

Plateau fractures.   Fracture of the articular surfaces, either femur or tibia, will cause serious impairment if there is any significant loss of anatomic position. Therefore, displaced fractures of the articular surface of the distal femur or proximal tibia plateau are treated by surgical open reduction with internal fixation in an attempt to begin early range of motion, active and passive. Significantly depressed fracture of the tibial plateau, 8 mm or more, usually involves destruction of the menisci. Despite bone grafting and internal fixation to elevate the plateau, the patient will be entitled to at least a 20-percent impairment.

§ 5.13   Knee Limitation Guidelines

Stiffness and loss of motion may result from serious infection or osteoarthritic changes. Total knee replacement often is associated with marked restriction of flexion and extension.

Mild limitation of motion.   Mild limitation of motion—0- to 110-degrees flexion—entitles the patient to about 5-percent impairment.

Moderate limitation of motion. Moderate limitation of motion—0- to 80-degrees flexion—entitles the patient to about 15-percent impairment.

Severe limitation of motion. Severe limitation of motion—0- to about 60-degrees flexion—entitles the patient to about 35-percent impairment.

If motion is markedly limited from about 15 degrees of flexion to about 90 degrees of further flexion, then 40-percent impairment is appropriate.

Ankylosis. Even in an optimal position of 15-degrees flexion, ankylosis entitles the patient to a 50-percent impairment and loss of physical function.

FOOT AND ANKLE

§ 5.14   Anatomy

The 26 bones of the foot include 14 phalanges, 5 metatarsals, and 7 tarsal bones (see **Figure 5–8**). The talus is the keystone of the foot. It is gripped by the medial malleolus of the tibia and the lateral malleolus (distal fibula) to form the ankle mortise. The talus works as a hinge joint within this mortise.

Ligaments. The ankle is further stabilized by multiple ligaments. These include the interosseous ligament (tibia to fibula) and the anterior and posterior tibio-fibula ligaments. These ligaments often are partially or completely torn in fractures and severe ankle sprains.

Muscles. Muscles acting on the foot can be divided into extrinsic (originating away from the foot) and intrinsic (originating and inserting within the foot itself).

§ 5.15   History

As in evaluating any alleged disability problem, the examiner should start with the history. The conscientious examiner always will be thinking and look-ing for inconsistency. The patient should be asked to indicate the site of pain. Is the pain related to a particular activity, motion, or position? Does the patient require custom-made shoe inserts, cane, or crutches? The examiner should be suspicious of the patient wearing high-heeled shoes or soft loafers that give no support whatsoever—and particularly suspicious of the patient who alleges substantial foot and ankle problems but wears jogging sneakers with a sweat suit to match.

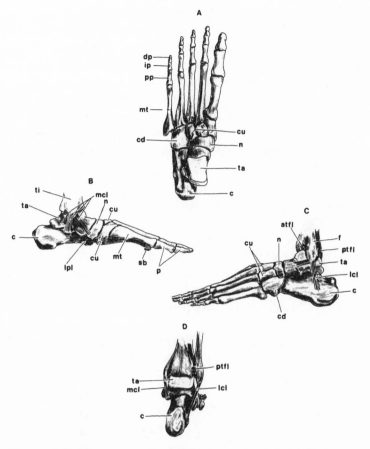

Figure 5–8. The osseous foot and primary ligaments. Shown are superior (A), medial (B), lateral (C), and posterior (D) views. The tarsal bones include the talus (ta), calcaneus (c), navicular (n), cuboid (cd), and the medial, intermediate, and lateral cuneiform bones, indicated collectively as (cu). Like the hand, each digit has a single metatarsal bone (mt); each of the lateral four digits has a proximal, intermediate, and distal phalanx (pp, ip, dp). The great toe, like the thumb, has only two phalangeal bones, proximal (pp) and distal (dp). Extending from the tibia (ti) and the fibula (f) to the bones of the tarsus are the medial and lateral collateral ligaments (mcl and lcl). Extending between the tibia and fibula, anteriorly and posteriorly, are the respective talofibular ligaments (atfl and ptfl). Also depicted is the long plantar ligament (lpl) of the foot.

The shoes should be carefully examined for inconsistent wear. If the patient walks on the lateral aspect of the foot when walking barefoot, the examiner would expect a corresponding wear pattern on the shoes. Inconsistency should make the examiner suspicious of exaggeration of complaints.

§ 5.16 Physical Examination

Circulatory status. The foot should be observed for visible varicosities and pitting edema, which imply venous insufficiency. The presence or absence of edema, dependent cyanosis, skin temperature, and blanching of the elevated foot are all criteria used to evaluate circulatory status. The physician should check the dorsalis pedis and posterior tibial pulses and compare the opposite side. The dorsalis pedis pulse is felt best on the dorsum of the foot between the first and second metatarsals. The posterior tibial pulse is felt best below and behind the medial malleolus.

Neurologic status. A safety pin can determine sensitivity to light touch and dermatome areas of hypalgesia or anesthesia. Any motor deficits should be observed and evaluated.

Skin. The physician should observe and palpate abnormal calluses. A dime-sized callus on the weight-bearing surface is a classic sign of prominent metatarsal head. Tenderness on deep palpation between the metatarsal heads, especially the third and fourth, suggests Morton's neuroma.

Muscles. The physician should measure the calf muscles at maximal circumference and compare with the opposite side. Atrophy clearly is consistent with increased use and impairment.

§ 5.17 X rays

X rays of the ankle demonstrate relationship of the talus in the ankle mortise. Widening of the mortise or failure to restore anatomic alignment after bimalleolar or trimalleolar fracture is readily demonstrated on X rays and is consistent with substantial impairment. Widening of the mortise also suggests torn deltoid ligaments or entrapment of the posterior tibial tendons. Similarly, narrowing or obliteration of the ankle mortise, as in severe degenerative arthritis, is consistent with markedly decreased range of motion and substantial impairment. Physicians always should look for loose fragments as well as for malignancy or osteomyelitis and observe the calcaneous for painful calcaneal spurs, usually associated with plantar fascitis.

§ 5.18 Common Disability Problems (see **Figure 5–9**)

Bimalleolar and trimalleolar fractures. Bimalleolar and trimalleolar ankle fractures usually require open reduction with internal fixation (surgery). Failure to restore anatomic alignment invariably will result in decreased movement and disability. Disability is measured by decreased range of motion.

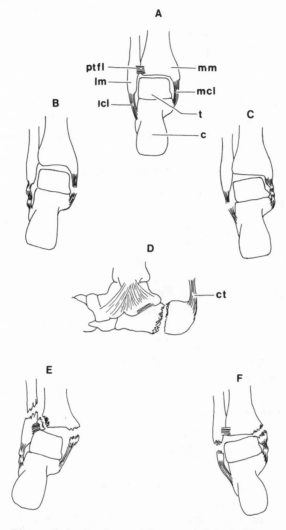

Figure 5–9. Sprains and fractures of the ankle. A depicts normal configuration of the ankle joint and the associated ligamentous structures. Indicated are the talus (t), calcaneus (c), medial malleolus (mm), and lateral malleolus (lm). Ligaments are the posterior talofibular (ptfl), the medial collateral ligament (mcl), and the lateral collateral ligament (lcl). View B depicts an eversion sprain, with rupture of the medial collateral ligament. View C shows rupture of the lateral collateral ligament attendent to an inversion sprain. View D depicts a fracture of the calcaneus with displacement of the fragment by the pull of the muscles acting on the calcaneal tendon (ct). View E is a trimalleolar fracture resulting from acute eversion; view F is a depiction of a bimalleolar fracture resulting from acute inversion.

Calcaneal fractures.   Calcaneal fractures are associated usually with a fall from a substantial height. These often are notoriously disabling, regardless of initial treatment, closed or open. Persistent chronic pain may require subtalar arthrodesis or even triple arthrodesis.

Ruptured achilles tendon.   Recent studies suggest that closed rather than open treatment is preferable if the tendon ends are adequately approximated. Calf atrophy after tendon rupture is consistent with impairment.

Ankle sprain.   Most sprains heal well with conservative treatment. On X rays, widening of the mortise suggests a torn deltoid ligament. Recurrent ankle sprains and varus instability suggest torn lateral ligaments. Usually, this is easily repaired by the Evans ligament reconstruction using the peroneous longus tendon.

§ 5.19   Ankle and Foot Limitation Guidelines
(see **Figure 5–10**)

Mild limitation of motion.   Mild limitation of motion of the ankle—90-degrees right angle to 20-degrees plantar flexion—entitles the patient to about 10-percent impairment.

Moderate limitation of motion.   Moderate limitation of motion of the ankle—motion limited from 10-degrees plantar flexion to 20-degrees plantar flexion—entitles the patient to about 25-percent impairment.

Severe limitation of motion.   Severe limitation of motion of the ankle—motion limited from a position of 20-degrees plantar flexion to 30-degrees plantar flexion—entitles the patient to a 50-percent impairment.

Ankylosis of the toe.   Complete ankylosis of the metatarsophalangeal joint of any toe equates to 50-percent impairment of the toe.

Ankylosis of the ankle and foot.   Ankylosis of the ankle and foot (partalar arthrodesis) entitles the patient to a 50-percent impairment.

Arthrodesis of subtalar.   Subtalar or triple arthrodesis entitles the patient to a 25-percent impairment.

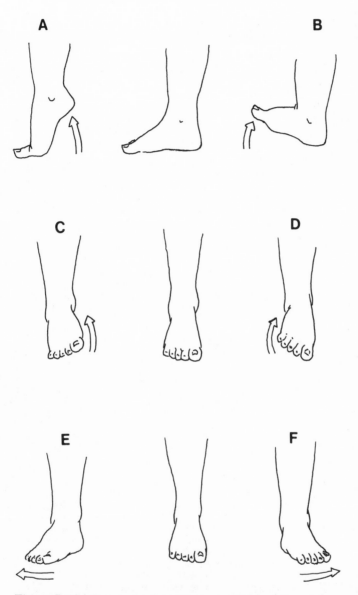

Figure 5–10. The six basic movements of the ankle and foot. A is plantar flexion; B is dorsiflexion. The latter is sometimes designated as extension, and while that is correct, it can lead to some confusion. C is inversion (the sole of the foot turned toward the midline); D is eversion (the sole facing laterally). E and F indicate the limited rotatory movements which take place at the ankle.

CHAPTER 6

PAIN AND IMPAIRMENT

§ 6.1   Introduction

The third edition of the AMA *Guides to the Evaluation of Permanent Impairment* provides an excellent framework in which to evaluate impairment and pain. It is important to begin with a definition of terms, including pain, impairment, disability, and handicap. Pain is part of any disability evaluation whether it is cardiac, orthopedic, or some other type. *Pain* has been defined by a committee of the International Association for the Study of Pain as "an unpleasant sensory and emotional experience which we associate with tissue damage or describe in terms of tissue damage."

§ 6.2   Health Status

Impairment means an alteration of an individual's health status that is assessed by medical means. *Disability,* on the other hand, means an alteration of an individual's capacity to meet social, personal, or occupational demands or to meet

111

regulatory or statutory requirements. Disability is assessed by nonmedical means, usually by nonphysicians. To put it simply, *impairment* is what is wrong with the health of an individual; *disability* is the difference between what the individual can do and what the individual needs or wants to do.

Obviously, an individual who is impaired is not necessarily disabled. Impairment produces disability only when the medical condition limits the individual's capacity to meet particular demands related to nonmedical fields and activities. For example, consider the effect of the loss of the fifth finger of the left hand. If the individual is a bank president, there is negligible occupational impact. On the other hand, a typist or concert pianist is likely to be totally disabled. A medical evaluation can reveal impairment, but the individual may not be disabled with respect to particular occupational requirements.

The term "handicap" is frequently used interchangably with the terms "impairment" and "disability," although handicap is really independent of both impairment and disability. Under the Rehabilitation Act of 1973,[1] to be described as handicapped an individual has an impairment that substantially limits one or more life activities, including work, has a record of such impairment, or is regarded as having such an impairment. This definition is so vague and broad that nearly any individual who desires to do so might be included in the class of the handicapped under this federal law.

It is far better to regard a handicap as an obstacle or barrier to functional activity. For example, an individual with a limited functional capacity is handicapped if able to perform certain life activities only by compensating in some way, such as by using assistive devices like crutches, wheelchairs, hearing aids, prostheses, or optical magnifiers. Similarly, modification of the environment or modification of tasks or activities, including increasing time for task completion, would also fit this definition. If such accommodations cannot be made to enable an individual to accomplish specific tasks or life activities, then the individual would indeed be regarded as disabled. Obviously, the converse is true in that an impaired individual who is able to accomplish a task or activity without accommodations is neither handicapped nor disabled. Disability is generally determined by judges, lawyers, and juries; impairment is determined by physicians, who do a medical evaluation of an individual's health status.

The concept of employability must also be understood. If an individual has the capacity, with or without accommodations, to meet the job demands and conditions of employment, the individual is obviously employable, not disabled. Even in the presence of impairment, if an individual can fulfill job requirements, then clearly the individual is not disabled for that job.

---

[1] 29 U.S.C. § 706.

§ 6.3 Pain

Any discussion about impairment, disability, and handicap requires an understanding of the concept of pain itself. Although chronic pain is clearly a common problem, the medical profession has been very slow to identify chronic pain as a specific medical disorder. Unfortunately there has been minimal research on the subject. This is surprising if one considers that $60 to $100 billion is spent annually in the United States on chronic pain syndromes. This represents approximately one quarter of the annual health care budget. Furthermore, 550 million sick days are lost annually because of chronic pain syndromes among the full-time working population. Thirty million individuals are afflicted with chronic lower back problems.

The Commission on the Evaluation of Pain has defined *pain* as a "complex experience, embracing physical, mental, social and behavioral processes which compromises the quality of life of many individuals." The Commission has gone on to recognize two categories of pain: acute and chronic. Chronic pain syndrome is also defined. Basically, pain is regarded as a subjective and unpleasant physical and emotional experience associated with the perception of physical harm.

Acute pain is an alerting mechanism or early warning signal that protects an individual from bodily tissue damage. By definition, acute pain is of recent onset and of short duration, seldom presenting a major diagnostic or therapeutic problem. A physical injury gives rise to a noxious stimulus, resulting in pain perception and pain behavior that are usually appropriate to the underlying causation. Appropriate treatment includes making a correct diagnosis and providing palliative measures such as oral medication and immobilization of the affected part. Because pain abatement accompanies tissue healing, impairment and/or disability rarely exceeds the underlying pathology.

More complicated is acute recurrent pain seen in conditions that cause tissue damage, such as arthritis and cancer. Acute recurrent pain is sometimes controllable with medication and immobilization. However, because of the long-term nature of the underlying disease process, the intensity and duration of health care and the resulting impairment and/or disability are usually greater in magnitude. Acute recurrent pain, however, should not be confused with chronic pain.

Chronic pain, also known as chronic intractable pain or chronic benign pain, is the entity usually associated with chronic pain syndrome. While acute pain obviously has some protective value, chronic pain is a destructive force. It is a pathological disorder in its own right associated with markedly abnormal pain behavior. This pain behavior is maladaptive and counterproductive. Both pain behavior and pain perception are out of proportion to any underlying noxious stimulus. Obviously, the tissue damage that originally generated the pain has healed and no longer serves as the underlying generator of pain. Instead, one has abnormal pain behavior that is in itself disabling. Chronic pain syndrome is essentially a bio-social phenomenon. It is important that this social aspect of pain be understood by any evaluator of disability.

§ 6.4   Relationship of Physiological and Social Factors

Emotions definitely can determine the degree of pain a stimulus can cause in a subject. It is well known that in World War II, soldiers were unaware of injuries at the time they occurred but sought medical attention hours later when fighting diminished. Among G.I.s at Anzio Beachhead in World War II, narcotics were requested less often than anticipated because having a wound meant that one would be shipped out of the combat zone back to the United States.

Dr. John Lieser, of the Department of Neurological Surgery of the University of Washington, has designed an excellent model incorporating the following four concepts (see **Figure 6–1**):

1. *nociception:* potentially tissue-damaging thermal or mechanical energy
2. *pain:* perception of nociceptive input to the nervous system
3. *suffering:* negative affective response
4. *pain behavior:* any type of output from the organism to suggest the existence of tissue-damaging stimulus.

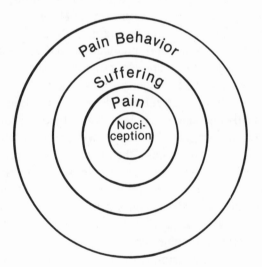

Figure 6–1.

The general concept of the model is that tissue damage leads to nociception, which leads to pain, which is one of the causes of suffering, which leads to pain behavior. Attorneys, physicians, and patients' families respond to pain behavior—the only observable aspect of the pain process.

To understand some pain behavior, one must look outside the individual organism. Loss of loved objects, anxiety, depression, or effects of medication can lead to suffering. The behavior the patient manifests will be indistinguishable from that caused by nociception. The poorly paid worker with little job satisfaction may well avoid an unpleasant job by low back pain. In such cases, the symptoms may be impossible to ameliorate by therapies directed only at presumed noxious stimuli.

There is no such thing as functional or psychosomatic pain; all pain behavior is real. The proper question is not, "Does the patient hurt?" but "What are the factors which lead to this patient's pain behavior?" It is crucial to consider family, job satisfaction, life-style, and the effects of narcotics.

§ 6.5 Body Area

Body area sometimes is a factor in determining a patient's reaction. Patients who complain clearly about headaches may be reluctant to describe rectal pain or genital pain. The patient, ashamed of painful hemorrhoids, may consider a headache more socially acceptable. Therefore, the examiner must ask specifically about such potentially embarrassing matters as incontinence.

§ 6.6 Psychological Conditioning

Many workers harbor a latent hostility toward their employer, especially in large companies. After a work-connected injury, this resentment may surface. Workers often feel their labors are undervalued and unappreciated. Often the injury is attributed to someone else's carelessness or inadequate safety provisions on the job site. Prolongation of symptoms allows the patient an honorable and socially accepted withdrawal from an unpleasant or hazardous task without criticism from either fellow workers or family. Yet when confronted with such a schema, most patients react with genuine indignation and astonishment. In such cases, lump-sum early settlement often is less costly than attempts at psychological evaluation.

§ 6.7 Hypochondria

There are definite characteristics that may be helpful in making the diagnosis of hypochondria. Hypochondriacs often are intelligent and may be subjected to substantial stress on and off the job. They will have seen many physicians and, with minimal urging, tend to be quite critical of each. Multiple hospitalizations are common for a variety of ills, most often affecting gastrointestinal, cardiac, chest, and musculoskeletal problems. There usually are few objective findings.

Hypochondriacs tend to embrace eagerly the latest treatment rage, be it gravity traction, acupuncture, or hypnosis. Irritability and nervousness are common, as seen in excess perspiration or tremor of the hands. A telephone ring may produce a dramatic startled reaction.

§ 6.8   Malingering

Actually, malingering is relatively rare. It is usually accompanied by some kind of secondary gain, such as in finances (Social Security income, workers' compensation) or perhaps a change in the job (less travel, less strenuous work, increased attention).

§ 6.9   Causalgia

Causalgia is a relatively rare clinical syndrome associated with incomplete lesion of a peripheral nerve containing sensory fibers. It is characterized most commonly by excruciating pain in the hand or foot. The patient usually describes the pain as throbbing, burning, pressing, aching, twisting, or crushing. In two-thirds of the cases, the pain begins immediately after the injury, but it also can be delayed in onset. Injuries to the median and tibial nerves are most commonly associated with causalgia.

Frequently the pain is limited to the cutaneous distribution of the affected nerve. The pain is extreme and may be exacerbated by psychological factors such as surprise, anger, or even the mention of a slick object such as a paper or sheet. The pain is often relieved by moisture; some patients will keep the affected extremity wrapped in a wet towel. The pain also is less severe on cool, damp days. Clinically, the skin of the affected area usually is cold and moist, but frequently it may appear dark red, dry, atrophied, and glossy. If the condition does not resolve spontaneously, surgical sympathectomy is the treatment of choice.

§ 6.10   Reflex Sympathetic Dystrophy

Reflex sympathetic dystrophy (Sudeck's atrophy) was first described in 1900 by Dr. Sudeck as an acute atrophy of bone with characteristic spotty decalcification developing after trauma. It is associated possibly with pain, edema, tenderness, sweating, coldness, and stiffness of the affected area. Etiology is not fully understood, but it may be caused by continuous vasospasm of the arteries, after even a minor injury, as part of the body's self-defense mechanism, much like the "fight-or-flight" reflex. Capillaries and venules become distended with sluggishly flowing blood, causing a cyanosis and coldness. The spotty decalcification seen on X rays may be explained by a similar distribution of capillary beds within the bone. Clinically, the mobility of joints is restricted and often never fully recovered. Treatment is notoriously unsuccessful. Sympathectomy sometimes is helpful in the early stages of the condition. It should be emphasized that this is a real but poorly understood entity and frequently may explain why an individual may have persistent pain, tenderness, swelling, and edema even in the absence of a fracture or significant X-ray findings.

CHAPTER 7

UNDERSTANDING SOCIAL SECURITY DISABILITY

§ 7.1 Background for the Attorney

Attorneys working with injured individuals will frequently be asked to assist them in obtaining Social Security disability. Those attorneys must understand the complexities of the system in order to help injured individuals obtain the disability benefits for which they are qualified. The Social Security disability system in the United States is the largest governmental program providing long-term payment for inability to work. More than four million Americans who are unable to work because of medical problems (medically impaired) receive support from the Social Security Disability Insurance (SSDI) and Supplemental Security Income (SSI) programs.

Every practicing attorney at one time or another may have to help a client weigh the advisability of applying for and obtaining disability benefits. Because the programs are extremely complex, an understanding of impairment and disability is essential. As discussed **Chapter 6,** *impairment* is a physical or mental limitation of function resulting from a disease process or injury. For example, a single disease like diabetes can result in varied impairments, ranging from none to blindness or kidney failure. On the other hand, *disability* is "the incapacity of an individual to meet certain standards of physical efficacy and/or social, occupational or economic responsibility." Obviously, disability involves multiple factors, including social and economic aspects of an individual's interaction with the disease.

Impairment and disease are usually measured by physicians, but disability, in the Social Security disability program, is assessed by the administrative agency

119

and not by the treating or consulting physician. It is in the attorney's interest and the client's interest to be certain that the treating physician provides the Social Security Disability Administration with adequate information. Concerned attorneys and physicians can obtain the manual, *Disability Evaluation Under Social Security*, a handbook for physicians published by the Social Security disability system. This handbook can help attorneys better understand each of the disability programs administered by the Social Security Administration. It explains how each program works and what kinds of medical information a physician must furnish to ensure sound and prompt decisions on disability claims. (Copies may be obtained by writing to the Superintendent of Documents, Government Printing Office, Washington, D.C. 20402.)

§ 7.2 Applying for Benefits

An injured individual who no longer feels able to work must take the first step toward obtaining benefits by applying at the local Social Security office. Attorneys should advise their clients that this is an important decision because of the relatively low level of payment (approximately $500 to $800 per month). The attorney should make clear that the applicant must be out of work for more than six months before receiving such benefits. The client should be advised that leaving the work force might affect his self-image and that the disabled role is usually permanent once an individual is so certified. If there is no qualifying disability, it would be best to counsel the individual appropriately to avoid a possibly frustrating exercise. Obviously, if a condition is progressive, then discussion of Social Security disability is a reasonable plan.

If a condition has a variable diagnosis with intermittent impairment, the magnitude of disability may change considerably from month to month. It may be appropriate to advise an individual to attempt other measures short of applying for permanent benefits, such as extended sick leave or part-time work. Furthermore, Social Security programs in the past have been regarded as permanent. Recent cost-saving measures, however, have resulted in disability reforms that provide incentives to resume work. Such incentives include continuation of health benefits and availability of work trials with expedited return of benefits if the disability recipient is unable to sustain gainful employment. Current policies include periodic reevaluation of individuals receiving benefits to determine whether the medical condition causing the disability has continued.

§ 7.3 Qualifying for Benefits

The process of qualifying for Social Security disability is complex and should be clearly understood. Once the individual applies for disability benefits, the Social

Security office will seek medical information from the applicant's personal physician and also obtain hospital records and other medical records. In about a third of applications, the local Social Security office will request and pay for a consultative examination performed by a physician other than the patient's doctor.

Once this information-gathering process is completed, a physician/administrative panel employed by the Social Security agency makes an initial decision. The applicant is informed of this decision and then has 60 days in which to request possible reconsideration. In the event of an appeal, the case is transferred to a different physician/administrative panel, using the same criteria for eligibility. Usually the applicant does not meet with the panel itself. Only 15 percent of initial appeals for reconsideration result in the applicants' being granted Social Security benefits.

The appeals process can continue to a third level—that of the administrative/law judge. This judge is a specially trained administrator, usually an attorney, who makes decisions concerning cases within the Social Security system. It is possible for the applicant to be represented by counsel at this appeal level and to present additional evidence concerning disability. Studies suggest that more than 50 percent of denials appealed to administrative/law judges are reversed in favor of the applicant. Even if an applicant's appeal is rejected at this level, the process can continue with appeals through the Social Security Appeals Council and the Federal District Court.

§ 7.4 Objective Evidence

Pain is a special case. To a physician in a clinical setting, pain is a cardinal indicator of disease or injury and responds to treatment. The Social Security disability system tends to downplay the role of pain and requires more "objective" evidence of disease and impairment in the evaluation of disability. In the all-too-common example of an individual with back pain, the Social Security impairment listings require pain to be present. However, pain is not a sufficient condition for the awarding of disability benefits. Neurologic abnormalities must also be documented. To the patient and the treating physician, the more disabling part of the nerve-root syndrome obviously is not the absent ankle-jerk reflex or the weak dorsiflexion of the foot but rather the chronic pain. A review of *Disability Evaluation Under Social Security* suggests that criteria for permanent disability from low back pain include the following:

1. Pain persisting for at least six months, despite prescribed therapy, and expected to last 12 months
2. Pain, muscle spasm, and significant limitation of motion in the spine
3. Appropriate radicular distribution of significant motor loss with muscle weakness and sensory and reflex loss.

In general, to succeed in getting Social Security disability payments requires fulfillment of complex objective criteria. The handbook's definition of *disability* is "inability to engage in any substantial gainful activity by reason of any medically determinable physical or mental impairment or impairments which can be expected to result in death or which have lasted, or can be expected to last, for a continuous period of not less than twelve months."

Impairment is defined as "a physical or mental impairment that results from anatomical, physiological or psychological abnormalities which are demonstrable by medically acceptable clinical and laboratory diagnostic techniques." Statements of the applicants, including their own descriptions of their impairments (symptoms) are, alone, insufficient to establish the presence of physical or mental impairments.

According to the Social Security handbook, in determining disability,

> primary consideration is given to the severity of the individual's impairment … age, education and work experience. Medical considerations alone (including the physiological and psychological manifestations of aging) can … justify a finding that the individual is under a disability where his impairment is one that meets the duration requirements and is listed.

Disability is determined not by the treating physician but by the nonphysician, clerks, and administrative/law judges:

> The function of deciding whether or not an individual is under a disability is the responsibility of the Secretary. A statement by a physician … shall not be determinative … . [T]he weight to be given such a physician's statement depends on the extent to which it is supported by specific and complete physical findings and is consistent with other evidences as to the severity and probable duration.

CHAPTER 8

THE EXPERT WITNESS

Steven Friedland

§ 8.1 Introduction

Expert witnesses are different from lay (nonexpert) witnesses in several important respects. Unlike lay witnesses, experts are generally permitted to offer opinions at trial and respond to hypothetical questions. Further, experts can base their conclusions on facts or data reasonably relied on by experts in the particular field, even if that information is not otherwise admissible. Perhaps the most significant difference, however, is the ability of experts in their presentations, through their aura of expertise and specialized knowledge, to persuade juries.

Lay witnesses are generally restricted to providing sensory observations—that is, sight, sound, smell, and touch—and very few opinions. The allowable opinions often are considered "shorthand renditions of fact" and include opinions within common knowledge, such as descriptions of a frown or a person jogging. Lay witnesses are at a disadvantage compared to experts because they often do not have the instant credibility with the jury that accompanies the expert's special background in education, experience, or training.

§ 8.2 Function of the Expert

An expert can serve two distinct functions. One function is as a witness at trial, providing specialized knowledge, skill, or training to assist the fact finder, whether it be jury or judge. The expert may also function as a nontestifying special assistant to the attorneys prior to trial. In this capacity, the expert serves as an educator, teaching the attorneys about various aspects of the case.

At trial, experts may play an important role in persuading jurors for various reasons. Given the advances in technology and science, litigation about related issues has become increasingly complex. Experts can make exceedingly esoteric or difficult issues understandable for juries and attorneys alike. In addition, experts are powerful witnesses. Because of their experience, they can explain the case to the jury often in a way that the lawyer cannot. By virtue of their specialized knowledge, moreover, experts are often held in high esteem and accorded a special deference, enhancing their believability. Finally, jurors are often fascinated by experts, perhaps a result of movies and television shows that create the popular culture.

In many courts the trend is toward increasing the admissibility of experts. The liberal admissibility of expert testimony offers several advantages, even permitting some witnesses to act as both a fact witness and an expert witness. In one court case, for example, investigative agents for prosecutors were permitted to testify about both their observations and their opinions.[1] Witnesses who wear dual hats, those of the fact witness and the opinion witness, provide extra

---

[1] *See* United States v. Young, 745 F.2d 733 (2d Cir. 1984) (permitting the investigative agents to provide their opinions about the nature of telephone conversations involving the defendants and about the transfer of packages).

versatility and impact to those who offer them. Yet, liberal admissibility and its resulting "invasion of experts" at trial have their critics. Some believe that experts have too great an impact on jurors and, in effect, take over trials they participate in.[2]

An additional distinguishing feature of expert testimony is the allowance of expert opinions based on otherwise inadmissible evidence, such as hearsay. When experts explain the reasons underlying their opinions, otherwise inadmissible evidence that could be reasonably relied on to form an opinion is often brought to the jury's attention. While this information is admitted only for the limited purpose of illustrating how the experts reached their conclusions, this subtlety often may be lost on the jury. Jurors accustomed to gossip and innuendo may be unduly impressed by such evidence, much like the old commercial that stated, "when ___ talks, everybody listens." Consequently, a huge "back door" for otherwise inadmissible evidence may be created by expert testimony. The applicable evidentiary rule minimizes this exception and maintains indicia of trustworthiness, however, by limiting such underlying information to that which is reasonably relied on in the expert's field or specialty.

PREREQUISITES TO ADMISSIBILITY

§ 8.3 Reliable Science

The first prerequisite that must be met for a person to testify as an expert at trial is that the subject matter of the testimony must be based on a reliable science. The concept of reliability has been defined in different ways. One of the most enduring formulations has asked whether the science is "generally accepted in the field."[3] *Frye v. United States* concerned polygraph evidence, but its test was expanded to embrace all forms of novel scientific evidence. The *Frye* test is still firmly entrenched in most jurisdictions. However, alternative formulations of reliability, such as whether sufficient independent indicia exist, are gaining grudging acceptance in some jurisdictions.[4] The battle over which test is used is crucial to persuading juries. Novel scientific evidence is used often in areas crucial to the outcomes of cases. Lie detectors, hypnosis, and expert psychologists all relate to the credibility of witnesses, an issue often dispositive of many types of cases. If the experts are allowed, the proffering parties' chances for a successful result will be significantly improved. Thus, what the courts permit may be the factor that determines the outcome of the case.

---

[2] As to the implications of such admissibility, *see* P. Bamberger, *The Dangerous Expert Witness,* 52 Brook. L. Rev. 855 (1986).

[3] *See* Frye v. United States, 293 F. 1013 (D.C. 1923).

[4] *See* United States v. Downing, 753 F.2d 1224 (3d Cir. 1985).

The *Frye* test has been used to exclude many novel forms of expert testimony. These include psycho-linguistics, hypnosis, spectrographic voice identification, bite-mark comparisons, accidentology, DNA print identification, and numerous forms of experimental and test data. The movement toward more liberal admissibility has been triggered in part by the difficulty of administering *Frye*: what does "generally accepted in the field" really mean, after all? The restrictiveness of *Frye* has also delayed the admission of important evidence. One illustration is the cautiousness with which DNA print identification evidence has been received in rape cases.

The reaction to *Frye* is not yet a counterrevolution. However, a greater number of courts are allowing novel expert testimony, particularly in certain types of cases. In these cases, juries can receive guidance on how to evaluate the evidence and even, by inference, what conclusions to draw about extremely difficult issues. For example, expert psychologists are slowly being permitted to testify in trials concerning child sexual battery, adult rape, and other cases in which the credibility of witnesses is crucial, particularly when there exists little, if any, significant corroborative evidence.

The downfall of *Frye* is being hastened by new scientific discoveries about judicial stalwarts such as common sense. Psychologists have found that the experience of laypersons, including jurors, may still be common, but often does not make sense. To illustrate, psychologists have discovered that just because an eyewitness is more certain about an identification does not make the eyewitness more reliable; that the perception of individuals is not a process equivalent to a camera snapshot but, instead, is highly selective and subject to suggestions from others; and that people tend to exaggerate estimates, particularly concerning duration. These conclusions indicate that even within the jury's common sense, many misconceptions may result. Thus, the concept of useful knowledge is being expanded so that experts in many different fields can testify about numerous types of subjects.[5]

§ 8.4 Expertise

Even if the underlying science upon which the testimony is based is reliable, the expert must also possess sufficient expertise in a particular field to be properly qualified. It behooves attorneys to obtain well-qualified witnesses because those witnesses will likely impress the jury the most. Although style counts a lot as well, there is no substitute for substance.

The qualification requirement has two components: a threshold level of expertise and a particular subject matter upon which the witness has the requisite

---

[5] For critiques of *Frye, see, e.g.,* Giannelli, *The Admissibility of Novel Scientific Evidence: Frye v. United States, A Half Century Later,* 80 Colum. L. Rev. 1197 (1980); Imwinkelreid, *The Standard for Admitting Scientific Evidence: A Critique from the Perspective Juror Psychology,* 28 Vill. L. Rev. 554, 557–60 (1982).

expertise. The first component involving quantity of expertise is broadly defined. Under the evidence rules of most states and the federal court system, a person may be qualified as an expert by the court as a result of experience, education, training, or otherwise. An expert need not possess academic degrees or special awards to qualify.

The second component is often overlooked. The expert must be qualified and offered on a particular issue or in a specific field or subject area. This will inform the jury that the expert knows about the salient question up for consideration. For example, a medical expert should not be offered simply as an expert in medicine, but rather as an expert in anesthesiology or forensic psychiatry. A farming expert, for example, may be qualified in tractor operation or corn grown in a special kind of organic soil.

§ 8.5 Helpfulness

Even if an expert is properly qualified and the scientific basis of the expert's testimony is deemed sufficiently reliable, the subject matter of the expert's testimony must be considered helpful to the jury in either understanding the evidence or deciding a fact at issue. "Helpfulness" is the linchpin of admissibility for experts. If the testimony is not helpful and it merely duplicates the jury's common sense or usurps the jury's responsibility to decide the facts, the expert will not be allowed to testify. In our current society, specialization is rampant, and expertise in a particular area is almost necessary to understand it. Thus, the threshold for helpfulness is extremely low: the more specialized society gets, the less people know about subjects other than their own area of expertise.

An expert is generally permitted to testify about the ultimate factual issue in a case. However, the testimony must not be framed in legal terms, particularly with respect to the mental state of an individual at the time of an event.[6] At least in this one area, courts have concluded that experts using legal jargon can overwhelm the jury's evaluative abilities, prejudicing the outcome. The ultimate issue area is a dynamic one, and courts struggle with drawing an acceptably clear line between exclusion and admissibility.[7]

Once permitted to testify, the expert may do so by relying on three different types of information:

1. The expert may testify based solely on hypothetical facts given to her at trial
2. The expert may testify based upon personal observations that occurred prior to trial
3. The expert may testify based upon personal observations during trial.

---

[6] See Fed. R. Evid. 704(b).

[7] See, e.g., C. Erhardt, *The Conflict Concerning Expert Witnesses and Legal Conclusions,* 92 W. Va. L. Rev. 645 (1990).

An expert who testifies based on hypothetical facts assists the jury by interpreting the facts presented. The hypothetical facts must not distort information or mislead the jury into an improper decision. This form of testimony is quite advantageous because the expert need not have any personal knowledge about the case, and the attorney's theory of the case can be presented in a clear and concise manner. The persuasive power of an expert testifying based on hypothetical questions is even greater considering that the attorney, in laying out the facts upon which the expert's conclusion is predicated, gets to repeat the theory of the case one more time. A second "bite of the apple" is almost always welcome and helpful in inculcating the jury with the party's theory.

An expert who acts as a fact witness, using personal observations made prior to trial, also has a special advantage—that of combining familiarity about the case with the ability to draw inferences from those observations. For example, a psychiatrist who has interviewed the defendant in a criminal case is more persuasive because she can testify about both her personal observations and the diagnosis that results from her observations.

The third form of testimony is probably not as persuasive or as common as the other two. The basis of this testimony is observations made at trial. This form occurs, for example, when a psychiatrist observes a defendant testify. The defendant witness may have interposed an insanity defense, or the defendant's competency to stand trial may be at issue. The psychiatrist subsequently testifies on these issues.

§ 8.6 Qualifications

Experts may become qualified in most jurisdictions in a variety of ways. These include education, training, and experience. It is a popular misconception that a witness must have a Ph.D., M.D., or equivalent degree to qualify as an expert. It is important to remember that whether the basis for expert testimony is education, training, or experience, the expert can provide significant assistance to the jury by shedding new light on the facts or assisting the jury in obtaining a different perspective about those facts. When explained properly by an expert, even subtleties and minor points may be enough to make a difference. The various ways a witness may qualify as an expert follow.

Education

Many expert witnesses are qualified by virtue of their education. An example is a medical doctor who has been awarded a medical degree or an engineering professor who has been awarded a doctorate in engineering. Juries are respectful generally of those called "professors" or of practitioners with advanced academic degrees. Other examples include a professor of education who has a doctorate in education; a social worker with a master's degree in social work or an advanced degree in a similar area; a mathematician who has an advanced degree in mathematics; an economist who has a degree from the London School of Economics; a biochemist who has studied genetic engineering; a microbiologist who can testify about a study she has performed as part of her academic education; and a computer expert who has completed advanced corporate education classes in computer software technology.

Training

Training is a common means of qualifying an expert witness. Trained individuals also impress juries, particularly if the training sounds rigorous or extensive. Fingerprint examiners undergo special training through the Federal Bureau of Investigation to learn how to identify the ridges and patterns that permit them to identify fingerprints. Doctors' residencies involve specialized training. Other examples of experience obtained through training are a document examiner who learned to identify handwriting; a police officer who trained to detect illegal narcotics; a photographer who apprenticed with a master photographer on lighting practices; a psychologist who apprenticed in a battered women's clinic; and a pilot trained by other pilots on how to fly a certain type of airplane.

Experience

Experts who qualify to testify based on experience include a vast assortment of persons. This group encompasses farmers who, by virtue of their experience, can testify as experts on farming and even burglars who can testify about the types of burglary tools often used in the commission of such crimes. Experts qualified by experience range from tool-mark examiners to motorcycle riders to sky divers. Several recent court cases provide additional illustrations:

1. In a personal injury action arising out of the alleged negligent placement of stop signs, a trial judge was found to have properly admitted expert testimony from a "human factors" consultant, who had experience in traffic device placement, and an accident reconstruction expert.[8]
2. In a murder prosecution in which a central issue was the identification of the defendant's truck on a dark street, the appellate court held that there was no abuse of discretion in permitting the testimony of an expert in photography who had extensive experience in the area of lighting.[9]
3. In an action to set aside a will in which most of the estate was left to the decedent's conservator and the attorney, the appellate court found that it was not an abuse of discretion to permit the chair of the State Bar Grievance

---

[8] *See* Cook v. State, 431 N.W.2d 800 (Iowa 1988).

[9] *See* Bowden v. State, 761 S.W.2d 148 (Ark. 1988).

Committee to offer an opinion on whether the attorney violated the Code of Professional Responsibility.[10]

Meeting the Prerequisites of Expert Testimony at Trial—A Checklist

1. Reliability
   - ____ a. If the expert is relying on a novel science, is that science generally accepted in the field or otherwise reliable?
   - ____ b. Based on what support or authority?
   - ____ c. Is the factual information used by the expert to form an opinion reasonably relied on by experts in the field?
2. Qualifications
   - ____ a. The expert is qualified in which particular field or subspecialty?
   - ____ b. Is the expert's qualification based on education, training, experience, or a combination of the three?
3. Helpfulness
   - ____ How is the expert helpful to the trier of the fact in either deciding a fact at issue or in understanding evidence?

THE EXPERT

§ 8.7 Why Hire an Expert?

Experts are not appropriate in every case. Sometimes juries or attorneys would not benefit sufficiently from experts to warrant their use. If the experts merely request the factual data or draw unsupported conclusions, juries may have even an adverse reaction. Counsel must decide early enough whether the case is suitable for an expert witness. In deciding this question, counsel, if possible, should construct a general preliminary theory of the case. Then counsel should ask two questions: (1) Would an expert assist counsel in understanding and presenting the theory of the case? (2) Would an expert help persuade the trier of fact (generally the jury) that the theory of the case is the correct one?

To help in determining whether an expert is warranted, counsel can acquire background information by reading various books about experts and the services experts can provide. For example, the National Forensic Center publishes a forensic bibliography covering many specialties. The bibliography can assist the attorney in learning about the kinds of experts that exist and the substance of the various experts' testimony.

---

[10] *See In re* Estate of Dankbar, 430 N.W.2d 124 (Iowa 1988).

Various considerations determine whether counsel wishes to hire an expert. One factor is the technical complexity of the facts or principles associated with a case. As technology advances and social scientists discover new and important insights about human behavior, even "slip-and-fall" cases can become complex. The attorneys cannot be expected to be fully versed about the scientific or technical underpinnings of a case without experience, training in a particular scientific area, or the consultation of an expert. Similarly, jurors and judges may have an incomplete understanding of complex or obscure scientific and technological principles. Thus, for example, an expert may serve to explain to the jury how an electric toaster works and why it becomes defective; how the drive shaft of an automobile spins; or why a particular children's product is flameproof except under certain circumstances.

Although experts often testify at trial, the expert may be quite valuable also in the preparation phase of the case. An expert psychologist may assist the attorney with general principles in jury selection, with a particular strategy that an attorney desires to pretest in a mock hearing, or with strategies counsel is developing for trial.

Pretrial assistance also includes various tests the expert can perform. Toxicologists perform blood and urine testing. Other experts re-create an accident or the operation of a machine that is the basis of a personal injury claim. Other experts may investigate the scientific reasons for a defect in a product or why a person was injured or became ill.

An expert may also serve to explain the customs or trade practices in a particular business. If the interpretation of a contract or bill of lading is relevant to litigation, the expert can provide important contextual information to allow the jury, as trier of fact, to resolve the dispute. Some jurors have the equivalent of a math phobia when it comes to business-related or scientific terms.

Additionally, an expert can help to explain the meanings of certain words that depend upon their cultural context or nonbusiness usage. Such words may constitute "terms of art" and require special explanation. For example, the word *bad* in certain contexts can mean good, as in "that person is bad." Without an expert, the jurors who lack a sufficient understanding of the context will be completely misconstruing important facts.

An expert accountant or actuary may provide estimates of potential economic damages in a particular case. They may create projections involving mathematical calculations based on the facts of the case. The losses involved in such calculations may be personal, involving psychological and physical injury, or business-related.

The presence of experts often sends a message to the jury that the case is a worthy one. It suggests that the case involves sufficiently weighty, complex, or difficult issues. The aura of expertise that accompanies such witnesses may have a spill-over effect on the rest of the case. While an expert should not be called simply because of the aura of expertise that the witness provides, such a factor may be relevant in deciding whether an expert will be helpful.

The testimony of experts applies in some situations more than others. For example, when a person's mental state on a particular occasion is relevant to the issues in the case, an expert is usually relied on to provide a diagnosis and treatment assessment. Although fact witnesses can testify about their observations at the time and may actually be the best source of information, an expert psychiatrist or psychologist can interpret that factual information and add a different dimension to the case.

§ 8.8   Helpfulness

The helpfulness of the expert is the primary factor in determining whether an expert should be retained, either to testify or for pretrial or sentencing purposes. Some of the considerations in ascertaining whether helpfulness exists include the following questions:

Helpfulness Checklist

_____ 1. How complex is the case? (The more complex it is, the more likely that an expert witness will assist the jury in understanding the issues to be decided.)

_____ 2. How much fact evidence exists in a particular area? (If sufficient independent fact evidence does not exist or is not easily organized in its presentation, an expert may provide assistance. While an expert is often not an evidence substitute, the quantity and quality of evidence in any one area may serve as a consideration.)

_____ 3. Does the jury expect an expert? (If it is likely the jury expects an expert based on the nature of the case, then it is preferable to hire one.)

_____ 4. Does the opposition have an expert witness? (It is often important to rebut expert testimony _with_ expert testimony. Cross-examination may be insufficient.)

_____ 5. How would the expert augment or supplement the existing testimony? (What would the expert be testifying on? The expert should not simply repeat a lay witness's testimony.)

§ 8.9   Nature of the Case

In certain types of cases, an expert is either expressly or implicitly required. In medical malpractice cases, for example, many jurisdictions require that an expert testify on the issue of the minimum acceptable standard of practice in the relevant community.

To determine whether an expert is necessary in a particular type of case, an attorney should check the law of the local jurisdiction as well as the common practice among the local bar. In some cases, it is not necessary to hire an expert, but it may be common practice to do so.

§ 8.10 Cost

In every case, cost is an issue. For example, in a personal injury case based on a contingency fee, cost may dictate whether an expert of marginal utility is hired. Even if counsel is paid on an hourly basis and money is available for experts, the cost of the expert still may be an important factor in the decision-making process.

The cost factor should be discussed with the expert prior to hiring. Counsel can review with the expert the parameters of the expert's anticipated participation in the case and seek an estimate of total costs. This approach will permit counsel to determine whether hiring an expert will be cost-effective.

SELECTING THE EXPERT WITNESS

§ 8.11 Resources

Once counsel decides to hire an expert, there are different ways to locate the most suitable one. Some experts advertise, but many others do not. Thus, locating an expert often depends on the ingenuity of the attorney.

One source of expert witnesses is academia. Many university professors have developed an expertise in a particular area. This expertise, often based on years of practice, training, or research, can be discovered by contacting a university or academic institution and asking which instructors are knowledgeable about the area in question.

In addition to academic institutions, expert witnesses may be located through the use of directories and registries. The *Forensic Services Directory*, for example, lists numerous forensic science experts. Other major directories are the *Technical Advisory Service for Attorneys (TASA)* and the *Expert Witness Index Service*. The *Forensic Services Directory* is published by the National Forensic Center, which is located in Lawrenceville, New Jersey. The *TASA* organization is located in Ft. Washington, Pennsylvania, and Phoenix, Arizona. The *Expert Witness Index Service* is located in Chicago, Illinois.

While some directories such as *TASA* provide a wide variety of listings, others focus on a particular area. For example, the Technical Assistance Bureau, located in Reston, Virginia, deals only with medical expertise; the *Aerospace Consultants Directory* and *Automotive Consultants Directory* deal with the subspecialties listed in the titles. (Both of these directories are published by the Society of Automotive Engineers located in Warrendale, Pennsylvania.)

In addition to clearing houses and the academic arena, a third source of expert witnesses is professional organizations. Many experts belong to various professional and trade associations. Attorneys are allowed to join some of these organizations, or they may be able to obtain membership lists from them. These groups include the American Academy of Forensic Sciences, the American Standards Testing Bureau, the National Safety Council, the American Bar Association, the Association of Trial Lawyers of America, and the American Society for Testing and Materials.[11] Numerous other groups exist, and by tapping into one of these organizations, an attorney can obtain a list of many experts in a particular field.

Magazines and other periodicals often contain advertisements by experts. This literature includes *Trial Magazine*, published by the Association of Trial Lawyers of America in Washington, D.C.; *The Expert and the Law*, published by the National Forensic Center, in Lawrenceville, New Jersey; *The Advocate*, published by the Los Angeles Trial Lawyers Association; *Consultants News*, published by Kennedy and Kennedy, Inc., of Fitzwilliam, New Hampshire; and the *Consulting Opportunities Journal*, published by J. Stephen Lanning of Gapland, Maryland.[12]

An additional method for locating the expert is through conferences or continuing education classes that discuss particular areas of expertise. A considerable number of experts in a particular area may gather at a specialty conference. A list of attendees may be made available for purchase or distribution, or attorneys can attempt to otherwise contact those persons attending the conference.

An additional and sometimes overlooked source of information is other attorneys who routinely work with or hire experts in a particular field. Attorneys who regularly use experts will likely maintain a list of potential witnesses, as well as evaluations about those witnesses. Of course, counsel must trust the other attorneys from whom advice is sought.

Modern technology, particularly the computer, can be utilized to speed up the location process. Computers can provide ready accessibility to numerous academic journals or reviews and can display and share additional information. The computer can be used as an organizing tool as well, maintaining records of names and phone numbers of experts or persons who may assist in locating experts in a particular field. Such a data bank may be invaluable in future cases.

Expert Witness Resource Checklist

____   1.   Other attorneys
____   2.   Other professionals

---

[11] *See generally,* D. Poynter, The Expert Witness Handbook (1987).

[12] *Id.*

_____   3.   Professional organizations
_____   4.   Academic institutions
_____   5.   Literature (magazines and other periodicals)
_____   6.   Clearing houses
_____   7.   Continuing education programs and specialty conferences
_____   8.   Other

§ 8.12   The Right Expert

An attorney who decides to hire an expert witness often has a choice between experts. Unfortunately, not all experts are equally diligent, dependable, persuasive, and ethical. The attorney can safeguard the selection in several ways.

When deciding between experts, the lawyer can seek the advice or confirmation of other lawyers who deal with experts in the same area. The approval or disapproval of other attorneys who have used the services of the expert may prove relevant or even determinative in the hiring process.

It is important for the attorney to discover which experts should be avoided. Some experts may disclose incorrect information, fail to disclose pertinent information, or present themselves in a fashion that would not promote the attorney's case.

It may be worthwhile to assess the work habits of experts. They are often asked to look through voluminous documents and spend a great deal of time pouring over minute details. If an expert appears to jump to conclusions or to avoid rigorous preparation, the cause may not be promoted even though the witness's opinions are compatible with the attorney's position in the case. It is important to remember that the attorney's initial impression of the expert may be quite similar to a jury's, and believing that the expert will change is often incorrect.

Prior to hiring an expert, it is useful to review as much as is possible of the expert's publications, presented papers, and other written materials and to explore the expert's history as a testifying witness either in depositions or at trial. This might be accomplished through special computer networks, by reviewing a lawsuit index if one exists, or by inquiring at the expert's place of business. The more information an attorney gathers about the expert, the more informed the hiring decision will be.

The expert's licensing status is also important. It is preferable not to take the expert's academic degrees and licenses at face value. A telephone call to the licensing institution or professional grievance committee in question may serve as a worthwhile check. It is also important to find out whether complaints have been lodged against the expert and whether any suspensions, revocations, or other information bearing on the expert's credibility exists.

§ 8.13 Credentials

Before commencing with the selection process, it is important for the lawyer to understand the credentials of the type of expert required. In a criminal case when insanity or competency to stand trial is at issue, for example, the attorney should know the difference between a psychologist and a psychiatrist. (A *psychiatrist* is a medical doctor who diagnoses and treats mental illness. A psychiatrist can prescribe medication to treat emotional or mental disorders. A psychologist, on the other hand, generally is a person with a master's or doctorate degree in psychology and clinical training in the area, but who cannot dispense medication.)

In essence, because some people are more "expert" than others or have very specialized focuses, it is important to review the expert's credentials carefully. Relevant considerations include:

1. Whether the expert has published in the field
2. The level of postgraduate training
3. Whether the person is certified in the particular specialty practiced
4. The expert's level of certification
5. Whether the expert testified as an expert before
6. If the expert has testified before, the number of times
7. In what court the testimony was given
8. Whether the expert has given any speeches or academic presentations
9. Whether the expert has held any positions in professional organizations
10. Whether the expert has written any treatises
11. Whether the expert has testified before in the particular court in which the case is pending
12. Whether the expert testified or was called to testify on behalf of plaintiff or defendant.

§ 8.14 Demeanor

Another important factor in selecting an expert is the person's demeanor. In essence, this issue concerns subjective believability. Does the individual look and act like an expert? Although some individuals may have impeccable credentials and may be extremely accomplished, if they do not present themselves well, juries may discount their testimony, or worse, disbelieve them. This is not to say that experts should be slick, only sincere and believable. Thus, it may be helpful to actually meet or study photographs of expert witnesses before hiring them.

§ 8.15 Communicative Ability

Although a person may be sufficiently qualified and have the look of an expert, if that person cannot adequately communicate with the jury, the value of the testimony may be severely diminished. If jurors do not understand it, the testimony is worthless. In a sense, the expert is a teacher, and the jurors are the students. Sensitivity to the "students" is important. If the expert can communicate difficult concepts easily, and in a form the jury will understand, it is likely the expert will be more effective.

Thus, before hiring an expert it may be helpful to consider whether this person can teach effectively. The answer might depend on the circumstances. Some experts are more comfortable explaining a diagram, chart, or model than discussing the substance of testimony directly. Still others may prefer to stand outside the witness box to present information, such as diagrams, than to sit in the witness box. These practical issues should be addressed in advance.

PREPARING THE EXPERT WITNESS

§ 8.16 The Interview

When interviewing an expert, as with most witnesses, the attorney should have three distinct objectives: to give information, to get information, and to establish rapport.

The attorney gives the expert a variety of information. It is important to inform the expert about why the expert has been called to testify and about the exact nature of the subject matter of the testimony. The lawyer may provide the expert with background information: about the case and the persons potentially involved; the layout of the courtroom; the length of time allocated for the expert's preparation and actual testimony; the identities of opposing experts, if any, who will testify for the opponent; and other pertinent information.

In addition to giving information, the attorney also should obtain information from the expert. This information should include the expert's qualifications and other pertinent data about the expert. At this stage of involvement, the expert may not be able to offer an opinion about the case or the facts at issue.

Giving and getting information in this way has the beneficial side effect of promoting rapport between the attorney and the expert. Establishing rapport is important to the attorney's professional relationship with the expert. The direct examination will go more smoothly if a good rapport exists.

Interview Checklist

A. Giving Information to the Expert
____ 1. About the case
____ 2. About the expert's role in the case
  ____ a. Pretrial advice
  ____ b. Experimental testing
  ____ c. Academic research (including economic evaluations of damages)
  ____ d. Written reports and/or evaluations
  ____ e. Creation and use of graphs, charts, models, diagrams
____ 3. Time and money—anticipated amount of time to be spent by the expert on the case, and manner and amount of compensation
____ 4. Opposing experts
____ 5. Other weaknesses or special circumstances

B. Obtaining Information from the expert
____ 1. Qualifications—education, experience, training, publications, professional organizations, other activities
____ 2. Familiarity of expert with particular subject matter
____ 3. Background of expert in similar cases
____ 4. Potential biases of expert
____ 5. Other weaknesses of the expert as a witness
  ____ a. Contradictions
  ____ b. Convictions
  ____ c. Prior bad acts
  ____ d. Testimonial capacities
  ____ e. Prior inconsistent statements

C. Establishing Rapport
____ 1. Communicative ability
____ 2. Demeanor

§ 8.17 Preparation for the Trial

It is the responsibility of the attorney to prepare witnesses for trial. This may mean actually rehearsing the witness as if the witness was on the witness stand. Experts are generally familiar with the litigation process, so a rehearsal is often unnecessary. A rehearsal may be useful, however, if only to familiarize the expert and the attorney with each other's style and habits. If a rehearsal occurs, the responses must be the witness's own words and not the lawyer's or those of someone else. It is important to note that if the testimony sounds rehearsed, it will be less credible. The quickest way to lose a jury is to read the opening or closing or to offer a witness who sounds rehearsed.

The Expert's Credibility

An attorney can prepare an expert in other ways. An expert can be informed to look like an expert—to dress conservatively and formally, if at all possible. First impressions count with jurors, and count for a lot. If the expert's appearance meets the expectations of the jury, it is reasonable to believe that the expert will have greater credibility at the outset.

It also may be necessary to politely but firmly remind the expert about the role she is to play at trial. Expert testimony is not a lecture in which the expert is given free rein. Nor is it a scientific inquiry where truth is valued more than public policy or individual rights. Rather, a trial or deposition is a formalized procedure governed and limited by legal rules. Experts must be informed that these rules and limitations are paramount, whether the expert approves of those rules or not. Thus, although an expert may desire to explain an answer on cross-examination, the court may not permit the expert to do so. If informed about such limitations in advance, the expert is less likely to become frustrated or argumentative while testifying, which would have an adverse effect on the jury. At the very least, experts are more persuasive when poised (as the commercial once said, "Never let them see you sweat").

Of particular discomfort to experts is the adversarial nature of the questions put by opposing counsel. The expert should be told that generally little is achieved by becoming angry or upset about the questions asked. The expert should be reminded that she is a professional and should always appear as such at either a deposition, a trial, or other proceeding.

It is also worth cautioning the expert not to get caught up in the adversarial nature of the deposition or trial. The expert should not shade, exaggerate, or otherwise provide incomplete answers just because those responses might disadvantage the opponent's position. In addition to the ethical obligations associated with testimony at trial, if an expert is perceived by the jury to be exaggerating or otherwise less than completely truthful, this will serve to undermine the expert's credibility. Thus, it is helpful if the expert endeavors to be objective and truthful.

The Expert's Presentation

The use of eye contact to promote rapport between the expert and the jury is a subject worthy of express attention. Some experts prefer to respond primarily and directly to the jury. Others, who may be less comfortable with such a technique, return eye contact to the attorney who is asking the questions. Some experts engage in a combination of both techniques. The options and approaches should be expressly explored prior to the expert's testimony.

Experts, like most people, often hear what they want to hear. Thus, it is extremely important for the expert to be reminded to listen carefully to the questions asked before answering. It is often a good idea to tell the expert to count to three before answering questions, especially on cross-examination, or to at least pause for one second. This will promote responsiveness and accuracy.

The way in which the expert speaks is also significant. Because many juries are not permitted to take notes, the jurors rely solely on the expert's presentation. The expert and the attorneys should be cognizant of how difficult it is to assimilate vast amounts of often complex information without notes (and why some courts permit jurors to take notes). Thus, the expert should speak slowly and carefully, particularly in areas that the expert wishes to emphasize. The expert is not permitted to ask the jury whether they understand what was said; thus, this suggestion becomes even more important.

A situation may arise when the expert does not understand a question put by either side, because it is poorly phrased or simply unfamiliar in the form asked. If this occurs, the expert should not attempt to answer the question but should ask the attorney to rephrase it. If the expert does not understand it, chances are the jury does not either. An alternative suggestion is to have the expert repeat what she thinks the question states before answering it, that is, "If I understand the question correctly, you have asked whether ... ."

A corollary to this suggestion pertains to traps set for the unwary expert by the use of hypothetical questions. Given a series of facts that are assumed, the expert is asked to draw inferences from them. If the expert has difficulty with one or more of the facts, she should say so and explain why. The expert should not simply ignore the problems with the hypothetical or attempt to answer the question as framed.

The Expert's Accuracy

If the expert says something and then realizes it is incorrect, she should immediately attempt to correct herself. Inadvertent errors are commonplace, but the harm is augmented if the expert appears to believe that mistakes are not allowed. If the expert treats such a mistake as human, the harm from the error should be minimized. Jurors realize that experts are human, and they may even warm to an expert who admits to being such (as long as these mistakes do not occur frequently during the testimony).

An expert should mean what she says. Thus, if the expert says that something is "highly likely," the expert should intend it and not simply be using words loosely. Similarly, the expert should be careful with all adjectives used because these are the kinds of opinion statements that attorneys often successfully attack on cross-examination.

Sometimes, despite the most attentive preparation, an expert will have a memory lapse while testifying. The expert should be told that there is no need to panic if such a thing occurs. Instead, the expert should say that the answer escapes her memory at the time. The expert's memory may then be refreshed through documents or any other form of evidence, admissible or not, that might assist in awakening the witness's memory. Juries like honesty and in many instances will forgive experts for human frailties.

Experts tend to speak at length on their area of expertise. It is especially important to remind the expert not to volunteer information. This is true on both direct and cross-examination. On direct examination, it is counsel's responsibility to control the nature and scope of the examination. On cross-examination, it is rarely helpful to volunteer information. Thus, the expert should be reminded to answer only the questions asked—no more and no less.

Preparation for Cross-Examination

It is important for counsel to prepare the expert for cross-examination as well as direct examination. Counsel can review all of the potential impeachment areas with the expert and actually perform a mock cross-examination with the witness.

During cross-examination, the expert may be requested to answer "yes" or "no" to a particular question. Such a technique may either distort a response, if the answer cannot be simply framed as either "yes" or "no," or may leave an unfair impression with the trier of fact. In these instances, if a "yes" or "no" is not possible or appropriate, the expert should say so. In such situations, courts will generally permit a limited explanation of an expert's answer. Even if the court does not permit an immediate elaboration, the proponent of the expert can follow up with questions on redirect examination.

On cross-examination, attorneys generally attempt to control the pace of the examination. Jurors are often impressed by the pacing or cadence of a cross-examination. The expert should be told not to be bullied into speaking before either understanding the question or taking the time to think of the answer.

In preparing the expert for cross-examination, the attorney should inform the person about often used impeachment tactics, such as questions that ask whether the expert is being paid for testimony in court (the responses include: "I am being paid for my time, not my testimony"; "I am being paid for my time just like you and the other lawyers in this case").

Checklist for Preparing the Expert Witness

For each expert witness, the following items should be reviewed.

_____   1.   Subject matter about which the expert can be expected to testify
_____   2.   Qualifications of the expert relevant to the case at bar
_____   3.   The general opinions of the expert on the particular issue at hand

_____ 4. The expert's rationale or basis for her conclusions

_____ 5. Any special information pertinent to important issues, deposition, or trial

_____ 6. Assistance used or offered by the expert, including graphs, charts, reports, models, or test results

EXPERT WITNESS AT DEPOSITION AND TRIAL

§ 8.18 Direct Examination

In many respects expert witnesses are like any other witness and can be examined in a similar fashion. However, the appellation of "expert" also distinguishes this category of witness, necessitating special considerations on both direct and cross-examination.

Of particular difficulty is the fact that many experts, based on their professional experience in the trial system, appear to be able to operate almost without the assistance of the attorney. Thus, there is a tendency for the attorney to let the expert lead while testifying, especially on direct examination. This approach can produce dangerous results. The expert does not know the case or the jury. The attorney does. As the case develops, it is the attorney who should be the "orchestra conductor," focusing the expert and emphasizing certain points consistent with the attorney's conceptualization of the case.

The Courtroom Atmosphere

Juries are especially impressed by charts, graphs, models, and other kinds of visual presentations. Simply put, jurors have become socialized to respond to visual aids. They will remember the testimony better with associated visual assistance, and a chart, graph, or other representative evidence offers attorneys the opportunity to repeat testimony. Further, experts often feel more comfortable explaining something tangible like a chart, instead of simply responding to questions. An expert in accident reconstruction, for example, would be much more effective if she was able to use a diagram explaining her conclusions, instead of forcing the jury to conjure up an image of the scene on its own.

There is also no substitute for enthusiasm. An unenthusiastic or tired expert's testimony will result in a jury who is disinterested in the subject, no matter how inherently interesting. An enthusiastic expert, on the other hand, can cause even an otherwise dull area of testimony to come alive.

Along these same lines, it is important to keep in mind that jurors are influenced greatly by popular culture, such as the television show "L.A. Law." Building drama or excitement into the testimony, even if it involves only the use of a graph or chart, feeds the jurors' expectations. While it is not the fault of lawyers or experts that cases are often dull, jurors may implicitly hold it against the parties and credit the expert's testimony less.

The Expert's Attitude

While the substance of the testimony is important to a jury, so are its form and the people presenting it. If it is presented by a person who is condescending, or confusing, the jurors will discredit the substance. There is nothing worse than an expert who says to the jury, "Let me explain this concept to you," and then grimaces. Making the jury feel unintelligent is a cardinal error.

Similarly, jurors credit the confident, personable witness who can talk with the jury, not down to it. Such experts offer the jurors eye contact, hold themselves erect on the witness stand without slumping over, do not constantly apologize for the opinions provided, and appear to believe in themselves. If a psychiatrist testifies in a criminal case about the defendant's sanity, the more disheveled the witness appears, the more the witness will be confused with the patient and the less the expert's presumption of credibility attaches. Thus, counsel should be aware that the appearance, demeanor, attitude, and nonverbal cues of the expert witness all play a major role in the effectiveness of that witness's testimony with the jury.

Additional Suggestions About Direct Examination

1. Every witness, including experts, should have three parts to the testimony—background, setting the scene, and action. Each part serves a distinct purpose. Do not omit the background of the expert; this personalizes and strengthens the expert's credibility.
2. As a general rule, do not stipulate to the expert's credentials when asked. (It is important to establish the credibility of the witness.)
3. Cover the expert's credentials precisely.
4. It is the expert's show; don't steal it.
5. Make sure the expert translates "expert talk" into plain English.
6. The expert is the teacher, her class is the jury, and the attorney is merely an off-stage facilitator.
7. An expert generally should look confident, be confident, and explain her answers.
8. Experts should not overreach; exaggeration always comes back to haunt you in the end.
9. A good question to ask experts on direct examination is "Why?".
10. Re-ask questions subjected to an overruled objection for the jury's sake, not the expert's.

11. Experts should leave the trial business to the lawyers and the judge.

12. Experts are professionals and should act the part (do not lose composure).

13. Never underestimate the lawyers, the judge, the jury, or even the elderly couple watching in the front row (prepare, prepare, prepare).[13]

§ 8.19   Cross-Examination

Cross-examination is a right, not a privilege.[14] To paraphrase Professor John Henry Wigmore, cross-examination is the greatest legal engine for discovering the truth. Thus, it is an important and often integral part of the case.

Cross-examination serves several diverse purposes. It can be used to attack the credibility of the opposing witnesses, to corroborate counsel's own case, or to elicit additional information not brought forth on direct examination. If these objectives will not be met by cross-examination, no cross-examination should occur.

All too often, an attorney may attempt to cross-examine a witness, expert or not, without having a preconceived "game plan." This is problematic. Asking questions for questions' sake simply does not serve the attorney or her case.

The Manner of Questioning

On cross-examination, an expert witness rarely will concede that the essence of her testimony was in error. Thus, frontal attacks on an expert are often futile and may simply create an appearance of arguing with the witness. This is risky because jurors will often take sides in a perceived argument, and it could prejudice the more substantive aspects of the case.

It is extremely important to ask experts simple and direct questions. Given the technical and scientific nature of many experts' testimony, it is important to maintain the impact of cross-examination while allowing the jury to understand the nature of the questions. If the expert provides an answer filled with jargon or technical terms, the attorney must assertively follow up with explanatory questions in language the jurors can understand. Otherwise, the impact of the cross-examination, no matter how stellar, will be lost. Jurors are used to media such as television commercials that highlight main points. In essence, jurors like, and remember, slogans or their functional equivalent.

Along a similar vein, the cross-examiner should take pains to highlight the key points on cross-examination. The late Professor Irving Younger suggested that the cross-examiner has very few points to make. Although these points may be small in number, an attorney can ask many questions about each point to highlight

---

[13] For a fine source of types of questions to ask experts, *see, e.g.,* E. Salcines, *Trial Techniques Predicate Questions,* National District Attorney's Association, Chicago (1977).

[14] *See, e.g.,* Davis v. Alaska, 410 U.S. 925, 93 S.Ct. 1392.

and emphasize the importance of that particular issue. For example, in a "driving-under-the-influence" case, an expert who is being questioned about the effect of six glasses of vodka on a person who is the size of the defendant could also be asked about the effect of one glass, two glasses, three glasses, four glasses, and then five glasses of vodka. This buildup allows the jury to get the message loud and clear.

Nonverbal Tools

Even on cross-examination, eye contact and body language are significant. It is not as important for the attorney to maintain eye contact with the witness, but rather to use eye contact to communicate a lack of belief in the witness's statements. This nonverbal message can result from eye contact with the jury, facial expressions, pacing, or a lack of eye contact with the witness. Looking at the jury during an important part of the question, or simply away from the witness, is a way of saying that the witness is incredible or only partially credible. The use of such nonverbal tools, however, may be most persuasive when understated and not presented in an overly dramatic fashion.

Nonverbal cues are important to experts as well. Jurors regularly use nonverbal cues to evaluate individuals in the courtroom. These hundreds of different cues are all used to weigh the credibility of the speakers. If the expert gives the impression to the jury that she does not care, or is inaccurate, the believability of the witness will be in doubt no matter what her words. But experts, like other laypersons, can be taught effective nonverbal communication.

The Difficult Witness

One particularly difficult expert is the "runaway" witness. This is the expert who refuses to answer questions that are asked but insists on answering other kinds of questions to the witness's own liking. When this occurs, the jury may lose respect for counsel's ability to maintain poise and control.

Such a witness may be dealt with in several ways. It is not helpful to ask the judge to control the witness. This can appear to be a sign of weakness, like a child asking a parent for help with a sibling. While such a request may be inevitable, it is often useful to first use body language. That is, if the witness insists on ignoring a question or not following up on it, the attorney can put up her hand in a stop motion. This often has the effect of stopping the witness from speaking. Another technique is to repeat the same question several times. After a while, the witness learns in a Pavlovian fashion what will not be tolerated and eventually provides a straightforward and simple answer.[15]

---

[15] *See generally,* L. Pozner and R. Dodd, *Controlling the Runaway Witness: Tried and True Techniques for Cross Examination,* Trial, Jan. 1991, at 110 (suggesting as well that it is often helpful if the court reporter is asked to read back a question).

If the "broken-record" technique does not succeed and the witness still persists in refusing to answer, it may be helpful to ask the witness a directly opposing question. The opposite question would suggest a contrary—and likely incorrect—proposition. For example, a witness who refuses to say that the earth's seas are rising each year might be asked whether she's saying the earth's seas are falling each year. Witnesses are often quick to dispel the inference that they have testified to a proposition that appears to be incorrect.

After the witness has been drawn back into the issue by such a technique, the initial question can be put to the witness once again. For example, if the expert is asked whether the defendant is suffering from schizophrenia at the time of the incident in question, the expert can be asked, "So are you saying that the witness was not suffering from any mental disease or defect at all at the time of the incident?" After the witness says, "No, I wasn't saying that," the attorney can then follow up with, "So you are saying the witness suffers from schizophrenia?"[16]

To combat the aura of expertise that envelops an expert witness, it is often useful to ask the witness about particular facts in the record that the witness may not recall. If the witness fails to recall enough of these small but pertinent facts, this may provide the inference that the witness is less than omniscient about the particular case.

One other useful technique on cross-examination is the "not" approach. An expert cannot be expected to have performed every test, or interviewed a person continuously, or to otherwise have "done it all." Thus, the expert can be asked about what she did not do, observe, or know. For example, counsel may suggest that the expert has spent only limited time in either interviewing witnesses or examining the issue in question—such as asking, "You did not see the defendant until three months after the incident, isn't that right, Doctor? You also have not seen her in the five months after that one visit?"

On cross-examination, as on direct examination, the attorney should re-ask a question for the jury after an objection is overruled. Even if the expert remembers the question, some of the jurors may not. The attorney should always remember that the cross-examination is being done for two audiences: the jury, that is, the trier of fact; and the record. Following are some additional suggestions regarding the cross-examination of experts.

Cross-Examination Pointers

1. Generally, attacking the witness directly is a "no-no" (if it is to be done, proceed with caution).
2. Particularly on voir dire of the expert, attack the expert's qualifications through the "not" method (for example, "You are not board-certified,

---

[16] For further suggestions of a helpful nature, *see generally*, M. Dombroff, *Cross Examining Witness: The Do's and Don'ts*, Trial, Feb. 1987, at 74.

Doctor? You did not graduate with highest honors from medical school? You did not write the treatise?").

3. If appropriate, attack the facts. Sooner or later the expert has to rely on some facts to support her conclusions.

4. Change facts in hypothetical questions put to experts.

5. Attack the expert with treatises in the field.

6. Permit the expert to become unprofessional.

7. Maintain control over the direction of the cross-examination; train the expert, if possible, not to speak nonstop and to only answer the questions asked.

8. Control the pace of the examination.

9. Look for the ambiguities, probabilities, or variables in the case and ask the expert to agree that they exist.

10. Use the expert to corroborate your case.

11. Do not mislead or unfairly attack the witness.[17]

---

[17] For additional information on the cross-examination of experts, *see generally,* Note, *Cross Examination of Expert Witness: Dispelling the Aura of Reliability,* 42 U. Miami L. Rev. 1073 (1988); John Bonina, *The Cross Examination of an Expert Witness,* The Practicing Law Institute (Oct. 1988). *See also,* C. Schmidt, *Cross Examination of an Expert Witness,* 13 St. Mary's L.J. 89 (1981) (emphasizing preparation as an extremely important part of cross-examination); M. Graham, *Expert Witness Testimony and the Federal Rules of Evidence: Insuring Adequate Assurance of Trustworthiness,* 1986 U. Ill. L. Rev. 43 (1986).

CHAPTER 9

VOIR DIRE

Stacey D. Mullins

§ 9.1   Trial by Jury

Perhaps it was best summarized by Thomas Jefferson when in 1788 he said, "I consider trial by jury as the only anchor ever yet imagined by man, by which a government can be held to the principles of the constitution." The Sixth

Amendment to the Constitution of the United States of America guarantees every criminal defendant the right to a trial by jury. Provisions for trial by jury for civil actions vary among the states.

Voir dire is the lawyer's opportunity to have a direct impact upon the fairness and the sanctity of the selection process and, ultimately, upon the process of trial by jury.

§ 9.2   Introduction to Jury Selection

The Bull and the Bullfrog

A young bullfrog was exploring the far end of the pond, when a bull walked up for a drink of water. The bullfrog was amazed by the bull's size. He had never seen anything so large before. Excited, he swam home to tell his father what he had seen.

"Father, I saw the most gigantic animal in the world," said the young bullfrog. "He was at the other end of the pond."

"Now son," his father replied, "everyone knows that I'm the biggest animal in this pond. Just watch me."

The old bullfrog took in a big gulp of air and puffed himself up.

"Was that animal bigger than this?" the father asked.

"Much bigger than that," said his son.

"How about now?" asked the father, puffing himself even bigger.

"I'm afraid he was much bigger still," said the son. "Well," said the father bullfrog, as he sucked in as much air as he could, "he couldn't have been much bigger than this!"

"But he really was *much* bigger than that," replied the young bullfrog.

"OK son, watch me now. He couldn't possibly have been bigger than this."

The old bullfrog began to puff himself up a little bit more when suddenly— BANG! He burst into tiny pieces.

—Aesop's Fables

As the old bullfrog in Aesop's fable learned in a most unfortunate way, "Be Yourself." Jury selection is generally the first time potential jurors have the opportunity to meet the lawyers. From the moment they walk into the courtroom, lawyers must always remember what the old bullfrog learned, be yourself.

Most jurors enter the courtroom with a plethora of preconceived notions about what lawyers are like, what plaintiffs with orthopedic disabilities are like, and generally what the entire process is like. The purpose of this chapter is to provide a useful guide to consider and consult when handling a case involving an orthopedic disability.

PREPARING FOR JURY SELECTION

§ 9.3 Juror Profile

In order to effectively conduct jury selection in a case involving an orthopedic disability, a juror profile should be established. A juror profile is dependent upon a number of factors. A tremendous amount of emphasis often is placed upon age, gender, occupation, and socioeconomic level. Such profiles often result in generalizations of stereotypical standards and beliefs.

Experts tell us that reliance solely upon age, gender, and occupation will likely produce unfavorable results. Dr. Amy Singer of Trial Consultants, Inc. recommends that the lawyer consider and evaluate the prospective juror's life experiences, value beliefs, and psychosyntricity.

Prospective jurors' life experiences will affect their willingness to find liability on the part of the defendant. For example, the lawyer who has a products liability case against Ford Motor Company would want to know that a prospective juror's family owns five Fords and they have been loyal customers of Ford for 20 years.

Prospective jurors' value beliefs will affect their willingness to award damages on behalf of the plaintiff. The lawyer handling a medical malpractice action will want to know whether a prospective juror feels that medical malpractice actions are the cause of the high cost of medical care.

Psychosyntricity is a third area of consideration that Dr. Singer highly recommends. Psychosyntricity tests a prospective juror's ability or willingness to empathize with the plaintiff. For example, two prospective jurors both may have lost their husbands. Juror One may feel that although she did not recover any money when she lost her husband, she can understand why someone should. Juror Two may feel that because she did not recover anything when she lost her husband, why should the plaintiff be entitled to recover. Juror Two is considered to be psychocentric and not good for the plaintiff.

§ 9.4 Demographics

It is very important to understand the demographics of the area from which jurors will be called. Sometimes predicting the potential jury pool is not that easy. For example, suppose a trial is scheduled to be held in a college community. The jury pool may consist of well-educated professors, students, and other university-related individuals as well as uneducated individuals from the surrounding rural areas that are so common to university towns. However, suppose the trial is scheduled to be held in a community such as Palm Beach, Florida, or Beverly Hills, California; to predict and plan for the likely jury pool is much easier.

§ 9.5 Juror Questionnaires

Well-tailored juror questionnaires can save attorneys, courts, and prospective jurors a lot of time. Questionnaires specifically designed to address potential prejudicial issues of a particular case will identify prospective jurors that should be disqualified for cause or, at the very least, identify potential prejudicial jurors. Juror questionnaires are not necessary in every case. They are most helpful when employed in a case involving controversial issues. The following is an example of a court motion for the use of a jury questionnaire.

MOTION TO UTILIZE JURY QUESTIONNAIRE

Plaintiffs, _____ , by and through their undersigned attorneys, respectfully move the Court for an Order permitting use of Jury Questionnaire (in the manner and form to be supplied to the Court) as a predicate to oral voir dire in this case. As grounds for this Motion, Plaintiffs would respectfully show unto the Court that:

1. This is a complex product liability case involving numerous technical and highly personal issues.

2. Having the advantage of general information covered by the proposed Jury Questionnaire will immensely shorten the amount of judicial time or court time necessary to conduct the oral voir dire examination.

3. Use of the Jury Questionnaire, or a variant thereof, will further the interest of justice in this case and will not prejudice any of the parties.

4. This case involves certain matters of a highly personal nature. These matters involve inquiry of jurors pertaining to breast problems, plastic surgery procedures performed on members of the jury venire, jurors' personal feelings regarding breast augmentation and breast enlargement, and more. It is absolutely essential that counsel for all parties know and understand the jurors' feelings with respect to these items. Yet, these are highly personal matters and questioning jurors in front of a full court on these matters would prove to be highly embarrassing and perhaps even humiliating.

5. Plaintiffs would state to the Court that it has requested the use of a Jury Questionnaire in the following cases and said request has been granted on each occasion: (list appropriate cases).

6. Plaintiff's counsel would also state to the Court that (list appropriate organizations) approve and recommend use of the Jury Questionnaire in cases involving issues such as medical negligence, medical device product liability, and cases of this nature.

Wherefore, Plaintiffs respectfully request that this Court enter an Order Granting their Motion to Utilize Jury Questionnaire.

§ 9.6 —Sample Juror Questionnaire

The following sample juror questionnaire was prepared by attorney John F. Romano of West Palm Beach, Florida, and accepted by the trial judge in *Weitz v. A.H. Robins*,[1] a products liability case in the United States District Court.

JUROR INFORMATION SHEET

Directions

The integrity of our legal system depends upon the fairness and impartiality of judges and jurors. This questionnaire has been prepared to assist the judge and the parties in determining whether or not you may have had personal experiences or knowledge about the issues to be decided by the jury in this case.

Please read all the questions carefully and thoroughly. Answer each question as best you can, even though some may not be worded quite correctly for your situation. (For example, we refer in some questions to "members of your family." If you live alone, this will mean just you.)

Indicate your answers to the questions by filling in the appropriate space or by circling the appropriate response number. On some questions, the most appropriate response might be "doesn't apply to me" (if, for instance we ask a question about your children, and you don't have any children.)

Confidentiality

The responses that you have given will be kept under seal in the strictest confidence. They will be reviewed by only the judge, the attorneys for the parties, and their staffs. If you are not selected as a juror, your questionnaire and any copies will be destroyed. If you are selected, the attorneys will be permitted to retain a copy but will be under order of the court to use the contents only for purposes of this case, and not to use or disclose the contents of the questionnaire you fill out for any other purpose.

1. Please enter your full name.

   _____   _____   _____
         first name   middle name   last name

2. In terms of your political outlook, do you usually think of yourself as:
   a. Very conservative
   b. Somewhat conservative
   c. Middle of the road
   d. Somewhat liberal
   e. Very liberal

---

[1] Case No. 81-6307 (S.D. Fla. 1981).

3. Please enter the names, ages, and your relationship with each person who lives at your current address:

    Name   Age   Relationship

    _____   _____   _____
    _____   _____   _____
    _____   _____   _____

4. Do you rent or own your home?
    a. Own or am buying
    b. Pay rent
    c. Other (Please describe) _____

5. About how long have you lived at your current address?
    _____ years (If less than 1 year, write "0")

6. Where were you born? _____ (If you were born in Florida, please go to question #10.)

7. You said that you were born outside of *Florida*. When did you move to *Florida*?
    19 _____ (year)

8. Why did you move to *Florida*?

    1. Job   4. Spouse relocation
    2. School   5. Retirement
    3. Family   6. Other (specify)

                                        _____

9. What is your current marital status?

    1. Married   4. Separated
    2. Widowed   5. Single/never married
    3. Divorced

10. If you are currently divorced or separated, how long were you married?
    _____ years

11. How many children have you ever had? (Please count all children that were born alive at any time, including any you had from a previous marriage.)
    _____

12. What are your children's ages and sexes?
    DAUGHTERS
    Name   Age

    _____   _____
    _____   _____
    _____   _____
    _____   _____

    SONS
    Name   Age

    _____   _____
    _____   _____
    _____   _____
    _____   _____

13. How many grandchildren have you ever had?

_____

14. Have you, a relative, or a close friend ever adopted or attempted to adopt a child?

   1. Yes   2. No

15. What is the highest level of formal education that you have completed?

   1. Grade 1–9
   2. Grade 10–11
   3. High School graduate
   4. Technical school graduate
   5. One year of college
   6. Two years of college or junior college graduate
   7. Three years of college
   8. College graduate
   9. Started graduate school
   10. Graduate degree

16. If you attended college, what was your major area of study?

17. If you attended graduate school, what was your major area of study?

18. Have you ever planned to become a doctor or a scientist?

   1. Yes   2. No

19. If you are married, what is the highest grade in school that your husband or wife has completed?

   1. Grade 1–9
   2. Grade 10–11
   3. High School graduate
   4. Technical school graduate
   5. One year of college
   6. Two years of college or junior college graduate
   7. Three years of college
   8. College graduate
   9. Started graduate school
   10. Graduate degree

20. If your spouse attended graduate school, what was his/her major area of study?

21. If you have children, what is the highest grade that they have completed? (Circle the appropriate grade for each child.)

   1. Grade 1–9
   2. Grade 10–11
   3. High School graduate
   4. Technical school graduate
   5. One year of college
   6. Two years of college or junior college graduate
   7. Three years of college
   8. College graduate
   9. Started graduate school
   10. Graduate degree

22. What is your current occupational status?
    1. Working full-time
    2. Working part-time
    3. Retired
    4. Unemployed/laid off
    5. Full-time homemaker
    6. Attending school part-time
23. What is your current occupation? (If you are retired, what was your last occupation?)
24. Who is your employer?
25. How long have you held this job?
    _____ years (If less than 1 year, write "0")
26. Where did you work before that, and what was your job there?
27. How long did you hold that job?
    _____ years (If less than 1 year, write "0")
28. What is the occupation that you have worked at for the longest period of time, if different from the one that you currently work at?
29. Have you ever gone to law school, or do you have any intention of going to law school?
    1. Yes   2. No
30. Have you ever workeed as a salesman?
    1. Yes   2. No
31. If you are married, does your spouse work?
    1. Yes
    2. No—please skip to question #34
    3. Not married—please skip to question #34
32. What is your spouse's occupation?
33. If your spouse works, who is his/her employer?
34. Do any of your children work?
    1. Yes
    2. No
    3. Don't have children
35. Do you have any relatives or close friends who work in the medical field, for instance a doctor, a nurse, or someone who works in a hospital?
    1. Yes   2. No
36. Have you, a relative, or a close friend ever worked for a pharmaceutical company?
    1. Yes   2. No
37. Have you, a relative, or a close friend ever owned stock in a pharmaceutical company?
    1. Yes   2. No
38. Have you, a relative, or a close friend ever had a financial interest in any insurance company?
    1. Yes   2. No
39. Have you, a relative, or a close friend ever worked in the insurance industry?
    1. Yes   2. No

40. Have you ever purchased or used any of the following prescription drugs manufactured by the A.H. Robins Company?

1. Yes	2. No
Dimetane	Reglan
Dimetapp	Robamox
Donnatal	Robaxin
Dopram	Robaxisal
Entozyme	Robicillin VK
Exna	Robimycin
Imavate	Rovinul
Phenaphen with codeine	Robitet
Pondimin	Skelaxin
Quindex	Tybatran

41. Have you ever purchased or used any of the following over-the-counter drugs manufactured by the A.H. Robins Company?

1. Yes	2. No
Adabee	Mitrolan
Albee	Pabalate
Arthralgen	Phenaphen
Dalkon Foam Contraceptive	Robalate
Dimacol	Robitussin Cough Syrup
Dimetane	Silain
Donnagel	Z-Bec Tablets

42. If you have used products of the A.H. Robins Company, was there anything about your experience with the product which would cause you to be prejudiced either for or against the defendant A.H. Robins Company?

    1. Yes   2. No

If yes, please explain _____

_____

43. Please tell us the names of any clubs, groups, or organizations that you belong to. Please also indicate whether you have ever been an officer or leader in any of these groups.

Club Name	Officer or Leader?	
_____	1. Yes	2. No
_____	1. Yes	2. No
_____	1. Yes	2. No

44. Has any of these groups taken a stand, one way or another, on abortion, birth control, or any issues having to do with sexuality?

    1. Yes   2. No

45. What kinds of things do you like to do in your spare time?

46. What magazines do you like to read?

1. Time	9. Readers Digest
2. People	10. U.S. News & World Report
3. Mother Jones	11. Ms.
4. Omni	12. National Review

5. Consumer Reports
6. Popular Mechanics
7. Playboy
8. Cosmopolitan

13. Rolling Stone
14. National Geographic
15. Playgirl
16. Newsweek

Others (Please specify): _____

_____

47. Which of the following newspapers do you subscribe to or read? (Place an "X" in the appropriate spaces.)

	Subscribe To	Read More Than 3 Times per Week	Read Less Than 3 Times per Week
Palm Beach Post Times	_____	_____	_____
Lake Worth Herald	_____	_____	_____
Miami Herald	_____	_____	_____
Wall Street Journal	_____	_____	_____

48. What are the last three books you have read?

_____

_____

_____

49. What are the three books you have enjoyed most in the last ten years?

_____

_____

_____

50. What television shows do you watch regularly?

_____

_____

_____

51. How would you rate your health?
    1. Poor
    2. Fair
    3. Good
    4. Excellent

52. Have you ever had a serious injury or illness that made it necessary for you to use a prescription drug or medical device for an extensive period of time?
    1. Yes (Please describe) _____

       _____

    2. No

53. Are you currently using any prescription drugs or medical devices?
    1. Yes (Please describe) _____

       _____

    2. No

54. Have you, a relative, or a close friend ever had a bad reaction to a prescription drug or medical device?
    1. Yes (Please describe) _____

       _____

    2. No

55. Have you, an immediate family member, or a close friend ever sued or been sued by any person or organization?
    1. Yes (Please describe) _____
    _____
    2. No

56. Have you, an immediate family member, or a close friend ever filed a claim that stopped short of a lawsuit against any person or organization or had such a claim filed against you?
    1. Yes (Please describe) _____
    _____
    2. No

57. Have you ever been in a courtroom before?
    1. Yes (Please describe) _____
    _____
    2. No

58. Have you ever served as a juror?
    1. Yes
    2. No (Please skip to question #64)

59. How many cases have you served on as a juror?
    _____ cases

60. In what kind(s) of case(s) did you serve as a juror?
    1. Civil   3. Both
    2. Criminal   4. Don't recall

61. Have you ever sat on a jury that deliberated to a verdict?
    1. Yes   2. No

62. Were you ever elected foreman of a jury?
    1. Yes   2. No

63. Have you ever heard of the Dalkon Shield?
    1. Yes   2. No

64. The jury in this case will be hearing evidence dealing with injuries to women's reproductive organs. Would this cause you a great deal of embarrassment or anxiety?
    1. Yes   2. No

65. Have you, a close friend, or a relative ever had a hysterectomy?
    1. Yes   2. No

66. Have you, a close friend, or a relative ever experienced a miscarriage?
    1. Yes   2. No

67. Have you, a close friend, or a relative ever experienced an abortion?
    1. Yes   2. No

68. Have you, your spouse, or a sexual partner ever used any form of birth control?
    1. Yes   2. No

69. To your knowledge, have you, a close friend, or relative ever experienced a serious problem with a method of contraceptive?

    1. Yes (Please explain) _____

    _____

    2. No

70. Have you read or heard anything suggesting that a particular form of contraception may be dangerous to the user?

    1. Yes   2. No

71. How would you describe your opinion of the following people?

		I've never heard of him/her	Favorable	Unfavorable
a.	Ralph Nader	_____	_____	_____
b.	Gloria Steinem	_____	_____	_____
c.	Phyllis Schlafley	_____	_____	_____
d.	Jane Fonda	_____	_____	_____
e.	William F. Buckley	_____	_____	_____
f.	Jerry Falwell	_____	_____	_____

72. Do you support the Equal Rights Amendment for women?

    1. Yes   2. No

73. Do you think that as a general rule, people are or are not given adequate information about the safety of the birth control methods they use?

    1. People are given adequate information.
    2. People are not given adequate information.

74. In a legal dispute between a private individual and a large corporation, all things considered, I would probably:

    1. Tend to side with the corporation;
    2. Tend to side with the individual;
    3. Not have an opinion one way or another.

75. Have you, any member of your family, or any acquaintance ever used an IUD?

    1. Yes   2. No

76. If so, please indicate, to the extent you know, if it was any of the following IUDs by marking the appropriate line:

    _____   Cu-7 or Copper 7   _____   Lippes Loop
    _____   Cu-T or Copper T   _____   Progestasert
    _____   Tatum T   _____   Dalkon Shield
    _____   Saf-T-Coil   _____   Other (specify)

77. If you, any member of your family, or any acquaintance have used an IUD, please indicate, to the extent you know, whether the experience was:

                         Favorable   _____
                         Unfavorable   _____
                         Other   _____

78. Have you, any member of your family, or any acquaintance ever used an IUD in the past but had it removed?

    1. Yes   2. No

79. If so, please describe the reason, as you understand it, for the removal of the IUD: _____

_____

_____

80. Have you, any member of your family, or any acquaintance ever suffered any adverse effect, however slight, which you believe may have resulted from using an IUD?

    1. Yes   2. No

81. If so, please describe the adverse experience as you understand it:

_____

_____

_____

82. Have you ever read or heard anything about the Dalkon Shield IUD?

    1. Yes   2. No

83. If so, please describe what you have read or heard about the Dalkon Shield:

_____

_____

_____

84. Has any physician or another person told you, a member of your family, or any acquaintance that there may be risks associated with using the Dalkon Shield?

    1. Yes   2. No

85. If so, please describe what you were told or what you have heard:

_____

_____

_____

86. Have you, a member of your family, or any acquaintance ever made a choice not to use an IUD?

    1. Yes   2. No

87. If so, what were the reasons that choice was made?

_____

_____

_____

88. Do you consider effective birth control important in today's society?

    1. Yes   2. No

89. Do you have any religious or moral objections to birth control for yourself or your spouse?

    1. Yes   2. No

90. Have you or your spouse at any time practiced any of the following methods of birth control (check all forms you have used):

_____	Birth Control Pill	_____	Spermicidal Foam
_____	IUD	_____	Rhythm
_____	Diaphragm	_____	Vasectomy
_____	Condom	_____	Tubal Ligation
_____	Withdrawal	_____	Hysterectomy
_____	Contraceptive Sponge	_____	Other (specify)

91. For each form of birth control you have checked, please state whether the experience in using it was favorable or unfavorable and, if favorable, why:

_____

_____

_____

92. Have you ever read or heard anything about the benefits and risks of birth control pills?

     1. Yes   2. No

93. If so, please describe what you have heard or read:

_____

_____

_____

94. Have you or has anyone you know ever had a miscarriage or spontaneous abortion?

     1. Yes   2. No

95. Have you or has any member of your family ever had any infection of the reproductive organs?

     1. Yes   2. No

96. If so, what was the medical result of such infection and what treatment was received?

_____

_____

_____

97. Do you have any moral, philosophical, or religious beliefs which you think might in any way affect your impartiality in this case?

     1. Yes   2. No

98. If so, please describe your belief that you think may affect your impartiality.

_____

_____

_____

§ 9.7 Mock Jury Selection/Trial

A mock jury selection/trial is an excellent opportunity to fine-tune a case prior to trial. There are a growing number of reputable firms that will organize a mock jury selection/trial for a lawyer. Generally, the firm will use people from the community where the trial will be held. It is important to make sure that the chosen firm does not use "professional" jurors. In order to get the most reliable feedback, the jurors selected must be typical of those who will actually sit on the jury. "Jurors" who have been involved in more than one or two mock jury selection/trials will likely not provide the lawyer with the most reliable and helpful information.

The mock jurors hear abbreviated arguments presented by two lawyers, one arguing for the adverse party. The presentation may include the use of demonstrative evidence. The jurors are then given actual jury instructions and told to deliberate on the issues and reach a verdict.

Most firms will videotape the jurors as they deliberate. This is extremely helpful in that the lawyers can see where the case was won or lost. Did one juror simply not like counsel's tie or suit? Was another juror offended by something counsel said during jury selection? Videotaping the jurors deliberate is preferred over watching the jurors as they deliberate. If the lawyers are present during the jury's deliberations, the jurors will likely say things they wouldn't ordinarily say and not say things that they ordinarily would say if they thought no one was listening.

In order to validate the results, consultants recommend that a minimum of three simulations be done. The consultant will then provide the lawyer with a suggested juror profile, voir dire questions, and litigation recommendations.

Trial Technologies, Inc., litigation consultants, conducted three jury simulations in a medical malpractice case in West Palm Beach to ascertain juror reactions to certain issues and themes. Six jurors were used in each of the three jury simulations. An abbreviated version of the case was presented and the jurors were then asked to deliberate and reach a verdict. Prior to deliberating, the jurors were permitted to ask questions. May of those questions revealed to the lawyer certain areas that needed further development. During their deliberations, the trial consultants noted, via videotape, certain key deliberation comments and themes. For example, although the lawyer was concerned about the hospital's allegation that the plaintiff had consumed cocaine prior to his admission, the jurors either were not very concerned about the allegation or felt that the hospital didn't run enough tests to determine positively that the plaintiff in fact had consumed cocaine.

In the simulations the lawyer learned a lot about the damages aspect of the case. The plaintiff was twelve years old when he was rendered a quadriplegic. At that time, the plaintiff was a behavioral problem in school and collecting disability. The jurors had no difficulty awarding him medical expenses. They had some difficulty calculating lost wages. They had a significant amount of difficulty calculating past and future pain and suffering. Some deliberation comments included: "I don't think future damages should be given. We provided that in the medical expense damage amount."; "I don't think money is an appropriate form of compensation."; "He probably wouldn't have any social life anyway because he was severely emotionally disturbed."; and "I've seen a show where paraplegics lead full lives."

The trial consultants suggested to the lawyer that the jurors would have been more comfortable if told exactly what kind of pain and suffering the plaintiff already had gone through and what he would experience in the future. The consultants felt that the jurors wanted some sort of guideline.

The lawyer also learned that although the allegation of cocaine use did not have a tremendous impact when deciding negligence, it was a strong factor when pain and suffering was considered.

In consideration of the pre- and postdeliberation questions and comments, the trial consultants then made certain litigation recommendations. For example, the lawyers were told to clarify certain issues, such as what is pain and suffering and loss of the enjoyment of life. The lawyers were also told to clarify the plaintiff's loss of earning potential, perhaps through the use of a vocational expert who could explain that even though the plaintiff was receiving social security disability, he could have done x, y, and z with his life.

Based upon the facts of this case, the juror consultants made certain juror-profile recommendations. Plaintiff-oriented recommendations included retired elderly people who may be afraid of being left alone with no care; people with arthritis or mobility problems not due to an accident; and people who were successful in a lawsuit after an accident. Defense-oriented people included anyone who did not like children; low- to middle-powered individuals; perfectionists because they tend to award lower amounts for pain and suffering; individuals who feel sorry for themselves; and those who believe in fate.

CONDUCTING JURY SELECTION

§ 9.8 Selecting the Format

Just as one person may say "toe-ma-toe" and another may say "toe-may-toe," one may say "vwa-dear" and another may say "vwar-dyer." However great the number of pronunciations, there are that many and more methods of conducting jury selection.

Voir dire is generally conducted in the courtroom. A certain number of jurors are called from the jury pool and are seated in the jury box or in the rows of seats behind the lawyers' tables. Each lawyer then has the opportunity to question the jurors, all in the presence of the other jurors. Although this is the generally accepted format of jury selection, other formats may be more appropriate under certain circumstances or simply preferable to the lawyers and judge.

Judge-Conducted Voir Dire

Certain jurisdictions require outright that the questioning of the potential jurors be conducted by the judge. In those jurisdictions, the judge may ask questions submitted by the lawyers. Often, a motion to permit oral voir dire in a jurisdiction that restricts or prohibits lawyer-conducted voir dire is granted. Lawyer-conducted voir dire is not permitted in federal court as a matter of course. However, in many instances the court will allow voir dire if the lawyer can persuade the court that it is necessary and will be conducted efficiently and effectively.

If provided the choice, the lawyer should seek to avoid judge-conducted voir dire. Voir dire is the only time the lawyer can converse with the individual jurors. Voir dire is critical to the lawyer when developing a rapport with the jurors. In addition to developing that rapport, the lawyer is in a better situation to identify prejudice. There are many facts in a particular case that the judge does not know about that are critical to the lawyer when selecting a jury. Judge-conducted voir dire is superficial by nature because the judge simply does not know about all the issues.

Private Voir Dire

Occasionally, the lawyer should seek to question jurors privately. In cases when there has been a tremendous amount of media coverage, questioning the jurors in private prevents contamination by a prejudiced juror of the remaining jurors. Private voir dire is also beneficial when personal questions must be asked. A case involving an orthopedic disability will likely not require questions of an extremely personal nature. However, a case involving incest or abuse may require that the lawyers ask some very personal and sensitive questions. Most jurors will feel very uncomfortable revealing such personal matters before 15 to 20 total strangers. Private voir dire provides the lawyers with the opportunity to develop a rapport of trust with the juror as well as provide a less threatening and cold environment.

§ 9.9 Personal Space

Men and women move about this world surrounded by an invisible wall known as "personal space." Personal space is the buffer zone between individuals maintained during the communication process in order to feel comfortable and at ease. Lawyers must always be aware of, and sensitive to, invading jurors' personal space. This often occurs when lawyers get too close to the jury box or even lean on the jury box. When one's personal space has been invaded, that person becomes apprehensive, uncomfortable, and defensive and most importantly ceases to pay attention to what is being said.

Personal space is just as it sounds, personal to every individual. There are, however, a number of generalized factors to be considered when evaluating a particular person's personal space. Of utmost importance is an individual's cultural heritage. Americans are known to be very noncontact oriented and prefer further distances than do Mediterranean and Latin American people. Gender also influences preferred personal space. Women are generally more comfortable closer to other women than are men to other men.

As a generalization, psychologists often tell us that 2½ to four feet is an appropriate and comfortable distance when discussing personal matters. Four feet to seven feet is an appropriate distance when discussions are more formal. Once a person's personal space is invaded, that person begins to feel uncomfortable and becomes inattentive.

A courtroom generally provides, at a minimum, approximately four feet between the lawyers and the jurors. Jurors' personal space is often protected by a barrier wall (jury box) between them and the lawyers. However, all too often lawyers will lean against the jury box or even lean over the box in order to grab the jurors' attention. That is all well and good for "L.A. Law," but for the real practice of law, lawyers must be mindful of jurors' personal space.

§ 9.10   Questioning the Panel

Voir dire is the lawyer's first and only opportunity to speak with prospective jurors directly. It is therefore essential that the lawyer use this opportunity to develop a rapport with the jurors. At the outset the lawyer ought to briefly introduce himself; educate the jury about the basic facts of the case; determine whether any jurors know the lawyers, witnesses, court personnel, or parties involved; and then move on to more detailed questions.

The best formulated questions are those that enable the jurors to do all of the talking; otherwise, not much is going to be learned from the panel. Preliminary questions such as those designed to determine whether any jurors know the witnesses or parties can be asked of the prospective jurors as a group and followed up individually if necessary. Questioning the group as a whole should be limited to preliminary questions. More specific questions should be posed to each juror individually, thereby giving each juror an opportunity to speak directly with the lawyer. In addition, the lawyer will learn a lot more about the truthfulness and sincerity of a juror when the juror is required to speak. When the lawyer asks questions only to the group as a whole, a juror who does not want to be identified as holding a specific opinion can avoid identification by simply not acknowledging when asked.

The following excerpt has been taken from a voir dire that was conducted in *Hall v. State Department of Health & Rehabilitative Services*.[2] This excerpt is an example of a sample introduction to voir dire.

> Hello, folks. My name is Joe Attorney. I'm from West Palm Beach. And I'm proud to say to you that I'm going to be trying this case with my partner Sam Attorney.
>
> We represent a young girl, a seven-year-old girl, from here in Fort Myers named Jane Doe. And the case is actually being brought by her grandmother on Jane's behalf. And you'll be hearing from them during the course of the trial.

---

[2] Case No. 83-4057 (Fla. Cir. Ct. 1983).

With that, I wanted to start off by introducing everyone to you that will be involved in the case and just check with you and see if you all know any of us or any of the courtroom personnel, and if you do, what you might know about us or think about us.

I'm assuming that no one in here has had anything to do with us and you don't know anything about us; is that right? Okay.

The defendant in this case is the government of Florida, the State of Florida HRS, and they'll be represented in this case by Mr. Attorney from the law firm of Attorney & Lawyer, P.A.

First of all, do any of you know either of the two of them?

Do any of you know any of the members of that law firm?

Has anyone here ever been represented by that law firm or, to your knowledge, have you ever had any kind of legal dealings with the law firm, perhaps real estate matters, wills, probate, anything like that? Okay.

The Court personnel in this case that we'll be working with, our bailiff, if I look around here, is Ms. Bailiff. Do any of you know Ms. Bailiff?

Or our court clerk, Mr. Clerk? Does anyone know Mr. Clerk?

Our court reporter for today is Mr. Reporter. Do any of you know Mr. Reporter? Okay. It's possible that our court reporter, it may—our court reporter may change from day to day throughout the trial.

Now, Judge mentioned to you a few minutes ago this process of jury selection or voir dire—and she told you that it means to speak the truth. And what we're trying to do, both sides are trying to find out enough about you so that a decision can be made so that we end up with people that are fair and impartial to try the case.

If I ask a question and perhaps move on to another juror and a few minutes goes by and you think, I would like to say something to him now about that because it just—something clicked off that you think we ought to know about, please feel free to put your hand up and tell us and we'll come back to you and get that information.

In this case, many witnesses will be called by each side. Some witnesses will be coming in from out of state, such as expert witnesses. Other witnesses will be testifying from here in the Fort Myers area. It may very well be that some of you know the local witnesses, so I'm just going to give you the names of the local people and I'll go through them one by one and I'll just ask you to put up your hand if any of these names ring a bell to you. Some of these are medical people or doctors. And it may be that you're being treated by some of them.

§ 9.11 Addressing Difficult Situations

Following are three situations about which the jurors may have preconceived opinions that could influence the awarding of damages at trial.

Jury Verdicts Are Too High

The communication media broadcasts what sells. A jury in Portland, Oregon, that awards Joe Smith $800 for the loss of his right hand due to the defective design of a saw does not draw public interest; therefore, it does not draw media coverage. On the other hand, a $10 million verdict to a California woman for the loss of her Beverly Hills husband in a boat-racing accident is "newsworthy." As a result jurors often think that plaintiffs are running away with unjust, tremendous verdicts.

Prospective jurors who have never served on a civil jury before do not understand that the monetary damages are quantifiable. The lawyer needs to educate the jury about its role in deciding damages. The following series of questions is an example of how to address the issue of damages:

Lawyer: Have you heard about verdicts on the TV or read about verdicts in the newspaper that you thought were too high?

Do you know who decided what that verdict would be?

Yes, the jury made that decision. Do you know how they came to that decision?

Do you understand that decision was based on testimony of witnesses and experts as to the present and future costs, present and future medical expenses, lost wages in the present and in the future, and other such similar expenses and damages?

Does anyone remember what a hamburger, order of fries, and a soda cost at Burger King only 15 years ago?

Does anyone know what a hamburger, order of fries, and a soda cost today?

If an economist told you that experts calculate a dollar today to be worth x cents in 2002 and x cents in 2022, could you understand why $500,000 may sound like an awful lot of money today but will not be such a great amount of money in 2022?

Do you think that you are required to award the damages that either I recommend or the defense lawyer recommends?

Do you think that once you have had the opportunity to hear all the evidence and the defense lawyer and I have made our recommendations you will be able to calculate damages? And if you think we've asked for too much, will you be able to award less, but if you think we've asked for too little, award more?

Tort Suits Affect American Businesses

During the 1992 presidential election, a common opinion heard within the administration was that this is a litigious society in which tort suits are adversely affecting American businesses. Many Americans were swayed by what was said and grasped it as an explanation for so much of this country's economic problems.

In the course of voir dire, the lawyer has the opportunity to use this campaign rhetoric to the plaintiff's advantage. For example, President Bush said that

Americans should care more about each other and stop suing. The following is an example of how to direct this theme to a desired response.

Lawyer: Ms. Williams, do you feel that plaintiffs are destroying American businesses and hurting the United States in world markets?

Thank you very much for your honesty, Ms. Williams. I take it then that you would agree with President Bush when he repeatedly said during the 1992 election campaign that Americans need to care more about each other?

Do you think a manufacturer has a responsibility to care about its customers?

Then would you agree with me that a manufacturer has a responsibility to its customers to care enough to tighten a screw if that manufacturer knows the screw is loose, knows x number of deaths will result because of the loose screw, but chooses not to fix the screw because of the cost, time, and effort of turning the screwdriver?

Another example using this theme is:

Lawyer: Ms. Williams, do you think that when someone chooses to get behind the wheel of the car that person should care about others on the road?

Insurance Premiums Affect Damage Awards

Although the existence or nonexistence of insurance is not admissible in the majority of cases, jurors cannot help but wonder whether a particular defendant is insured. Often jurors will feel more comfortable about awarding damages when they know that they are not going to be putting Defendant Grandpa Jones out on the street with their verdict because he has no insurance. However, on the other hand, jurors are often fearful that an award of damages will somehow affect their own insurance premiums and may volunteer that information to the lawyer.

The lawyer should, therefore, consider addressing in voir dire if brought up by a prospective juror why there will be no evidence given during the course of the trial as to whether or not Defendant Grandpa Jones has insurance. The following series of questions can help to turn the lack of evidence regarding insurance to the plaintiff's advantage:

Lawyer: Ms. Smith, did you mention that you were concerned that an award of damages would somehow have an effect on your insurance premiums (on insurance premiums in general?)

If you were to remain on this jury and because of your fear of the effect of an award of damages on insurance premiums you did not render a judgment in favor of my client, who do you think would be responsible for paying for my client's future medical expenses and rehabilitation if he was unable to?

The government, right?

Where does the government get the money to provide such services to those who cannot afford them?

Do you agree with me that someone ought to be responsible for his or her own acts?

Why do you feel that someone ought to be responsible for his or her own acts?

Do you think that someone ought to still be responsible for his or her own acts even if he or she did not intend the result?

Do you think that if someone chooses to contract with an insurance company to transfer risk of this kind and the insurance company accepts premiums from the insured, then the insurance company should have to pay rather than the public especially when the public did not enter into a contract to accept the risk nor did the public accept premiums?

Someone will have to pay for my client's injuries and damages. From whose pocket that money comes is not for you to decide. You will only be asked to decide whether Defendant Grandpa Jones was negligent, and if so, the amount of my client's injuries and damages. Whether or not Defendant Grandpa Jones has insurance is not relevant. Do you all therefore understand why you will not hear any evidence as to the existence or nonexistence of insurance?

§ 9.12 Final Question

The last question should be designed to elicit any information the jurors may have not had the opportunity to tell the lawyer. Many times jurors are disappointed at the end of voir dire because there was something that they were hoping to talk about, but the lawyer either never asked the jurors about the particular subject or a juror was overlooked and not questioned about the particular subject.

Attorney John Romano suggests the following question:

Lawyer: I would venture to guess that there are many of you sitting back and saying to yourselves, "Wow, if he'd just ask me this question," or "Wow, I bet he'd be surprised if he knew what I know about the plaintiff." I don't know whether or not what you have to say will have any bearing on your ability to sit as impartial jurors, but it very well could.

If any of you have anything at all that you would like to say, please feel free to raise your hand and I will do my best to get to all of you.

If you feel that what you have to say may prejudice the jury or is something you simply do not want to discuss in front of the rest of the jurors, please raise your hand and we will simply go into the judge's chambers where we can discuss anything you want in private.

THE SELECTION PROCESS

§ 9.13   Social Psychologists

> The common eye sees only the outside of things, and judges by that, but the seeing eye pierces through and reads the heart and the soul, finding there capacities which the outside didn't indicate or promise, and which the other kind couldn't detect.
>
> —Excerpt from Mark Twain's "Joan of Arc"

The use of social psychologists and trial experts ("seeing eyes") has been increasing over the last 10 or 15 years. Trial experts help the lawyer to determine before trial the impact of the lawyer's trial story and presentation. They offer a wide variety of services including focus groups, jury simulations, case analysis and trial strategy, coordination of demonstrative evidence, voir dire consultation, witness preparation, trial story surveys, and trial theme ideas.

§ 9.14   Primary Modes of Communication

The lawyer does not need a social psychologist or trial expert to understand and use some basic concepts of the communication process. According to leading neuro-linguists, people relate on either a visual, auditory, or kinesthetic level. What that means is people either see what you're saying, hear what you're saying, or feel what you're saying. In order for the lawyer to sell his client's case and himself to the jury, he must be cognizant of people's primary modes of communication.

Visually oriented people are persuaded primarily by things that they see, and they like charts, pictures, and graphs. The use of visual aids during jury selection is most beneficial to the visually oriented jurors.

Auditory oriented people are most affected by the use of the voice. The use of inflection, pitch, and tone interests the auditory oriented jurors. Auditory oriented people look for sincerity in the way that the lawyer sells his case.

Kinesthetic oriented people are those jurors who develop real feelings one way or the other about the lawyer and the client. Such feelings are often referred to as one's gut reactions. Kinesthetic people want to become a part of what is happening. Although the Golden Rule prevents lawyers from asking jurors to put themselves in the shoes of the client, a lawyer who makes jurors feel as though they are somehow a part of what is happening in the client's life will be most successful with kinesthetic jurors.

It is important to realize that no juror is either strictly visual, auditory, or kinesthetic but is primarily visual, auditory, or kinesthetic and a little bit of the other two. In order best to sell the case to jurors during jury selection, the lawyer must seek to identify each juror's primary mode of communication and tailor his presentation accordingly.

There are certain characteristics common among those individuals who share a primary mode of communication. Visually oriented people's eyes generally move about as someone speaks to them. They create images and pictures in their minds of what they are being told. Visually oriented people also tend to speak very fast without regard to how they sound. Auditory oriented people, on the other hand, speak slowly and deliberately with tremendous regard to the pitch and rhythm of their speech. Kinesthetic oriented people often make judgments very quickly and phrase their judgments in terms of "I feel."

Based upon these basic common characteristics, the lawyer can identify each juror's primary mode of communication and phrase his questions accordingly. For example, the lawyer would want to ask a kinesthetic oriented person how he *feels* about a certain subject, whereas the lawyer would want to ask a visually oriented person how he *sees* a particular issue or subject.

§ 9.15   Body Language

A gorilla bangs its chest communicating its dominance; a dog wags its tail communicating joy to its master; a fish swims a ritual dance communicating its desire to mate. Just as these animals communicate a message without the use of any words, body language, also known as nonverbal communication, is fundamental to the communication process between people.

Eye Contact

Constant and natural contact conveys sincerity and trustworthiness. A juror's verbal response to the lawyer's question is only one aspect of the whole picture of what the juror is really saying. A juror who consistently looks away when responding to the lawyer's questions may not be completely honest in his response. A lawyer who detects such behavior should question that juror more thoroughly to determine the juror's true position on the particular issue or subject.

Posture

Posture often reveals attitudes. For example, an interested listener often leans forward, whereas an uninterested listener often slumps and may support his head with his hand. Defense attorney William Kunstler was aware of such postural cues when participating in the trial of the Chicago Seven. Following closing arguments, Mr. Kunstler objected and argued that during the prosecution's closing statement the judge leaned forward but during the defense's closing statement, the judge leaned back in his chair.

Attention to posture can cue the lawyer when to speed up, slow down, or somehow heighten interest among the jurors. Similarly, it is important to remember that while the lawyer is paying attention to postural cues of potential jurors, these jurors are subconsciously, if not consciously, paying attention to the lawyer's postural cues. For example, if the lawyer sits up and leans forward during a selected portion of opposing counsel's questioning of the panel, potential jurors will be given the impression that opposing counsel has just said, or is about to say, something of great importance. The lawyer should always appear attentive but be careful of appearing too attentive.

Gesture

Gestures enable a speaker to emphasize certain things, as well as provide a picture for the listeners. Gestures should be used only when they have meaning. Many people subconsciously speak with their hands. Such gesturing is often distractive and adds little if anything to the message. Although often uncomfortable at the outset, the most natural looking standing position when speaking to a panel of jurors is with hands at the sides. Then, when gestures are used they have much more meaning and emphasis value.

Inflection

The pitch and tone of the lawyer's voice convey a message in and of itself. The lawyer who questions the prospective jurors in a constant flat, monotone voice will not convey to the prospective jurors that a particular question or statement is any more important than any of the other questions or statements.

Martin Luther King is praised as one of this country's best orators. His message was so effectively conveyed through the use of inflection and pitch that he very rarely gestured.

Appearance

The manner in which potential jurors dress and present themselves communicates a lot about their personalities, social statuses, and attitudes. For example, a very conservative woman will often wear skirts or dresses below the knee and pull her hair back. A very liberal woman often wears more trendy clothing and more natural hairstyles. A lawyer can make certain generalizations about these jurors regarding their social views, status, and personalities. However, it is important to keep in mind that every generalization has twice as many exceptions.

The manner in which the lawyer dresses and presents himself is also important during jury selection. As previously mentioned, jury selection is generally the first time the potential jurors meet the lawyer and is often the time period when potential jurors develop opinions regarding the believability and sincerity of the lawyer. He should coordinate his attire in accordance with acceptable local standards; therefore, the lawyer must be cognizant of the attitudes and values of the city or town where the trial is being held. For example, if selecting a jury in New York City, the lawyer would be accepted in a trendy suit with accessories such as a watch, maybe a bracelet, and/or a ring. However, if the lawyer is selecting a jury in a rural town such as Fort Pierce, Florida, he would be better accepted and trusted in a traditional suit without the accessories of jewelry and such.

The lawyer should also consider the color of his clothes. Social psychologists tell us that there are certain colors that convey trust and sincerity, in comparison to certain colors that create a sense of unease. For example, it is commonly believed that blue is the best and most effective color when trying to convey a sense of trust. It is also thought that the three worst colors are black, purple, and yellow.

§ 9.16   Challenges to the Jury

Once voir dire has been conducted, the lawyer must review all the information retrieved during the selection process and try to eliminate those jurors most likely to be adverse to the client's case and position. Every state provides for three basic challenges to the jury pool as a whole or to individual jurors.

Challenge to the Array

A jury pool must be representative of the community from which it is pulled.

Challenge for Cause

A lawyer may challenge as many jurors in the jury pool for cause as is justified. Challenges for cause are brought before the court, and then the judge decides whether or not cause exists. Cause is found to exist when a juror has expressed bias toward a party or advocate to the case. However, a general, abstract bias about a particular class of litigation will not, in itself, disqualify a juror when it appears that the bias can be set aside.[3] Mere assurance by a prospective juror that the juror can decide the case on the facts and law is not determinative on the issue of a challenge for cause.[4] Although the trial court properly is given discretion to evaluate responses given, close cases involving a challenge for cause of a prospective juror should be resolved in favor of excusing the juror. Cause is also found to exist when a juror is unable to serve due to a physical limitation such as sickness. Cause will not be found based upon the grounds that a lawyer does not like a potential juror.

---

[3] *See* Mantecristi Condominium Ass'n v. Hickey, 408 So. 2d 671 (Fla. Dist. Ct. App. 1982).

[4] Club West, Inc. v. Tropigas of Florida Inc., 514 So. 2d 426 (Fla. Dist. Ct. App. 1987), *rev. denied*, 523 So. 2d 579 (Fla. 1988).

Once the lawyer has identified the possibility of exercising a "for cause" challenge to a prospective juror, the lawyer must embark on a very methodical and detailed line of questioning to establish cause for the court. A lawyer must know the law before he will be able to excuse a juror for cause. The following memorandum of law was prepared by Orlando attorney Roy "Skip" Dalton, Jr. Mr. Dalton highly recommends that a memorandum of law, such as the following, be submitted to the court prior to jury selection in every case:

Memorandum of Law Regarding Challenge for Cause During Voir Dire

The purpose of the voir dire is to determine whether the prospective juror is qualified and will be completely impartial in his judgment. The impartiality of the finders of fact is an absolute prerequisite to our system of justice. Its length and extensiveness should be controlled by the circumstances surrounding the juror's attitude in order to assure a fair and impartial trial by persons whose minds are free from all interests, bias or prejudice.[5] Counsel has the duty to interrogate jurors before they are sworn and cannot expect relief afterward merely by explaining that he had overlooked doing so earlier.[6] Therefore, thorough examination of each potential juror is a right to which counsel must pursue zealously.

To insure the impartiality of each juror, Rule 1.431 (c)(1) and Florida Statutes, Section 913.03(10) provide that an individual juror may be challenged for cause for bias or prejudice. The juror's voir dire responses are the fundamental source for grounds of impartiality. The testimony or opinions derived from the potential juror's own consciousness is relevant, competent, and primary evidence on the issue of impartiality.[7] The individual juror is not, however, the judge of his own freedom from bias.[8] That question is a matter of the court's discretion, which will not be disturbed absent a showing of manifest error.[9] According to the decision in *Singer v. State*, the fundamental test for the finding of cause to excuse a juror is when there is a basis for reasonable doubt that the juror's state of mind is such that he cannot render a verdict based on impartiality and according to the evidence of the law.[10]

In recent Florida cases, the courts have consistently held that a juror's ability to be fair and impartial must be unequivocally asserted in the record; without such assertion, the juror should be excused.[11] Cause cases should be resolved in favor of excusing the juror rather than leaving a doubt as to his impartiality.[12]

---

[5] Barker v. Randolph, 239 So. 2d 110 (Fla. Dist. Ct. App. 1970).

[6] Ferrell v. State, 34 So. 2d 220 (Fla. 1903).

[7] 33 Fla. Jur. 2d *Juries* § 68 (1982).

[8] 47 Am. Jur. 2d *Jury* § 210 (1969).

[9] Singer v. State, 109 So. 2d 7 (Fla. 1959).

[10] *Id.*

[11] *See* Villorin v. State, 578 So. 2d 738 (Fla. Dist. Ct. App. 1991); Moore v. State, 525 So. 2d 870 (Fla. 1988); Price v. State, 538 So. 2d 486 (Fla. Dist. Ct. App. 1989); 501 Auriemme v. State, So. 2d 41 (Fla. Dist. Ct. App. 1986); Robinson v. State, 506 So. 2d 1070 (Fla. Dist. Ct. App. 1987).

[12] Sydleman v. Benson, 463 So. 2d 533 (Fla. Dist. Ct. App. 1985).

In *Sikes v. Seaboard Coastline R.R. Co.*,[13] the trial court erred by refusing to excuse a juror for cause on the basis of the juror's testimony that she would "try to be fair" notwithstanding her friendly relationship with an attorney who appeared in the courtroom only at the beginning of the trial and who did not participate in the actual trial. Citing the *Singer* opinion, the court held that if there is a basis for any reasonable doubt as to any juror's possessing that state of mind that will enable him to render an impartial verdict based solely on the evidence submitted and the law announced at trial, he should be excused.[14] Furthermore, it is an error for a trial court to force a lawyer to exhaust his peremptory challenges on persons who should be excused for cause because it has the effect of abridging the right to exercise those challenges.[15]

Current decisions indicate a policy shift towards stricter standards regarding the juror competency test by redefining the nature of rehabilitating a partial juror. Courts no longer seem satisfied that a juror is able to "lay aside" his prejudice, and the fact that the trial judge extracts a commitment from a prospective juror that he "will try to be fair" or even will be fair does not eliminate the prejudice or the grounds for the challenge.[16] In *Club West v. Tropigas of Florida, Inc.*[17] the court noted, "Where a juror initially demonstrates a predilection in a case which in the juror's mind would prevent him or her from impartially reaching a verdict, a subsequent change in that opinion, arrived at after further questioning by the parties' attorneys or judge, is properly viewed with some skepticism."[18]

In summary, if a reasonable doubt can be presented as to the juror's ability to set aside his prejudice, the trial courts have received a clear message that they must excuse the juror. Courts are no longer presuming the jury's impartiality the way that they require the jury to presume innocence. Higher standards are placed on the caliber of the juror's preconceived biases, on the juror's ability to overcome his own prejudices, and on the court's duty to safeguard the integrity and impartiality of the jurors.

The following sample line of questioning was used in *Fields v. Cambron*, a medical malpractice claim, for the purpose of establishing the grounds for a "for cause" challenge to a juror:

Lawyer: Do any of you know Mr. Jones, who is seated at Doctor Smith's right. Mr. Jones is with the law firm right here in Townsville. Do any of you know any of the members of that law firm?

Juror: Yeah. Mr. Frank's my lawyer for my estate, my husband's estate.

---

[13] 487 So. 2d 1118 (Fla. Dist. Ct. App. 1986).

[14] *Id.* at 1120. *See also* Jefferson v. State, 489 So. 2d 211 (Fla. Dist. Ct. App. 1986); Graham v. State, 470 So. 2d 97 (Fla. Dist. Ct. App. 1985).

[15] Jefferson v. State, 489 So. 2d at 212.

[16] *See* Leon v. State, 396 So. 2d 203 (Fla. Dist. Ct. App. 1981); Sikes v. Seaboard, 487 So. 2d 1118; Robinson v. State, 506 So. 2d 1070.

[17] 514 So. 2d 426 (Fla. Dist. Ct. App. 1987).

[18] *Id.* at 427.

Lawyer: Okay. Is that a matter that was handled recently or some time ago?

Juror: It's in litigation now. My husband just died.

Lawyer: How do you feel about it, sitting in judgment in a case where your lawyer is basically involved in the representation of the defendant in this case through one of his partners?

Juror: That doesn't make any difference except I've been a patient of Doctor Smith's. I don't know if that will enter into it or not.

Lawyer: How long have you known Dr. Smith?

Juror: Well, I guess indirectly I have known him for—I don't know how long he's been in Townsville; but he used to be on Delaware, and I had been to him years ago for my eyes, and I took my mother in there, and he took a cyst off my eye just a couple of years ago. I had my son in there, too.

Lawyer: When you need an ophthalmologist, is that the office here in the Townsville area you go to?

Juror: Right.

Lawyer: I assume that you go to that office of your own choice?

Juror: Right.

Lawyer: And you go to them because, over the years, you personally have come to want to go to that office for your own medical care and treatment?

Juror: Right.

Lawyer: You like the doctors there in the office?

Juror: Yes.

Lawyer: In this particular case, if you end up sitting on this jury, you may be very well sitting in judgment of your doctor. How do you feel about that?

Juror: I don't know.

Lawyer: In trying to be as candid as possible, do you think it would be fair to say that you think that you would tend to lean with your own doctor?

Juror: I don't think I want to go against him too much, plus I have another doctor in my family, my son married a doctor's daughter; so —.

Peremptory Challenges

Every state provides each side with a particular number of challenges to the jury. The lawyer may challenge a juror for any reason whatsoever aside from discrimination-based challenges. The lawyer generally need not even express the reason for the challenge unless questioned by opposing counsel regarding potential discrimination.

§ 9.17 Conclusion

Our system of justice provides for the most effective means of holding the government accountable to the principles of the United States Constitution, trial by jury. It is jury selection that allows the lawyers to ensure that the trial by jury be everything that Thomas Jefferson envisioned it would be over 200 years ago, a fair and equal process.

The Seven Sins of Jury Selection

1. Legalese—Speak to jurors in a language they understand, plain English.
2. Exaggeration—Fairly and accurately present your synopsis of the case.
3. Embarrassment—Always remember the Golden Rule, "Do unto others as you would have them do unto you."
4. Weakness—Beat opposing counsel to the punch and address weaknesses in your case from the beginning.
5. Yes/No—The best formulated questions are not those that require a yes/no response but rather those that enable the prospective jurors to speak.
6. Belief System—Understand and accept that prospective jurors' preexisting belief systems will not be changed during jury selection. Identify potential harmful belief systems and eliminate those jurors.
7. Be True Unto Thyself—Learn from the old bullfrog in Aesop's Fable, "Be Yourself."

CHAPTER 10

DIRECT EXAMINATION OF AN ORTHOPEDIC SURGEON*

J. Craig Currie, Esq.
Samuel D. Hodge, Jr., Esq.

* The authors are members of the Philadelphia Bar. They wish to express their appreciation for critical reading of the manuscript to Andrew Newman, M.D., of Philadelphia.

§ 10.1   Introduction

Personal injury litigation requires medical documentation to support a claimant's assertion of injury. Diagnostic test results, physical findings, and the diagnosis are supplied through the health-care provider's testimony that must be based upon reasonable medical certainty.

Good trial technique requires the discussion of at least the following topics by the physician:

1. Qualifications of the witness
2. Prior medical history
3. History of present injury
4. Complaints of the patient
5. Physical examination
6. Results of diagnostic tests
7. Diagnosis
8. Treatment plan
9. Prognosis
10. Past and future medical costs
11. Causation.

This chapter focuses on the direct examination of the plaintiff's medical expert. Although the presentation deals with the questioning of an orthopedic surgeon, the principles utilized and trial tips suggested apply to the direct examination of any health-care provider. The hypothetical case presented involves a claimant who is injured at work and sustains a herniated disc at the L_5-S_1 vertebral level.

§ 10.2   Guiding Principles

The likelihood of a jury finding in favor of the plaintiff and awarding substantial damages is directly proportionate to the degree to which the jury likes the plaintiff and understands the presentation of the plaintiff's case. The treating physician can be most helpful in both regards. First, the doctor's testimony constitutes what will be perceived as a neutral or impartial description of what the plaintiff has gone through and, thereby, will automatically enhance the credibility of the plaintiff and other lay witnesses who will testify about the injury and its effects. Again, most importantly, detailed testimony concerning the plaintiff's problems by the physician and others helps mitigate the need to have the plaintiff talk at length about not being able to do this and that. Second, if the jury is able to understand both the mechanism by which the injury was inflicted and the reasons for continued problems, both on a intellectual and a visceral level, the jury once again will be more likely to find in favor of the plaintiff and to increase the award.

The trial testimony of a treating physician may be presented in one of three ways. The preferred method of presentation is to produce the doctor in person at trial. Second is by way of a videotaped deposition. Third is to read the deposition of the physician to the jury. Because the use of a videotaped deposition is now the rule rather than the exception, this discussion will focus on that manner of presentation. Older trial lawyers lament this change, but it is an unavoidable fact of modern trial practice. On the positive side, there are a number of important advantages to presenting damages testimony by videotape.

§ 10.3   Videotaped Depositions

There are several advantages to the plaintiff's counsel conducting a videotaped deposition of the medical expert. One is that the trial lawyer is given more control over the order of presentation of witnesses. It is usually more desirable to present the testimony of the physician *before* the plaintiff. This can be accomplished with a videotaped deposition so that when on the stand, the plaintiff's testimony about the medical aspects of the case will sound more credible because it has already received the imprimatur of a physician. (The plaintiff can say, for example, "Like the doctor said, I had trouble sleeping for three weeks.") It is also desirable to have testimony concerning the plaintiff's pain and suffering presented by someone other than the plaintiff so that the claimant avoids appearing like a complainer or "whiner."

With the doctor's videotaped deposition in her briefcase, the plaintiff's lawyer can present the testimony when wanted and is not dependent on the schedule of the doctor. Because the videotaped deposition often is taken a few weeks before the trial starts, counsel for the plaintiff has one less problem to worry about, one less source of stress to deal with. The trial lawyer, therefore, does not have to spend hours trying to accommodate the doctor's schedule with the trial schedule or worrying about how to properly prepare the doctor. Rather, counsel can concentrate on aspects of the case that cannot be addressed beforehand, such as preparing the plaintiff or other important witnesses.

Because the video deposition is usually conducted several weeks or months before trial, the defense attorney may not be as well-prepared as when the medical witness is presented during the trial. In addition, cross-examination expectations may be thwarted. Effective cross-examination generally involves some minor theatrics on the part of the cross-examining lawyer; defense lawyers, therefore, lose a lot of cross-examining "punch" on a videotape because they are off camera.

By the same token, because the lawyers are not seen on the tape, counsel for the plaintiff can write out the questions, read them, and not be concerned how this lack of spontaneity might appear to the jury. Additionally, cross-examination may reveal a serious flaw in the case. Armed with this information in advance of trial, the plaintiff's counsel has the opportunity to repair the defect by eliciting properly corrected testimony either from the medical witness at a later time (for example, from a subsequent deposition of the doctor) or by another medical witness.

Conventional wisdom on videotaped depositions suggests that juries do not respond as favorably to them as live testimony. A number of studies, however, dispute this impression. In fact, the disenchantment with videotaped deposition is probably restricted to judges and lawyers. Jurors are used to obtaining important information from a television, so a videotaped deposition in some cases is more credible than a live witness.

A main disadvantage of a videotaped deposition is that without a judge present to make rulings and to keep obstreperous counsel in line, a defense attorney intent on "trashing" a deposition can do so by repeatedly making hypertechnical objections and forcing numerous interruptions. Good planning, however, can reduce this risk. Handling objections is discussed in § 10.10.

The possibility of using a deposition at trial without video should not be rejected out-of-hand. There are certain circumstances when it is advantageous. Counsel might wish to use this method when the treating physician makes a poor personal impression. A physician from another country whose English, although technically correct, is extremely difficult to understand is a good example. Another occasion to use a deposition without video is when the video of the primary treating physician has been conducted but a brief supplementation is needed.

PREPARATION

§ 10.4   Time

Preparation is the key to a successful videotaped deposition. This includes not only the usual preparation associated with any trial witness but also heavy emphasis on the "production" of the anticipated videotape. Experience dictates that the optimum length of a video deposition is about one hour. The deposition must be relatively short to maintain the interest of the fact finder. Therefore, it is more important than with live testimony that the lawyer and the doctor be "in sync" so that the testimony and presentation of the exhibits flow smoothly.

Because the treating physician is rarely able to spend as much time with the lawyer as the lawyer would like in preparing for trial, points must be made with the doctor in preparation quickly and effectively.

Busy orthopedists usually meet with the lawyer either half an hour or an hour before the deposition. This is frequently disastrous because the doctor may be running late with patients or may be busy in the operating room. Accordingly, unless counsel has had substantial experience with the doctor and knows that the physician will have completely reviewed the file, the lawyer should attempt to schedule a meeting with the doctor before the day of the videotaped deposition. This will better guarantee sufficient time for preparation by the physician.

However, if the doctor's schedule is unaccommodating, counsel has no alternative but to meet with the physician for a short time before the deposition, and the lawyer must be prepared to do two things. First, counsel must know the medical file in intimate detail and be prepared to "lead" the doctor through the chart not only in preparation, but in the course of the deposition. Second, counsel must keep the opposing attorney waiting as long as necessary until the physician has been adequately prepared and an acceptable level of rapport has been developed. As a practical matter, counsel for the plaintiff is in control because the defense lawyer really has only one option. Opposing counsel may leave and thereby run the risk that should plaintiff's counsel proceed with the deposition, a trial judge may later rule that the defense attorney's departure was unjustified and that the deposition is admissible without cross-examination.

§ 10.5   Items to Review

Counsel should have an outline prepared for the pre-deposition meeting with the orthopedist and take control of the meeting. The first items to review with the doctor are the critical questions about which the physician *must* testify in order to make out a prima facie case on the medical aspects. These include the following:

1. An opinion as to the causal relationship between the alleged tortious conduct of the defendant and the plaintiff's diagnosed injury
2. An opinion as to the causal relationship between the original injury and the plaintiff's various physical problems since the time of injury
3. The doctor's opinion as to prognosis
4. The doctor's opinion as to the necessity and reasonableness of the medical treatment and bills.

The doctor should be forewarned that there will be certain critical phases in the questioning about which there can be no equivocation on the doctor's part. If necessary, counsel can tell the doctor specifically what those questions will be. For example:

Q: Doctor, based upon the history that you have taken, the physical examination, your review of the diagnostic studies, and, of course, all of your training and background, have you formed an opinion, with a reasonable degree of medical certainty, as to the cause of plaintiff's herniated disc at L_5–S_1?

In this context, it may be important to discuss the doctor's understanding of the critical language, "with a reasonable degree of medical certainty," or whatever the applicable standard is. From time to time, a doctor may balk at rendering an opinion with the degree of certainty required by the prevailing evidentiary standards. It is then incumbent upon counsel to give alternative interpretations of the standard, finding one that the doctor will be most comfortable with and that will still satisfy the required evidentiary standard. This should be discussed at length with the doctor, so that if the physician is asked on cross-examination what she means by "reasonable degree of medical certainty," the doctor will be prepared to give an answer that will be consistent with the required case law.

In the advanced meeting with the doctor it is important to ascertain how the physician likes to discuss her qualifications. For example, should it be one opening question ("Doctor, can you tell us about your training and background?") or does the doctor want a steady stream of specific questions? Are there certain models and drawings that the doctor is most comfortable using? Are there certain analogies that she intends to rely upon?

Prior Videos of Doctor

To make the most of the brief amount of time that the lawyer will spend with the doctor in preparation for the videotape, counsel should view other videotapes that the physician has given and speak with other lawyers who have taken the doctor's deposition. This will provide the attorney with a better sense of the style of the doctor, how the doctor likes to present testimony, and the manner in which the doctor is most comfortable. Some doctors relish depositions and need only one or two questions to begin their testimony, then they proceed on their own through the various phases of the testimony. Others need to be prodded and directed. It is helpful to know this in advance.

The Doctor's File

The pre-deposition meeting with the doctor requires counsel to review the doctor's file and to understand the contents before the start of the deposition. It is customary before starting cross-examination for the defense attorney to ask to see the doctor's file. Because this is a videotaped deposition, the camera will stop and defense counsel will have much more time than would be the case in a courtroom to review the doctor's file. Accordingly, it is important that the plaintiff's lawyer be fully acquainted with the contents of the file in order to anticipate any question that might arise and to discuss the issue with the doctor so that no one will be surprised by a question during cross-examination based upon a letter or report in the file.

A medical file will frequently contain a letter discussing the doctor's fee. Often, it is good to allow this information to be elicited on cross-examination. First, the question is often *not* asked on cross-examination. This becomes helpful because plaintiff's counsel can then ask the question on cross-examination of the defense doctor. In other words, the jury will hear about the fee only from the defense doctor. Second, if properly forewarned, the orthopedist can answer questions about the fee deftly with, "Of course, I am charging a fee for these services, and the fee charged represents what I would have earned if I did not have to cancel out my patients for this morning's deposition."

Vocabulary

In preparing for the deposition, the claimant's attorney should think carefully about vocabulary. Certain words and phrases can add a decidedly pro-plaintiff flavor to the testimony. For example, it is prudent to avoid having the doctor talk about the plaintiff's "chief complaints." "Complaint" is a word with a negative connotation. Similarly, it is better to talk about a plaintiff "suffering" injuries rather than "experiencing" injuries. In this particular case, although the disc is technically "herniated," the term "rupture" will generate a more visceral reaction on the part of jurors.

§ 10.6 The Set

During the pre-deposition meeting with the doctor, it is important that the plaintiff's lawyer attend to the production details of the deposition. Where in the physician's office will the deposition be conducted? Will there be a view box available for review of X rays? What will be the visual background of the deposition? It is helpful if the deposition can be done at the doctor's desk in front of rows of medical books or with the physician's various diplomas in view. *Caution:* A seasoned defense attorney will object to this format as well as to the doctor's wearing a white coat during the deposition, on the grounds that the doctor would have none of these "props" if testifying in a courtroom.

Special attention must also be paid to background noise that might arise during the course of the deposition, such as air conditioners, telephones, beepers, and loudspeaker systems. All efforts should be made to eliminate these potential distractions. Counsel should be especially mindful of the rustling of papers, such as counsel's notes, which the microphones pick up quite easily. To reduce this problem, it is best to have all the medical records in one notebook (rather than in separate file folders) carefully indexed and tabbed so that counsel can flip quickly and quietly from record to record as needed. The use of a notebook becomes even more important if the deposition is conducted in a room where there is no desk or table to spread out the papers. A well laid-out notebook serves as an efficient laptop desk.

§ 10.7 The Props

At the pre-deposition meeting, counsel should discuss the use of visual aids. Ordinarily, a combination of anatomical models, schematics, and drawings is desired. If diagnostic films are to be used, it is valuable to present both the film itself and a reverse positive of the film or picture.

Depending upon the point to be made concerning the anatomical description of the parts involved, the doctor should have available the following for illustration:

1. A complete model of the spine with nerve roots protruding
2. Schematic drawings showing the interrelationship between the spinal nerve and the lower extremities
3. A dermatome chart
4. Anatomical drawings to give a "flesh-and-blood" quality to the presentation of the testimony
5. If X-ray or magnetic resonance imaging (MRI) films were taken, these should be used in conjunction with positives made of the same
6. If surgery or a myelogram is to be discussed, the doctor should show the jury the surgical saw or the myelogram needle.

With the foregoing in hand, the doctor can refer back and forth to the various materials, depending upon the point to be made. *Caution:* When using models, the jury often will not be oriented as to which is the front and which is the back of the model or exactly how it represents the human body. Care must be taken to elicit this from the witness. Schematic drawings and dermatome charts are helpful to convey conceptually what the doctor is discussing. Anatomical drawings are also helpful to complete the explanatory phase of the testimony. The jury develops a feeling for how the spine works, its relationship to muscles, and ultimately what will be involved in terms of penetrating the tissues and the bones if surgery is to be discussed.

In describing any one particular point, it is helpful to have the doctor explain it by referring to the model, the schematic chart, *and* the anatomical drawing. Using these visual aids in a cumulative fashion significantly increases the likelihood that the jury will understand the precise point the doctor wishes to make. For example:

Q: Doctor, can you stand up and show us how the model of the spine corresponds to your own back? Now can you show us on this drawing, which has been marked "Johns. Exhibit 2," where the L_5–S_1 disc is located?

If diagnostic films have been used, such as a myelogram or a MRI, it is very effective to have the physician place the original or duplicate film on a view box and point out precisely that area of the film that corroborates the diagnosis. The doctor should circle the area in question with a grease pencil. Then, the doctor holds up a positive of the same X ray or film, testifies that the positive is the same as the original X ray, and then circles the filling defect or abnormality on the MRI with a red pen. This is an important technique because ordinarily it is not sufficient simply to talk about what the diagnostic films show; the jury will be much more convinced if they see the actual film itself or at least know that the film exists. On the other hand, because the X rays are difficult to read and the jury may well not have a view box available to examine the X rays during deliberations, the positives are very helpful. These are easier to read and will become an exhibit at the time of trial that can be carried into the jury deliberation room.

Coordination with the Video Technician

In using any of these models and visual aids, it is important to discuss their use both with the doctor and the video technician. The doctor must be instructed to pause for a sufficient period of time when referring to the exhibit or drawing so that the technician can zoom in on the exhibit and get it into focus. It is this ability to zoom in that eliminates the time-consuming need of obtaining large blowups of any of the visual aids.

Selecting and Using Visual Aids

An expeditious use of visual aids begins by scanning the literature for schematic drawings that will be relevant to the testimony anticipated from the doctor. For anatomical drawings, reference should be made to Netter's *Atlas of Human Anatomy*.[1] (It is available in softback edition for about $50.) If there is enough time, copies of these different drawings should be sent to the doctor in advance so that she can select which ones to use at the time of the deposition. Then, prior to the deposition, the selected drawings should be blown up to approximately 11" x 17" (blowups of this size work well with the zoom-in technique described previously and are easy to handle) and mounted on foam board. Alternatively, if there will not be sufficient time for the doctor to select the drawings in advance so that these can be professionally mounted, counsel can enlarge a variety of different drawings and take them to the prep session, at which time the doctor can select the pictures she wants to use. The drawings can then be mounted within a matter of seconds on blank, precut pieces of foam board by using just a dab of glue in the corners.

---

[1] F. Netter (1989).

Just as with the positives of the X-ray and MRI films, it is important for the doctor during the course of testimony to refer to the drawings, especially the anatomical drawings and mark them in some way (with an arrow or a circle) to explain the testimony. It will then make sense to the jury watching the video at the time of trial because they will understand when the exhibits are submitted that there is something on the drawings that they should be examining. One should not rule out the possibility of supplying a model spine for the deposition, having it marked as an exhibit, and moving it into evidence at the time of trial so that the jury can develop a tactile as well as visual feeling for the medical evidence.

§ 10.8 Medical Expenses

In most jurisdictions in order for the plaintiff to recover medical expenses, a physician must testify that those expenses already incurred by the plaintiff were both necessary and reasonable. There are various ways that this can be done. One way is simply to have each bill marked as an exhibit or to have them marked collectively, then ask the doctor whether she has reviewed them and finds them to be reasonable and necessary. This method is potentially fraught with problems because the bills may not describe the treatment rendered and may make reference to the fact that the bill has been paid by or submitted to an insurance company.

There is an alternative approach. At the time that answers to interrogatories are prepared, a medical chronology/itemization list can be formulated that includes the date of treatment, the doctor or medical facility providing the treatment, a brief description of the treatment, and the amount charged. The format is illustrated in **Figure 10–1**. Depending upon the amount of treatment that the plaintiff has received at the time that the interrogatories are answered, the document may be several pages long (especially if a separate entry is made for each visit to the physical therapist). This document is updated periodically so that by the time the trial arrives, it will be current. This then becomes a separate exhibit for the videotaped deposition and the trial itself. It is an effective exhibit because it efficiently summarizes in a visual way the amount of treatment that the plaintiff has received, the duration of the treatment, the type of treatment, and the medical expenses. The following is an example of how the document would be used at the doctor's deposition:

Q: Doctor, before this deposition did you and I have an opportunity to review Exhibit C, which is a medical chronology and itemization of Bill Smith's medical care?

A: Yes we did.

Q: Does it, in your opinion, fairly summarize the medical treatment that he has received to date?

A: Yes it does.

Medical Chronology/Itemization
Michael Smith

Date	Services Rendered	Doctor/Hospital	Amount
2/20/92	Office visit, initial exam Dx: lumbar strain and sprain	Dr. David Allen	$ 100
2/28/92	Follow-up office visit Dx. Possible HNP L_5–S_1	Dr. David Allen	$ 50
3/3/92	Office visit, initial exam Dx: HNP L_5–S_1	Dr. Wilma Jones	$ 175
3/3/92	R Percoset Ibuprofen	Thrift Drug	$ 25
	Back brace	Williams Medical Supplies	$ 120
3/4/92	X rays	Center City Imaging Center	$ 225
3/10/92	MRI	Center City Imaging Center	$ 950
3/13/92	Follow-up office visit	Dr. Wilma Jones	$ 75
3/20/92	Physical Therapy (Posture training, etc.)	Back to Work Rehabilitation Clinic	$ 125

Figure 10–1. Medical chronology/itemization document.

Q: In your opinion, Doctor, was all of the medical treatment listed reasonable and necessary?
A: Yes it was.
Q: Are the amounts charged for the treatment rendered fair and reasonable?
A: Yes they are. If anything, they are somewhat low.
Q: And, Doctor, what is the total amount that is set forth at the bottom of the last page?
A: $14,556

Caution: If there are medical bills in the itemization from physical therapists or from hospitals, some doctors may become particularly fastidious and say that they really do not know what reasonable charges are for these services. First, it is important to review this document with the doctor prior to the deposition to learn whether she will be able to give testimony as to all of the expenses. If the doctor cannot or will not, then counsel should simply highlight with a yellow marker those expenses about which the doctor can testify and restrict questioning to those highlighted entries. The admissibility and recoverability of the other entries may then be established either by a request for admissions or by brief follow-up, in-person depositions of the physical therapist and the hospital administrator. The chronology/itemization exhibit becomes admissible at the time of trial when the plaintiff identifies the document as an accurate summary of the medical treatment he has received and an accurate itemization of his medical bills.

It is important to note that this type of exhibit may not be suitable if it tends to highlight what might be perceived as overtreatment or large gaps in treatment, particularly if the gaps are toward the end of the treatment and there is a flurry of treatment activity just before trial. Furthermore, to reduce the risk of the defense attorney objecting repeatedly to the use of the exhibits at the time of the deposition and otherwise disrupting the flow of the testimony, it is a good idea to let opposing counsel know prior to the deposition that the exhibits will be used and to supply the defense with copies if they are available.

§ 10.9 Involvement of Plaintiff

In meeting with the doctor, a critical concept to keep in mind is that of "coordination." In other words, the doctor's testimony must be coordinated or rendered consistent with testimony from other witnesses. These include liability witnesses who will talk about the manner in which the plaintiff contends the injury was inflicted, other physicians, a vocational expert, and, most importantly, the plaintiff.

It is advantageous to have the plaintiff visit the treating physician shortly before the videotaped deposition so that the physician's testimony will accurately reflect the plaintiff's current condition. This is especially important if the defense medical examination will be conducted shortly before trial. A particularly effective technique to neutralize a defense examination is to schedule the plaintiff for an appointment with the treating orthopedist within a day or two of the defense physical or, best of all, on the same day. *Caution:* In scheduling the plaintiff for a pre-video deposition exam, however, the plaintiff's lawyer must prepare the treating orthopedist for cross-examination by the defense attorney to the effect that the most recent appointment was not for purposes of treatment, but was merely in anticipation of the videotaped deposition. This could become a vulnerable point, for example, if as a result of the most recent examination, the doctor's notes suddenly paint a direr picture than earlier reported.

Before meeting with the doctor to prepare for the deposition, it is critical to speak with the plaintiff to get an updated, detailed picture as to his current complaints and restrictions. This is important so that at the time of the deposition of the doctor, counsel will be able to elicit testimony from the doctor confirming anticipated testimony of the plaintiff at the time of trial. For example:

Q: Would the injury that you have described, Doctor, be consistent with or otherwise explain why Michael Smith has difficulty standing or sitting for more than 15 minutes at a time? Or why he has difficulty walking more than a city block before having to sit down? Or why he has trouble bending over in the morning to brush his teeth, tie his shoes, or make his bed?

Q: Doctor, would Mr. Smith be entitled to pain and discomfort in driving long distances?

Q: Would he be entitled to pain and discomfort in attempting to lift items over 15 or 20 pounds? What about throwing his three-year-old son up in the air?

§ 10.10   Objections

Before the deposition begins, counsel should reach an understanding as to how objections will be handled. This issue is usually addressed in the controlling rules of civil procedures or local county rules, and these should be reviewed before the deposition. The rules will ordinarily permit the following arrangement: opposing counsel will simply say, "Objection," at which point the video camera operator will announce that they are going off the video record. However, the court stenographer will continue to transcribe the ensuing colloquy concerning the objection. This way, there is a record as to the basis for the objection, but it does not clutter up the videotape and will not require editing out at a later time, if so ruled. Also, it should be agreed by counsel that if the objection is merely to the form of the question and the nature of the objection will be obvious, the objecting lawyer should simply say, "Objection, as to form," or "Objection, leading." Under these circumstances, it would be understood that the video camera operator would continue to keep the video running. This will reduce the number of interruptions and the number of times that the video camera operator announces, "We are now going off the record." The fewer interruptions of this type the better.

It is anticipated that sometimes there will be one portion of the testimony that will be subject to serious objection and that its admissibility may be questionable.

For example, a witness's testimony may exceed the scope of her report, or a witness will testify about medical bills of uncertain admissibility because of certain no-fault laws relating to motor vehicle accidents. It is important to conduct the questioning in this area in a confined manner so that, if determined later on that the testimony is not admissible, that portion may be edited out without losing any other admissible testimony and without interrupting the basic flow of the deposition.

DEPOSITION

§ 10.11   Physician's Qualifications

How much time counsel should spend on qualifications depends upon the degree to which the injury is disputed and the period of time the doctor has treated the plaintiff. If the injury is not seriously disputed or if the doctor has treated the plaintiff over a substantial period of time, counsel need not dwell on the qualifications. It is important to remember that a videotaped deposition requires counsel to be selective in the points that are to be made. The customary areas discussed in qualifying a doctor are as follows:

1.   Undergraduate and medical school education
2.   Postgraduate training including residency, fellowships, and service in the military
3.   Clinical experience at various hospitals
4.   Duration, nature, and location of present private practice
5.   Affiliations with local hospitals
6.   Memberships in various medical societies
7.   Teaching positions
8.   Lectures given
9.   Articles written
10. Attendance at continuing education courses
11. Frequency and nature of surgery performed
12. Honor/awards
13. Board certification.

Ordinarily, a jury will not understand immediately what is taking place in the videotape deposition if counsel begins immediately with qualifications. It is better to begin the deposition with an introductory statement to help orient the jury:

Q: Dr. Johns, from reviewing your file on the plaintiff, I understand that you have treated him approximately eight times over the last 10 months. In a minute, I am going to ask you questions about the care and treatment you have rendered to this man. Before we do that however, it is important that the jury know a little bit about your background and training.

If an experienced witness, the doctor should be able to proceed through most of the pertinent testimony with only a few questions. If this is likely, it is helpful to begin this part of the testimony with a question:

Q: Doctor, for the benefit of the jury I would appreciate your putting modesty aside and telling us about your educational background and professional training, particularly as it relates to the treatment of the plaintiff.

More specific questions may be helpful, depending upon the responsiveness of the physician as a witness:

Q: Doctor, can you tell us from what medical school you graduated and the year of graduation? What postgraduate training did you pursue thereafter? At what point in your postgraduate training did you begin to specialize in orthopedics?

At this point it will be helpful to have the doctor explain just what the medical specialization of orthopedics is; after the doctor does that, ask if that includes diagnosis in management of problems associated with the lumbar spine because some jurors (who know what an orthopedist does) may believe that this is the sole province of neurosurgeons.

It is also important to deftly bring out certain facets of the doctor's training and background that may be more likely to create rapport with the jury. For example, if the doctor happened to have grown up and gone to high school in the area where now practicing, but went away to college and medical school, one would ask the following question:

Q: Doctor, you went basically halfway across the country for both college and medical school. How is it that you ended up in Philadelphia for your private practice?

A: Well, I grew up in this area and went to Central High School and have always enjoyed this area. When an opening arose at the hospital of the University of Pennsylvania, I thought it would be good for me and my family to be back in my hometown.

The Doctor's Curriculum Vitae (CV)

By the time the videotaped deposition for trial is to be taken, plaintiff's counsel will ordinarily have already received the report from the defendant's doctor and that doctor's CV. Of course, both the report and the CV should be reviewed carefully during the preparation session with the doctor. If the defense doctor's CV reveals weaknesses or the CV of the plaintiff's doctor is strong, emphasis should be placed on those distinguishing qualifications. This is particularly effective, for example, when the defense doctor is not board certified and the plaintiff's doctor is. Other areas of contrast are whether the physicians have written in peer review journals, how often they perform surgery, what type of operations they perform, whether they teach, and whether the profile of their patient population corresponds to that of the plaintiff (for example, mostly industrial or work-related injuries).

If the doctor has a lengthy curriculum vitae, it is counterproductive to go through all of the entries. A more effective approach follows:

Q: Doctor, you have handed both counsel a copy of your resume, which is about 15 pages in length. I do not wish to go through each and every entry but would like you to set aside modesty and discuss some of the highlights. For example, I have counted some 17 articles of which you have been an author or coauthor. Is that correct? Are these articles exclusively devoted to the subject of orthopedics? In fact, I note that at least three of these articles discuss low back injury and the herniation of discs. Is that correct?

When the medical issues will be bitterly contested, it is helpful to take this type of examination a step further and stress academic qualifications, such as whether any of the doctor's articles have appeared in peer-reviewed journals.

The same approach may be taken with respect to lectures given or teaching experience. For example:

Q: Doctor, have you been invited to lecture at various hospitals here in the metropolitan area? If I counted 15 lectures in the last five years, would that be accurate? And again, these are all in the field of orthopedics?

If the doctor is an active faculty member at a local medical school or has teaching responsibilities through a hospital in association with the local medical school, this qualification can be effectively touted:

Q: Doctor, have you also been invited to be a member of the staff at the University here in town? And among the courses that you teach, do those include diagnosis and treatment of low back conditions? Do those also include the diagnosis and management of herniated discs? Do you teach residents and fellows as well as medical students?

On the other hand, if the plaintiff's doctor does not have academic qualifications, he can be portrayed as a "hands-on" surgeon who is more interested in treating patients than writing articles. If this direction is taken, the number of patients seen per week and the frequency of the doctor's surgery should be stressed. References to continuing medical education courses will add the appropriate academic balance.

It is effective to end the qualification phase of the testimony with a high point, which is usually board certification. Most doctors with even a minimal amount of testimonial experience can effectively describe what is involved in board certification. The important point to stress is that not all orthopedists are board certified; some have never subjected themselves to the rigors of the exam; others have, but have failed. Therefore, after the doctor describes the board certification process, to the extent of not mentioning the percentage of practicing orthopedists who are, in fact, board certified, the following questions are helpful:

Q: Doctor, what percentage of practicing orthopedists are board certified? I take it, therefore, it is not necessary to be board certified in order to practice orthopedic medicine? Only those orthopedists who have achieved certain levels of accomplishment are entitled to this recognition, is that correct?

In some jurisdictions there is an ambiguity as to whether the treating physician is actually an expert or a fact witness. However, the use of experts routinely involves a review of their qualifications and the opportunity for opposing counsel to cross-examine them on qualifications. The use of the same format for a treating physician creates the opportunity to treat the doctor as an expert for certain purposes, such as making a transitional statement from the qualification to the substantive testimony after the defense attorney has cross-examined the doctor:

I now offer Dr. Jones as an expert in the field of orthopedics, and specifically as it relates to the diagnosis and treatment of low back injuries.

§ 10.12 Physician's Involvement with the Plaintiff

This is the point that the jury has been waiting for. The leadoff question typically goes as follows:

Q: Doctor, I am now going to ask you some questions about the care and treatment that you have rendered to Michael Smith over the past 10 months. You have in front of you your file, and please feel free to refer to it at any time that you wish during the course of the testimony. Please tell us when and under what circumstances you first met Michael Smith.

Use of Notes

Caution: Under most rules of evidence, witnesses may rely exclusively on written notes only when they have no present recollection of the incident and the notes do not refresh their recollection. Technically, under those circumstances, witnesses may read the notes to the jury, and they become substantive evidence. On the other hand, if after reviewing notes their recollection is refreshed, witnesses then testify from refreshed recollection. Ordinarily, however, in recognition of the practicalities of this situation, compliance with this rule of evidence is not insisted upon by defense attorneys or judges.

It would be particularly hard for a defense attorney to insist upon strict compliance with this rule of evidence at a videotaped deposition because there is no judge to enforce it at the time. However, should a defense attorney make such an objection during the course of the testimony, the doctor should be prepared to answer by stating that her recollection is refreshed as to some aspects and in others she must rely on the notes.

History

At this point the doctor recites the manner of first contact, either through referral from another physician or as the initially treating physician. In either case, the testifying physician will have an opportunity to recite an understanding of how the injury was inflicted. If cause of the injury is a serious issue, this portion of the doctor's testimony must be approached carefully because there is a risk that the liability version advanced by the plaintiff may be inadvertently contradicted. Conversely, it is an opportunity to strengthen the credibility of the plaintiff's version, especially if the history appearing in the doctor's chart was recorded soon after the accident.

In eliciting the history from the doctor, it is important to lay the foundation for what will ultimately be the doctor's opinion as to diagnosis and causation and also to provide testimony that will subtly strengthen the plaintiff's case for pain and suffering. For example:

A: Michael Smith was referred to me by David Allen, a general practitioner in Mr. Smith's neighborhood. When I met with the patient 10 months ago, I determined that he was 45 years old, married, a father of three, and working at the time of the accident as a maintenance man for the Jamestown Company, which sold and maintained industrial floor scrubbers. He had worked for this company for 10 years, and his job was to go out to the customers who were using the floor scrubbers and conduct repairs. Because these machines are operated by batteries, a fair amount of his work apparently involved lifting the batteries out and putting them back into the floor scrubbers. The position for the batteries on these machines was at about waist level. He told me that while servicing one of his customers at an office building, and working in the room that they had assigned him for repair of the machine, he was lifting one of the batteries that weighed about 60 pounds. While turning to set the battery down, his left foot slipped on some grease, causing his body to twist suddenly at the waist. He apparently managed to catch his balance before falling to the ground, still holding on to the battery. He said that he felt a sharp twinge in his low back at the time, but did not feel any immediate sense of pain or discomfort. He finished his job, but that night, by the time he got home, his back had started to ache. The following morning he had great difficulty getting out of bed, and his low back felt extremely painful. He took some Tylenol®. The next day, because of the severe pain that he was experiencing in his back, he called his employer and obtained permission to treat directly with his own family doctor. That afternoon he saw Dr. Allen, who suspected a sprain or strain of the ligament in the back and recommended complete bed rest for a week. Dr. Allen also prescribed some anti-inflammatory medication along with Tylenol 3® with codeine.

   Mr. Smith maintained strict bed rest except for necessary trips to the bathroom. He ate his meals in bed. After a week of bed rest, Mr. Smith felt better and returned to Dr. Allen, who decided that Mr. Smith could try light-duty work at his place of employment. For Mr. Smith this meant working in the parts department, distributing light parts to other employees. However, after a few days of even light duty, the pain returned in the same spot. Only this time it was more of a stabbing nature, and he began to experience what we call radiation—that is, movement of the pain in a path down his left leg. He reported these symptoms to Dr. Allen who, at that point, decided to refer Mr. Smith to me. I saw Mr. Smith two days later on March 3rd. After giving me this history, he stated that the pain had remained persistent and he noticed that it got worse when he strained, such as by coughing or sneezing.

Q: Doctor, based on only the history that you received from Mr. Smith, did you form some preliminary impression as to the cause of this pain?

   It is helpful to the plaintiff's case if the treating orthopedist will discuss the working diagnosis based upon history alone for two reasons: (1) it demonstrates that the contended mechanism of injury—sudden torsional forces on the spine area while holding a heavy object—is a well-recognized mechanism of injury and therefore increases the likelihood of the plaintiff's version of events and complaints; and (2) the easier the diagnosis is to make because of its classic features, the harder it will be for the defense to challenge the diagnosis.

Q: Doctor, how, based on history alone, could you form such a diagnosis?
A: First, as a result of extensive training in the area and my opportunity to examine hundreds of patients who have suffered trauma to the low back, it was my opinion that given the plaintiff's description of the traumatic incident and his symptomatology, the mechanism of injury and the symptoms were classic for a herniated disc, especially at the L_5–S_1 juncture. Sudden torsional forces exerted on the low back at the L_5–S_1 juncture, such as that described by Mr. Smith, is a well-recognized mechanism of causing rupture and herniation. Further, the intermittency of the pain after bed rest with eventual flare-up, especially with the radiation and the pain, and the distribution of the pain as described by the patient are also classic symptoms.

§ 10.13   Anatomy Explanation

The doctor has rendered a tentative impression of a herniated disc at L_5–S_1. It is at this point that the doctor then refers to the models, schematic drawings, and anatomic drawings that lead up to an explanation of a herniated disc. Thus, the doctor establishes the following:

1. The purpose of the spine as support for the entire back and also as protection and a channel for the spinal cord with the various roots running off at the different levels
2. The spine is made up of four distinct areas: cervical, thoracic, lumbar, and sacral
3. The description of a vertebral body in its relation to those above and below
4. A description of the intervertebral disc as well as an explanation of its function (weight bearing and cushioning effect)
5. Different nerve roots provide sensory and motor input to different parts of the body, depending upon the level at which they leave the spine.

Ample time should be spent here with the visual aids including the model, the schematic drawings, and the anatomical drawings.

The physician should discuss two other points at this time: (1) the concept and importance of lordosis (or natural curvature of the spine) and the clinical significance of its absence (presence of muscle spasm), and (2) the importance of the juncture at L_5–S_1 as a location where, because of the angling of these regions, trauma is more likely to have serious consequences. The doctor should also explain that because of the increased pressures placed on the low back in the lumbar region, as opposed to the cervical or thoracic region, injury is more likely to occur in this region.

The doctor can then explain what is meant by a herniated disc by describing the rupture of the outer casing of the disc or the annulus and the process by which the inner material, the nucleus pulposus, extrudes out. (This can be memorably demonstrated by use of either a jelly donut or a caramel candy with a soft vanilla inner candy.) It is also important to stress that once the pulposus is forced out, it cannot be placed back in again. In other words, the injury has a significant, permanent component to it.

In discussing a herniated disc, it is also helpful in developing jury rapport to talk about other terminology used to describe the same phenomenon, such as a slipped disc, a ruptured disc, or sciatica. With a greater variety of descriptive names, more jurors will understand the phenomenon because either they have experienced it themselves or know of others who have had the same problem, but with a different name.

§ 10.14   Mechanism of Injury

The doctor should describe the types of forces exerted upon the lumbar spine that will lead to herniation. In this particular fact scenario, the mechanism of injury involved a slipping without actually falling while the plaintiff was holding a heavy object, causing a twisting or torsional movement. The doctor should be asked to actually twist the model with her hands to demonstrate an understanding of the torsional force. The doctor then explains how a tear of the annulus can eventually lead to a herniation of disc material and how this disc material at some point will impinge upon the nerve root leaving through the foramina. It is this impingement that causes the pain, particularly the radiating aspect, and by now the jury will understand that the nerve root impinged upon at L_5–S_1 is the S_1 nerve.

Again, with the use of the appropriate visual aids, the doctor can trace the first sacral nerve as it leaves the foramina (because a lumbar disc protrusion usually does not affect the nerve existing above the disc, but rather the one below it). Further, the doctor should show how this nerve merges with nerves from L_4–S_4 to travel through the sciatic notch and form the sciatic nerve and how these nerves innervate the lower part of the body.

Because counsel is off camera during the course of the deposition, there is a tendency to focus on the written materials, such as questions that have been written out, an outline, or the records. Often, counsel is thinking of the next question to ask while the doctor is testifying. This is dangerous. It is imperative that counsel, as the producer/director of the deposition, pay close attention to the doctor's answers to make sure of two things: (1) that the doctor is actually covering the important points that counsel wants made, and (2) that it is being done in a way that will be understood by the average juror. For example, if the doctor, while glancing at her notes during direct testimony, overlooks an important positive test result or a significant complaint of pain by the plaintiff, counsel should jump into the deposition as follows:

A: Doctor, let me interrupt you for a second. Before you finish talking about the neurologic tests, I see from your office notes that you also performed the ankle-jerk test on Mr. Smith, but you did not mention this in reciting your clinical test results. Could you tell the jury about this?

Likewise, throughout the course of the doctor's testimony, when an explanation is unclear, or esoteric, the attorney must again jump in and attempt clarification for the jury. For example:

Q: Doctor, as a risk of surgery you have mentioned something called adhesions? Just what are these?

Or

Q: Doctor, you have talked about a torsional force on the spinal column. By that are we simply talking about a twisting? Can you demonstrate that with this model?

Close observation of the testimony is especially important when the doctor is using the models. Even though counsel knows exactly what the doctor is talking about, counsel must try to view them from the position of a juror who has never seen these drawings or models before.

§ 10.15 Physical Examination

Once the doctor has explained the anatomy and physiology of the spinal column and the spinal nerves, an explanation of the physical examination will make more sense to the jury. The doctor at this point will explain that there are certain tests and maneuvers that may be performed in the doctor's office that are helpful in confirming or ruling out the doctor's working diagnosis and otherwise pinpointing the precise location of the problem. For example, the doctor explains that if she is able to detect certain phenomenon associated with those areas of the body innervated by the S_1 nerve root, those findings will confirm some injury to S_1. The highlights would include the following:

1. Decreased lordosis—forward curvature of the lower spine
2. Palpation of the suspected area—this should produce an intense pain radiating into leg
3. The straight-leg raising test—this should produce pain at a lower degree than in the nonaffected leg especially if pain radiates into the lateral foot, indicating S_1 nerve root irritation
4. The Ely's test—the patient's heel is forced against the buttock
5. The Fabere-Patrick test—the thigh and knee are flexed and the outer side of the ankle is placed on the patella of the opposite knee.

The doctor describes the results of each of these tests and again, referring to the anatomical models and drawings, demonstrates how the movement causes a pulling or exerts a strain on the S_1 nerve and therefore results in pain. The question at this point would be as follows:

Q: Doctor, with the clinical tests that you have described, you have been able to establish that there is, in fact, pain with the sciatic nerve, correct? But because this sciatic nerve is made up of various nerve roots from different levels, is there any technique to determine which level of the sciatic nerve is actually being impinged upon?
A: Yes, with a neurologic examination we can determine, by the presence of certain abnormalities, just which nerve root is being impinged upon because specific nerve roots affect specific motor and sensory functions.

The doctor then recites aspects of the neurologic exam:

1. The knee-jerk—this relates to primarily the L_4 nerve and would reflect a lesion at that location in the spine if there were a loss or diminution in the degree of reflex.

2. Ankle-jerk—by tapping the Achilles heel the foot should experience a plantar or downward flexion if those nerves coming through the L_5–S_1 and S_2 segments are not injured. An absence or diminishment of reflex is indicative of injury at the L_5–S_1 level.

3. Muscle weakness—weakness in the peroneal and calf muscles is also suggestive of a lesion in L_5–S_1. This can be understood by also looking at the dermatome.

4. Sensory changes—with the use of a pin, the doctor checks the sensitivity of the skin in certain portions of the leg. Diminished sensation in certain portions, corresponding to the dermatome distribution, is generally indicative of a lesion at the corresponding level. For example, diminished sensation on the back, outside of the calf, and outside of the foot and the fifth toe are suggestive of an L_5–S_1 herniation.

It should be pointed out by the doctor that insofar as any of the neurologic signs are inconsistent with the doctor's working diagnosis of a herniation at L_5–S_1, the neurologic examination is not always precise because of anatomical variation between individuals that result in an overlap of nerve supply from adjoining nerve roots. Also, there is the possibility that herniated material from the ruptured disc may actually fall from its ordinary level down to a site below the actual site of herniation, thereby impinging upon a different nerve root.

Objective versus Subjective Signs

Depending upon the degree of other confirming evidence of a herniated disc, such as an MRI or a myelogram, counsel may or may not wish to address the issue of subjective versus objective signs. If there is strong diagnostic imaging evidence (myelogram or MRI) to support the final diagnosis, the lawyer should not waste time on this issue and should allow the doctor to handle it on cross-examination if a defense attorney chooses to venture into that area. However, insofar as the myelogram or MRI may not yet have been performed or the results are ambiguous, it is appropriate to discuss the distinction. The experienced orthopedist has little difficulty in handling this distinction.

Q: Doctor, in describing some of the clinical tests that you performed on Mr. Smith, such as the straight-leg raising test, does that depend upon a statement of pain by the patient? You yourself really have no way of knowing whether it is, in fact, painful, do you?

A: Yes, you are correct that it is subjective in the sense that I cannot tell for sure whether or not it is painful, but as a result of having done hundreds of these examinations, I believe I have developed the ability to distinguish between those who genuinely experience pain with certain movements and those who do not. Also, I work into the tests that I perform a particular test that is designed to eliminate would-be malingerers. On the other hand, there are certain test results over which the patient has no control, such as the reflex tests that I talked about earlier. There is no way someone can fool a physician with those tests. It is the same with the sensory test because the patient is lying down and cannot see where I am moving the needle.

Confirmation of Preliminary Diagnosis by Physical Examination

Q: Doctor, what effect did the results of the physical examination you just summarized for us have on the preliminary diagnosis that you made based solely upon history?
A: This simply confirmed my diagnosis and increased the extreme likelihood that the problem was located at the L_5–S_1 level.

This question at this time enhances the credibility of the medical witness if the physician is able to speak confidently about the results of findings independent of any reports or records that came from elsewhere. Further, the jury will appreciate the fact that the doctor is working on an essentially inductive basis, refining the analysis and diagnosis with each additional piece of evidence. This creates interest on the part of the jury because they will sense that the doctor is moving step-by-step towards a definitive diagnosis. A sense of anticipation is created.

Review of Other Records

If the doctor became involved in the management of the plaintiff after the claimant had seen other physicians, it is, of course, important that the doctor have those other records available for review. Frequently, however, the doctor will not look at the other records until after taking a history and conducting an examination. If these other records either explicitly or implicitly suggest a herniated disc, the testifying doctor's opinions will have greater weight if the same conclusions as those of the earlier physicians are reached. Therefore, the discussion of the input of the records, if any, is effectively left to this point in the direct examination.

When the treating physician makes reference to reports of other physicians, the defense may object on the grounds of hearsay. However, the law of evidence in most jurisdictions permits a physician to refer to and rely upon medical reports prepared by others if those are the types of reports ordinarily relied upon in conducting her practice. Therefore, should an objection arise on this basis, counsel should simply proceed as follows:

Q: Okay, Doctor, let's straighten this out. These reports from Dr. Allen: are these the type of reports that you routinely receive upon referral? And are these the type of reports that you routinely rely upon in helping you form a diagnosis and plan of treatment?

With these questions and affirmative answers from the doctor on the record, the basis of the defense objection will have been eliminated.

§ 10.16 Diagnostic Studies

In addition to a history and physical examination, an orthopedic surgeon will usually rely on certain diagnostic studies to rule out or confirm a diagnosis. These include X ray, myelogram, electromyography (EMG), and MRI.

X ray

Because X rays reveal only bony structure and not soft tissue, they are not diagnostic of a herniated disc. However, they are routinely requested in order to rule out alternative explanations for the low back pain, such as fractures and dislocations. They can provide indirect evidence of disc damage by showing that there has been a narrowing of the space between the discs at L_5–S_1. Spinal X rays also will show a change in the lordosis or curve of the spine, which may be further indicative of disc injury.

Myelogram

Before the advent of MRI, a myelogram was recognized as the best means of affirmatively diagnosing a herniated disc. The process involves injecting radiopaque dye into the subarachnoid space. With the use of X ray, the dye forms a silhouette around the spinal cord and nerve roots. If there is a herniated disc, the herniated portion of the disc will itself create a silhouette. This is routinely referred to as a "filling defect." A CAT scan is now often combined with a myelogram to increase the accuracy of the test.

A myelogram is considered a quasi-surgical procedure with distinct risks; it is not to be undertaken lightly. Accordingly, if in fact a myelogram has been performed or will be performed on the plaintiff, counsel should elicit substantial testimony from the doctor about the procedure—the type of preparation, the pain, and the certain risks that are involved. These risks include anaphylactic shock occurring as a result of an allergic reaction to the radiopaque dye. Additionally, just as with a spinal tap (a certain amount of fluid must be withdrawn from the subarachnoid space before the dye is injected) the patient may also experience severe headache, pain, and stiffness, as well as nausea and vomiting. Another complication, now fairly rare, is *adhesive arachnoiditis*, a condition resulting from the irritation of the arachnoid membrane by the radiopaque dye. The irritation leads to inflammation, which in turn causes the formation of scar tissue.

It is very effective at this time to show the jury the size of the needle used for the procedure. This will elicit a visceral reaction from most, if not all, members of the jury.

Electromyography

EMG is a technique of measuring the rate of nerve impulses transmitted through muscle fibers. If the nerve supply to a muscle is impaired because of a herniated disc, there will be a change in the electrical impulses given off by the nerves. The electrical impulses themselves are recorded on a cathode ray oscilloscope or on an ink-reading oscilloscope (for permanent record). The impulses are also transmitted to a loudspeaker for simultaneous auditory analysis. This technique is not highly diagnostic for intervertebral disc herniation because it will indicate only abnormal functions somewhere along the pathway of the nerve; moreover, it is restricted only to motor nerves and not sensory nerves. Therefore, if the herniation is affecting only the sensory portion of the nerve as opposed to the motor portion, the test will not be diagnostic. If the test has been performed, the doctor should describe in detail the mechanical aspects by which the test is implemented because it does involve sticking pins into various muscles of the plaintiff and is generally considered to be an unpleasant test, if not downright painful.

Magnetic Resonance Imaging

MRI is the latest and most sophisticated diagnostic imaging technique and by far the most preferred for evaluating herniated discs. Its method of operation is by and large too complicated to explain in detail to a jury except to explain that it uses electromagnetic forces with a computer reassimilation. Perhaps most important to mention to the jury is that the machinery costs more than $1 million. Juries will be familiar with CAT scan and will appreciate the significance of the MRI when they are told that the MRI has basically displaced CAT scans and other diagnostic tests for giving extremely high-resolution definition of soft tissue structure, including especially disc material. Also attractive about the MRI is that it is noninvasive and, unlike X rays, produces images without exposing the patient to ionizing radiation.

If an MRI film has been interpreted to be diagnostic of a herniated disc, this should provide the most convincing evidence and confirmation of the doctor's diagnosis. As with X rays, the doctor's testimony is enhanced if the actual film can be shown to the jury on a view box with the doctor highlighting those slices that show the herniation. It would be especially beneficial to have those slices blown up and colorized to further dramatize the physical evidence.

The testimony, therefore, concerning the diagnostic studies is as follows:

Q: Doctor, did you refer Michael Smith for any diagnostic testing?
A: Yes, I sent him initially for X rays and an MRI. Although the X rays would not be specifically diagnostic of a herniated disc, they would be valuable to rule out other, alternative explanations for low back problems, such as a fracture or congenital abnormality. Also, if there was a narrowing of the disc space between L_5 and S_1, that would be indicative of injury in that area. The MRI, on the other hand, is quite effective in diagnosing herniated discs, and the information from this would be valuable to my plan of treatment.
Q: How soon after your visit, Doctor, did you get the results?
A: I had the results within two weeks.
Q: And, Doctor, can you tell the jury what the results were?
A: Well, the X ray was mildly diagnostic. It confirmed a low back problem as indicated by muscle spasm, which results in a loss of the lordotic curve. There was also a distinct narrowing of the space between L_5 and S_1. On the other hand, there was no indication of bony abnormality that might explain the patient's symptoms of radiating pain. By contrast, the MRI results were quite helpful and confirmed precisely my clinical impressions based on history and physical examination. It showed a herniated disc at L_5–S_1 impinging upon the nerve root at the left-hand side. This would explain the radiation of pain down the left leg. I have the films here, and I have placed them on the view box. If the video camera operator would focus in on this one slice here and enlarge it for the jury, I can show you exactly where the herniation is. I have circled it here. This film has been marked as Doctor's Exhibit 3. Doctor's Exhibit 4 is a blowup of this particular slice, and it has also been colorized to better visualize the herniation I am talking about.

§ 10.17 Plan of Treatment

Because the defense physician will not have treated the plaintiff or, in all likelihood, proposed any plan of treatment, this area of the direct examination helps to strongly distinguish the testimony of the treating physician:

Q: Doctor, after you first had an opportunity to meet with Mr. Smith and learn firsthand about the discomfort and pain he was suffering, did you propose a plan of treatment?
A: Yes I did. Although I was highly confident of my diagnosis, I wished to await final confirmation with the diagnostic studies. Therefore, in the interim I prescribed certain pain medications, anti-inflammatory medications, and strict bed rest. This had not been successful before, but I believed that until I had a definitive diagnosis that we should try it again. Indeed, even after I received the results of the diagnostic films confirming the diagnosis, I was determined to take a conservative approach to therapy and exhaust all possibilities before proceeding to the next step, which is surgery.
Q: What did you have in mind doctor as far as continued, conservative therapy?
A: Basically, continued bed rest with moist heat and analgesics along with anti-inflammatories. In fact, I recommended two additional weeks of this with

the use of a back support and a return to part-time light duty to see how this would work. The bed rest is helpful to reduce pressure on the nerve root, which in turn reduces swelling and inflammation. Actually, before he went back to work, I proposed that he engage in a light exercise, strengthening program involving a gradual resumption of activity by walking short distances and beginning simple exercises.

The purpose of the muscle relaxant is to reduce muscle spasm, because muscle spasm is often a cause of pain in the low back. I also recommended some postural training, and I encouraged this by also prescribing a corset. The corset does not really relieve the pressure on the disc but does force the patient to walk in an upright position, and this posture in turn tends to reduce pressure on the nerve.

Q: Over what period of time, Doctor, did you attempt what you called "conservative therapy"?

A: Actually, this lasted for many months. After the bed rest phase and the resumption of light activity, Mr. Smith asked me if he could go back to work, at least light duty. I thought that as long as he practiced proper posture and truly did restrict himself to light duty, that this should be tried. I agreed with this only because he was so insistent on going back although he was in significant discomfort. In fact, he went back to work for about three months, but the pain became increasingly more severe; he began to experience a greater loss of sensation and a greater weakness in his lower leg and foot. This is what I called a "progressive neurological" sign, and at this point I felt that he should definitely consider surgery.

In discussing surgery the doctor should stress that this is basically an elective procedure with a significant amount of risk associated with it. In other words, the doctor's testimony should make clear that the plaintiff is agreeing to undergo this only because the pain and discomfort have reached a point where they are unbearable. First, the doctor explains the surgical procedure itself, that is, to excise the disc, particularly the extruded portion, and thereby relieve the pressure on the nerve. In explaining the mechanical aspects of the procedure, it is very advantageous to make use of anatomical drawings so that the jury gets a feel and full flavor of the procedure itself, involving the surgical incision through various layers of skin and tissue. Reference should be made to Netter's drawings[2] as well as those from surgical textbooks that graphically illustrate the various steps and procedures involved in a laminectomy. The doctor should attempt to describe in as vivid detail as possible the instruments used to cut through the soft tissues, the use of retractors, and especially the surgical saws used to cut through the laminae.

Extensive discussion should be given to the hazards associated with the surgery that arise even in the best of hands. These include not simply the general risks associated with anesthesia but those unique to the operation, such as injury to the spinal cord or the nerve root, as well as the formation of scar tissue or

---

[2] F. Netter, Atlas of Human Anatomy (1989).

adhesions. The picture that must be painted by the physician at this point is that although the plaintiff is a strong candidate for surgery, there is no guarantee that the surgery will be successful, and there is the possibility that the plaintiff could end up being worse. Testimony to this effect will be powerful, indirect evidence as to the severity of the plaintiff's complaints: anyone willing to undergo such a procedure must undoubtedly be experiencing great discomfort.

§ 10.18 Postsurgical Convalescence

To build further the plaintiff's case for pain and suffering as well as loss of income, the doctor should discuss the contemplated convalescence—how long it will last and what restrictions will be imposed upon the plaintiff. This usually includes a period of time with bed rest, a gradual increase in activities, and then some physical therapy to strengthen the muscles that will assume additional support of the back in lieu of the removed disc and laminae.

If a spinal fusion is required, the doctor will, of course, be required to explain the reason for this and the mechanics of the procedure. A spinal fusion may be required when the doctor concludes that after removal of the protruding disc and part of the laminae, the spine will be unstable. In that case, the uncontrolled movement of the spine causes pain. Description of the fusion procedure can be dramatic in that it requires the harvesting of a bone from another part of the body, either the pelvis or the lower ribs.

§ 10.19 Defense Doctor's Report

Whether plaintiff's counsel should elicit a rebuttal by the treating physician to the defense doctor's report is a tactical decision. On the one hand, direct confrontation of the report tends to undermine the otherwise subtle aura of independence that is created by the status of the physician as a treating doctor. In other words, asking the doctor whether she has read the defense doctor's report and agrees with it converts the doctor from an ostensibly impartial witness into an advocate.

Effective rebuttal can be achieved without specifically referring to the defense doctor's report by simply picking out the critical features in that report and repudiating each of them in the direct examination of the plaintiff's doctor. For example, where the defense doctor attempts to attribute the plaintiff's problems to preexisting degenerative disc disease or to prior trauma, the issue may be handled as follows:

Q: Doctor, your history does indicate that Mr. Smith was involved in an automobile accident before and also that, according to the X rays, he did have some preexisting degenerative disc disease. In your opinion, is either of those factors responsible for the pain, discomfort, and limitation that Mr. Smith has

A: experienced since the day he was caused to slip on grease left on the floor of the defendant's warehouse?

A: No. Those other factors are not responsible. The fact of the matter is that Mr. Smith has degenerative disc disease like most of us do at that age. However, he was not symptomatic; that is, those disc problems were not causing him any pain or discomfort as reflected by the fact that he sought no medical treatment anywhere. Also, the automobile accident was so long ago and his recovery was so quick, that it would not have played any role in bringing about Mr. Smith's present problem, except for the possibility that the trauma might have weakened the disc and made it somewhat more vulnerable to later trauma.

The alternative approach is simply to ask the doctor whether, after reading the defense doctor's report, she agrees with it and if not, why not. The countervailing advantage to an explicit rebuttal by name of the defense doctor's report is that it will undermine the effect of the defense doctor's testimony. By the time the defense doctor's testimony is presented, the jury will be able to specifically recall repudiation of this doctor by name and will be more suspicious of the testimony from the outset.

Either directly or indirectly, the treating physician should provide rebuttal testimony of the defense doctor's report in the course of her direct examination.

§ 10.20 Treating Physician's Definitive Diagnosis

With the review of the diagnostic films, the doctor has completed the workup of the patient and is now ready for the "payoff" questions:

Q: Doctor, based upon the history and physical examination of the plaintiff in your office, your review of the other records, and your review of the diagnostic studies, have you formed an opinion, with a reasonable degree of medical certainty, as to the cause of Mr. Smith's persistent lower back pain that radiates down his left leg?

A: Yes I have.

Q: And what is that opinion, Doctor?

A: Based upon the workup that I have reviewed here and especially including the MRI test results, it is my opinion, with a reasonable degree of medical certainty, that Mr. Smith is suffering from a herniated disc at L_5-S_1 that is impinging or pressing against the S_1 nerve root on the left side.

Q: Again, Doctor, with a reasonable degree of medical certainty, have you formed an opinion as to what caused this disc to herniate or rupture?

A: Yes I have.

Q: And what is that opinion, Doctor?

A: It is my opinion, also with a reasonable degree of medical certainty, that Mr. Smith suffered this rupture of his disc at L_5-S_1 when he slipped and stumbled while carrying the battery, and specifically, that this twisting motion under weight exerted torsional forces on the spine at L_5–S_1, and that it was this sudden torsional force that caused the disc to rupture.

§ 10.21 Final Prognosis

With a herniated disc, no matter what the results of either conservative or surgical treatment have been or will be, there is a significant component of permanency to the injury, and this must be fully exploited by the plaintiff's attorney. It is generally recognized among practitioners that it is the aspect of permanency that provides the key to larger verdicts. Thus, the doctor should be prepared to say that even if the plaintiff has enjoyed or can expect to enjoy a complete recovery, at a minimum his spine is now more vulnerable to future injury and he is undoubtedly an "industrial risk," meaning his ability to get hired for almost any type of work other than sedentary or light duty will be impaired. (Testifying to this conclusion may cause difficulty if the physician has not been involved in preemployment physicals or in screening potential applicants based upon their physical capabilities.)

The doctor can also opine that even with a successful laminectomy, the plaintiff should not continue with his pre-injury level of strenuous employment. If at the time of trial counsel intends to present testimony from a vocational expert about the plaintiff's diminished earning capacity because of his injury, it will be important to elicit from the doctor testimony that will provide a proper basis for the vocational expert's own opinions. For example, if the doctor is able to testify that following surgery the plaintiff should be restricted as to the amount of weight that he can lift and the number of repetitions of such weight, the vocational expert will then be in a position to testify as to the categories of work that have been put beyond the reach of the plaintiff as a result of this injury. (Of course, the vocational expert will also be able to testify that with a preexisting history of spinal injury, a worker seeking new employment of anything but the most sedentary type of work will have, in effect, suffered a loss of earning capacity because he will have more difficulty in getting hired.) The doctor should also discuss the fact that following a laminectomy there will be greater stress on the posterior joints that can lead to degenerative changes, and this itself may necessitate a spinal fusion (if not already contemplated).

The concluding question and answer should have been carefully discussed with the doctor ahead of time. Whatever can be offered by the doctor to enhance a sense of dread should be shared with the jury at this time:

Q: Doctor, as a 45-year-old man who has made his living repairing floor scrubbers, what does Mr. Smith have to look forward to for the rest of his life as a result of this injury?

A: Well, as I indicated earlier, he has ahead of him surgery to repair this herniated disc. Under the best-case scenario, with a perfect result, he will have trouble continuing on with the type of work he was doing, carrying heavy batteries and the like. He will also be more prone to recurrence of injury at that location. Then there is an intermediate result, if the surgery is not 100-percent effective, that will leave him with still restricted ability to carry on with his job and intermittent episodes of discomfort and pain. In a worst-case scenario, if the surgery is not successful, he basically will have to learn to live with the pain that he has now and the restrictions on his ability to work.

§ 10.22 Conclusion

The foregoing discussion of direct examination of the doctor does not purport to be the only or definitive means for presenting the medical testimony. It should, however, be of assistance to younger practitioners who are still developing their own styles and techniques. Few of the suggestions here are mutually exclusive with other approaches. What is critical and universally applicable, however, is the importance of maintaining the focus of the deposition on the three goals:

1. Fulfilling evidentiary requirements
2. Creating a "halo" effect for the plaintiff
3. Winning the jury over to the plaintiff's side by effectively communicating the medical aspects of the case, thereby inviting the jury to reward those who have explained to them a common but misunderstood phenomenon.

CHAPTER 11

GUIDELINES AND STRATEGIES FOR CROSS-EXAMINING ORTHOPEDIC EXPERTS

Mark R. Kosieradzki

§ 11.1 Medical Summary

Essential to the cross-examination of a medical expert is a thorough understanding of the injured plaintiff's medical condition, medical history, and associated medical principles. By understanding the medical facts of the case, the trial attorney will be able to identify admissions that may be gained from the adverse physician, the fallacies in that examiner's analysis, as well as potential avenues of impeachment. By thorough preparation, it is possible to gain insight into the heart and soul of the witness's testimony. With that understanding, it is then possible to systematically identify the deficiencies in the witness's analysis and, if necessary, impeach credibility.

An understanding of one's own case and the associated medical principles involved is the initial task in preparing an attack on any contrary medical expert. This establishes the strengths and exposes the weaknesses of the case on its merits, before the adverse witness enters the arena.

The attorney must have an intimate understanding of the foundation that the expert has or should have available to the development of an opinion. This includes scrutiny of the plaintiff's accident-related medical records as well as the records comprising any historical medical problems. The sources of medical information are not limited to medical records. Characterizations of physical capability or complaints are reflected in the plaintiff's deposition, employment records, military files, school records, insurance application, and in the testimony of lay damage witnesses.

Once all of the plaintiff's records are secured, they should be organized chronologically by provider. Thereafter, using simple word processing programs, it is possible to develop a medical summary that can be reorganized chronologically. This summary enables a trial attorney to move between medical providers in preparation for the cross-examination and have a clear understanding of the temporal relationships between the various complaints and treatments over the course of the plaintiff's life.

SAMPLE MEDICAL SUMMARY:

10/21/79   *MERCY MEDICAL CENTER:* Acute left ear pain with upper respiratory infection.

01/05/81   *DR. WOLFE:* Chiropractic treatment. Acute PNT left lumbrosacral area.

01/19/81   *DR. WOLFE:* Chiropractic treatment. Recurrence of low back pain and numbness. Whole foot involves all toes pain 50% better than numbness.

02/27/81   *MINNEAPOLIS FAMILY PRACTICE:* Acute upper respiratory infection.

06/21/85   *MINNEAPOLIS ORTHOPEDIC CENTER:* Discomfort approximately one month ago. Twisted foot and noted funny feeling. Restriction of motion comment does not appear to have any neurological deficit.

09/07/85   *MERCY MEDICAL CENTER:* X ray right ankle: avulsion and fracture of the distal fibula. Soft tissue swelling seen over the lateral malleolus.

10/28/85   *MINNEAPOLIS ORTHOPEDIC CENTER:* Cast removed. Fibers union of the small avulsion fracture at tip of fibula.

09/13/91	*SUBURBAN AMBULANCE:* Chief complaint: neck and back pain. No loss of consciousness. Complaints of middle neck pain and back pain at shoulder blades.
09/13/91	*MERCY MEDICAL CENTER:* Driver of car seat belted, no loss of consciousness, has neck pain. Complaints of back and shoulder pain.
09/16/91	*CANFIELD PHYSICIANS:* MVA 9/13/91—rear ended. Considerable cervical spasm more laterally in neck and in left front lumbar pain.
09/18/91	*KEL RIVER PHYSICAL THERAPY:* Initial evaluation. Referred for treatment of low back and neck pain. Range of motion limited, paraspinal spasm noted to the left.
09/20/91	*CANFIELD PHYSICIANS:* Continued cervical spasm, range of motion limited.

§ 11.2 Understanding Medical Principles

After developing this universe of information as completely as possible, the next, and the most important step, can be taken: understanding the medical principles behind the physical findings and recorded complaints. The knowledge of what can cause the objective findings or the subjective complaints to occur is critical. If the mechanism of injury to the plaintiff appears inconsistent with the findings present to any examination, one has identified a causation issue in the case or an oversight in a physician's analysis that will need clarification. With this knowledge, the attorney may prepare a cross-examination to gain admission relative to the case.

An understanding of the medical principles to a given medical problem starts with the understanding of the medical vocabulary contained within the record and the broad medical principles related in the literature. Begin with a review of the language contained in the records to ensure an understanding of all that is contained therein. Any unfamiliar words should be identified through the use of a medical dictionary. Thereafter, an understanding of the general subject matter should be pursued through medical texts or literature. A review of general textbooks used at the local medical schools, medico-legal treatises, and a systematic search of the *index medicos* or computerized data bases such as *Medline* may yield citations to articles of interest in the subject areas needed for study. By generally understanding the broad subject, the trial attorney becomes armed to focus on the core issues of the case.

Once the background information is established, it is advisable to confer with the testifying physician or with an expert, retained under Rule 26(b)(4)(B) of Federal Rules of Civil Procedure, who will not be called at trial but who will merely advise as to the nuances of the information contained within the medical records. It is always best to provide these experts with the historical medical records inasmuch as, more often than not, those witnesses will not have had access to that information. The experts can also suggest seminal articles or literature that may be of assistance in establishing the issues that are significant in the case.

Having a firm understanding of the strengths and weaknesses of the case, the attorney can analyze what needs to be proven and/or disproven through cross-examination. With an understanding of the medical principles, the trial attorney can gain those admissions that are necessary, determine what areas of weakness are subject to attack, expose the evidence in the medical records, and impeach the witness.

§ 11.3 The Adverse Expert

The next step is to address the soul of the adverse witness. Who the adverse expert is—his background and experience—will affect not only the nature of the opinions offered at trial, but the respect the trier of fact may accord them. Scrutiny of the expert's background is thus the start of the cross-examiner's task. Beginning with the doctor's resume or curriculum vitae, the credentials listed in terms of the educational achievements, board certification, employment, and teaching positions should be verified. Inconsistencies must be checked out. Publications written by the doctor may indicate there is a focus or subspecialty within his field that may or may not be consistent with the area of expertise for which he appears at trial. Most medical schools have access to *Medline* and can undertake a literature search to indicate articles the doctor has authored or co-authored. A *Medline* search will also reflect any letter-to-the-editor or other opinion statements by the doctor that may yield potentially useful impeachment information. Although an initial list of publications may be impressive as to its size, those publications that are in an area of subspecialty different than that which is the focus of the trial might be irrelevant to qualifying the doctor as an expert in the specialty area that is the focus of the trial. The same is true for the presentation of papers or the participation in seminars by the doctor, whether as a speaker or attendee. Prior testimony of the doctor is also revealing in terms of the nature of the cases in which he was formerly deemed an expert.

Prior testimony of the doctor will also yield revealing admissions that can be helpful in the preparation of cross-examination. Past concessions to prior cross-examiners or medical principles advocated on direct examination should yield at least a minimum number of admissions on basic information or medical issues that can form the framework of a cross-examination at trial, creating the appearance that the expert is conceding to the cross-examiner's perspective and committing the witness to general medical propositions that help support the case.

Preparation should include a careful examination of the doctor's notes and file compiled with regard to the individual case. The foundation of the doctor's opinion must be clearly understood by the cross-examiner. Often, doctors will acknowledge that the medical history plays a significant role in the formation of an accurate diagnosis. The absence of any critical medical history can be a devastatingly persuasive argument, apart from the legal significance, of whether enough foundation remains for the doctor to render an admissible opinion.

Particularly useful is an understanding of the nature of the tests and examinations performed by the plaintiff's physicians in the formulation of their diagnosis. Many tests are undertaken not only to confirm the existence of a condition, but to rule out the presence of other conditions. Thus, the presence of "normal" findings on a particular examination are not necessarily an indication that the plaintiff's problem is unproven, but rather may simply be an indication of the validity of the diagnosis reached by the examiner. Similarly, the examiner's failure to conduct or reference important diagnostic tests can reflect oversights that raise issues about the validity of opinions the expert seeks to offer. Certainly, any positive findings on examination by a physician must be stressed, to the extent that they are either contrary to the adverse examiner's findings or would tend to refute the adverse examiner's opinions and conclusions.

§ 11.4 —Impeachment and Bias

A final area of preparation must be that of impeachment and the demonstration of the witness's bias. If the adverse witness will not concede to the admissions previously made or that are justified by the medical principles governing the injury, the witness may then be challenged personally with a demonstration of bias. Prior medical reports issued by the same doctor may reveal repeated use of the same language to summarize findings. To the extent that this repetitive pattern can be demonstrated to a jury, the weight that they may accord the doctor's opinions can be reduced by confronting the doctor with past reports using the same phrases to describe the doctor's findings and conclusions.

Some techniques to prepare for impeachment based on bias or credibility include the examination of any professional reprimands against the doctor by the State Medical Society under which the doctor holds a license, as well as a review of past testimony reflecting the income generated by the doctor as an expert witness and his unique relationship with the particular attorney, law firm, or insurer that is employing the doctor in this case.

A further source of impeachment is the witness's potential reliance on outmoded medical principles. *Lexis* or *Westlaw* can be used to search the various jurisdictions in which the doctor has appeared as a witness and determine whether he is mentioned in any of the reported cases in the jurisdiction. This is particularly useful in the event that the appellate court determined either the doctor was insufficiently qualified to render an opinion, or that the opinion offered was against the weight of the evidence.

Cross-examination does carry risks that a careful attorney must weigh before undertaking the examination in front of a jury. One does not cross-examine a witness simply because it is expected or because emotions have kindled the desire to beat the witness into submission. Success for such goals is highly unlikely. The successful examination must have a specific purpose to be accomplished and an analysis of the likelihood of achieving the goal. Accordingly, the threshold question is "Do I need to cross-examine this witness?"

The answer to the threshold question is usually yes. If the witness wouldn't hurt the case, the probability of that witness being called would be negligible. However, occasionally a witness does not deliver as expected and therefore the question must be asked every time. Once it is determined to proceed with cross-examination, then strategy regarding area of focus must be identified and prepared.

Credibility is everything in the trial of a lawsuit. All efforts must be made not only to enhance the credibility of the attorney and witnesses, but also to highlight the lack of credibility of one's adversaries. Although the most effective persuasive technique is to take on the expert on the merits of the claim, the stage must first be set. The attorney can expect that the seasoned adverse orthopedic expert will not necessarily concede every point by the attorney. The jury expects adversity, and therefore they must understand the bias of that witness at the outset.

Based on the extensive research that has gone into the preparation of the cross-examination, the trial attorney will hopefully have sufficient information to proceed by taking control of the witness early in the cross-examination and establishing the bias:

Q. So there is no question in a jury's mind, I would like to focus on the role of the various doctors in this litigation. You did not see Mr. Smith for medical care, is that correct?

A. No, I did not.

Q. You saw him on one occasion, on May 4, 1992?

A. That is correct.

Q. And that would have been for medical legal purposes?

A. Yes.

Q. And that means for litigation.

A. Yes.

Q. It had nothing to do with treatment?

A. No, it did not.

Q. And this isn't the first time you performed a medical legal exam, is it doctor?

A. No.

Q. You have been involved with the litigation-type examinations since 1971, isn't that true?

A. Yes.

Q. The vast majority of these litigation exams are for the defense interest.

A. That is true.

Q. Probably at least 95%, correct?

A. Probably.

Q. And at this time you are performing 11 medical legal exams a week, isn't that true?

A. Yes.

Q. And you charge $1,000 per exam?

A. Yes.

Q. And that's $11,000 a week for litigation exams, isn't that true?

A. I guess that's what the math would be.

Q. In addition to charging for the exam, you charge for depositions, isn't that true doctor?

A. Yes.

Q. And the deposition cost is $500 per hour, isn't that true?

A. Yes.

Q. And we have now been here two hours, isn't that true?

A. Yes.

Q. So that would tell us that this deposition cost is already up to an additional $1,000?

A. Yes.

Q. You claim you receive referrals from other doctors for review of patients for similar conditions, isn't that true?

A. Yes.

Q. Do you charge those patients $1,000 for a comparable examinations?

A. No, those are different.

Q. And the truth is you charge $250 for that exam, isn't that true?

A. Well, that's true but that is a different type of exam.

Q. Well, those patients are coming to you for care and treatment for their health problems.

A. Yes.

Q. Treatment is certainly important to a sick patient, isn't it?

A. Yes.

Q. You would want to give them your best medical efforts for taking care of them, wouldn't you, Doctor?

A. Yes.

Q. And when your exam is for care and treatment you charge $250.

A. Well, those are different exams. In an independent exam we write reports and review medical records.

Q. Isn't it true you write a letter to your referring physician?

A. Yes.

Q. And you don't charge that physician do you?

A. No.

Q. But you charge a lawyer $1,000 for a medical legal exam?

A. Yes.

§ 11.5 —Admissions

Once the stage has been set establishing the relative roles of the physicians who will be testifying, the attorney may then use a cross-examination to reaffirm the uncontroverted facts of the case by obtaining as many admissions as possible from the adverse witness. This technique is accomplished by stringing admissions together with a series of "yes" responses. The attorney establishes his own credibility through the appearance of fairness to the witness while controlling the testimony case. When the witness attempts to vary from a direct response, a polite reminder of "Is that a yes or a no?" establishes discipline with the examination.

Q. It is true, is it not, Doctor, that Mr. Smith is at an increase risk for post traumatic arthritis in the area of the joint that has been damaged?

A. The development of arthritis is always a questionable thing. One never knows what will happen in the future; however, there is certainly medical literature which can be argued in both ways. Disruption of a joint is something that we always look to as a physician; however, I cannot predict with any certainty what will happen in the future.

Q. Is that a yes or is that a no?

A. That is a yes.

Not only is control established politely, but credibility is established by having the doctor agree with the proposition as set forth. Further, the doctor now appears evasive for failing to respond to a simple yes or no question. After this type of interchange is repeated on several occasions throughout the cross-examination, the witness will no longer appear to be the neutral conduit of facts and opinions but rather an advocate for the side that retained him.

When formulating a series of questions to establish a point through admissions, one may wish to consider the "mountain from a molehill" technique. This technique utilizes a series of short questions to emphasize a point in lieu of a single question that would include a response containing the same information. The use of multiple questions will increase the likelihood of recognition and retention by the jury. The repetition reinforces the theme throughout multiple and repeated communications. However, it is the theme to be repeated, not the words to describe the theme.

The technique can be used how ever the witness has become vulnerable—as the result of some deficiency in testimony such as inadequate qualifications or by overlooking some molehill fact. The effect is compounded if it appears the fact was material based on the witness's own admissions about critical elements of a diagnosis, determination of causation, or prognosis. An inconsistency with prior testimony in the absence of changes in medical literature can also form the basis of this technique. Sources of prior inconsistent statements include not only past depositions or trial testimony, but potentially include medical records and reports or other documents.

For example, on occasion the adverse witness will have questionable qualifications, such as failure to have board certification in the area of expertise. A simple question could eliminate the information necessary for argument:

Q. Is it true doctor that you are not board certified in the specialty of orthopedics?
A. That is correct.

However, the same point can be made for argument and ingrained in the understanding and memory of the jury by building the mountain from a molehill:

Q. There are a number of medical specialties in the area of medical practice, are there not?
A. Yes, there are many specialties.
Q. In fact, one of the specialties is orthopedic surgery, isn't that true, Doctor?
A. Yes.
Q. The American Board of Orthopedics has a certification process for certifying physicians as specialists in orthopedics, isn't that true?
A. That is correct.
Q. And the American Board of Orthopedic Surgery is recognized by the American Medical Association, is it not?
A. That is true.
Q. They have a certification examination?
A. Yes.
Q. And the purpose of that examination is to certify physicians as competent in a specialty area, isn't that true?
A. Yes.
Q. In addition, they have oral examinations, isn't that true?
A. Yes.
Q. And they require minimum requirements of practice in the area of specialty?
A. That is correct.
Q. Orthopedics isn't the only specialty area of medicine, that's true isn't it?
A. That is correct.
Q. Neurology has a specialty certification, does it not?
A. Yes.
Q. Obstetrics and gynecology has a specialty certification, does it not?
A. Yes.
Q. Internal medicine has a specialty certification, does it not?
A. Yes.
Q. Ophthalmology has a specialty certification, does it not?
A. Yes.
Q. Dermatology has a specialty certification, does it not?
A. Yes.
Q. Even family practice has a specialty certification, does it not?
A. That is correct.
Q. And you are not certified as a specialist in the area of orthopedics, are you?
A. I have not taken the test, that is correct.
Q. And in fact, you are not certified as a specialist in any area of medicine, are you?
A. I am not certified as a specialist in any area of medicine.

§ 11.6   Medico-legal Issues

Every case and every type of injury involve different medical legal issues and, therefore, different cross-examinations. However, as a general proposition, most medical cases involve diagnosis of injury, causation, and prognosis. Prognosis addresses the impact on the individual's life, whether the condition/symptoms are permanent, and whether the patient is at risk for future problems. Orthopedic injuries involving objective findings seldom involve disputes of diagnosis. Rather, the focus of litigation shifts to areas of causation, prognosis, functional impairment on life, permanent nature of the condition (as opposed to permanency ratings), and future risks.

The use of admissions is an important step because the doctor may admit that the plaintiff was injured, that the injury is significant, and that the injury is verified at least in part through objective findings during the course of the defense examiner's own examination or in medical records that the adverse examiner has reviewed.

In cases in which the diagnosis is undisputed, credibility is gained by first focusing on areas of agreement. In this fashion, the attorney can reinforce the testimony of his own physician, gain credibility with his case, and appear not to be concerned with the testimony of this particular witness.

Q.   You would agree, would you not, that my client, Mr. Jones, was injured in the collision of December 5, 1989?

A.   Yes, I think he was.

Q.   In your opinion, that injury would be known as a femoral neck fracture?

A.   That is correct.

Q.   A femoral neck fracture means that the head of the leg bone in the hip was broken off. Is that correct?

A.   Yes, that is one way you could describe it.

Q.   A femoral neck fracture can result in a disruption of the blood supply to the hip. Isn't that true, Doctor?

A.   Yes, that is one of the risks.

Q.   If there is a loss of blood supply to the hip, the patient is at risk for avascular necrosis. Isn't that true, Doctor?

A.   That is true.

Q.   Avascular necrosis means death of the tissue. Correct?

A.   Yes.

Q.   In the case of avascular necrosis of the femoral head, the bone in the hip actually dies. Isn't that true?

A.   That is true.

By focusing on the accepted medical principles associated with the patient's injury, the attorney highlighted the injured condition and thereby corroborated his own case.

§ 11.7 Learned Treatise Doctrine

Although the injury may not be in dispute, the sequelae or future risks of the injury may be hotly contested. At a minimum, the trial will then be faced with a "battle of the experts." In order to reinforce the testimony of one's own physician and to impeach the adversary's expert, the **learned treatise doctrine** can and should be utilized. The use of learned treatises in cross-examination is a grossly underutilized tool in establishing either that the doctor's opinion is at variance from popular views, or that such literature establishes a framework for the fair assessment of the facts in the case.

The learned treatise exception to the hearsay rule is a powerful tool for the trial lawyer. In any civil controversy involving a medical or scientific question, adequate preparation requires research into the authoritative literature on the subject. It is helpful to think of the use of learned treatises on direct examination of one's own witnesses so as to lay the foundation for their later use in cross-examination. To establish the authority of a learned treatise under the rule, one may take three approaches:

1. Through the statement of a qualified expert on direct examination
2. Through the admission of the expert being cross-examined
3. Through judicial notice.

The treatise itself must meet three criteria:

1. It must form part of the basis of a favorable expert's testimony or be called to the attention of an adverse witness
2. It must be established as a reliable authority by one of the experts or through judicial notice
3. It must contain written statements in a subject of science or art that is relevant to the matter in controversy.

The treatise cannot be admitted if this foundation has not been laid.

The persuasive quality of confronting a witness with an established contrary treatise loses its impact if the adverse examiner is permitted to dodge the point to be made with a long expository reply. The witness can be controlled in the scope of the reply at the end of the reading aloud of the passage in the issue by simply being asked the question, "Did I read that correctly, Doctor?"

Inasmuch as the Federal Rules provide that the learned treatise be established as reliable by any source, if your own expert witnesses on direct exam have or will establish the treatise as reliable, it is not necessary to have the witness whom you are confronting establish the reliability of the work. It is best not to ask that question inasmuch as the witness could often disagree with the reliability of the given article. Notwithstanding, it is appropriate to establish that the physician relies on journals, textbooks, and periodicals for the ongoing development of his practice to lend credence to the concept of the ongoing medical research:

Q. It is true, isn't it, Doctor, that Mrs. Jones is now at a serious risk for complications because of the Type III femoral neck fracture that she suffered in this collision?

A. Well, I don't know if anyone can really say that.

Q. Are you familiar with the *Journal of Trauma*, Doctor?

A. Yes, I am.

Q. In fact, I see that the *Journal of Trauma* is on your shelf at this time. Isn't that true?

A. Yes, it is.

Q. You subscribe to that *Journal of Trauma* as an orthopedic surgeon. Correct?

A. Yes.

Q. You read the *Journal of Trauma* to provide you with ongoing developments of information and risks relative to orthopedic injuries to your patients.

A. Yes.

Q. From time to time you have relied on information contained in the *Journal of Trauma* with respect to the care and treatment of your patients.

A. Yes.

Q. It is a reliable source of information with respect to orthopedic injuries, is it not?

A. Yes, it is.

Q. Calling your attention to Volume 26, Number 4, the *Journal of Trauma*, an article entitled "Displaced Hip Fractures in Children and Adolescents." I would like you to read along with me, "Fractures of the proximal femur in children have a high incidence of complications because of the unique osseous and vascular anatomy of the femoral head and neck region in a growing child. . . . (Type III) fractures are a result of high velocity trauma and the artery can either be torn or kinked over fracture fragments." Did I read that correctly?

A. Yes.

Q. Calling your attention to Volume 26, Number 10, of the *Journal of Trauma*, an article entitled "Complications of Femoral Neck Fractures in Young Adults." I would like you to read along with me. And on the first page of that article, I would like you to read along with me.

When the condition is undisputed but the diagnostic testing from the onset does not necessarily establish the injury, the adverse testimony will often argue that there is no causal relationship between the trauma and the condition. Alternatively, if there is a history of prior traumas, conditions, or treatments, the focus can again shift to the issue of causation. An intimate understanding of the medical records, as set forth in the medical summary, enables the examiner to utilize the medical records to highlight the obvious temporal relationship between the trauma and the onset of symptoms:

Q. Doctors can look at the same patient and arrive at different opinions, isn't that true?

A. It is possible that might happen.

Q. In fact it does happen. Isn't that true?

A. Certainly.

Q. Different doctors can look at the same patient and arrive at different conclusions as to the cause of the condition. Isn't that true?

A. They may. Yes.

Q. In the instant case, Doctor, I would like to try and determine on what we agree and what we disagree. Is that fair?

A. That is certainly fair, Counsel.

Q. Do you agree that my client, Mr. Jones, has a herniation of the disc in his neck between the fifth and sixth vertebrae?

A. Yes, I would agree that he does have a herniation of the disc at that level.

Q. You agree that the treatment he has received for that herniation has been fair and reasonable and appropriate up to this time. Correct?

A. Yes.

Q. That treatment would include the operative procedure in which Dr. Smith operatively removed the disc from his neck and fused the bones of his neck together.

A. Yes, that would be an appropriate treatment.

Q. As I understand it, where we disagree is that you believe that the condition for which he received the surgery was caused by an auto accident that occurred in 1982 and not the collision of September 10, 1991. Correct?

A. Yes, that is my opinion.

Q. You have received copies of all of Mr. Jones's medical records, have you not?

A. Well, I listed the records I have received from the defense lawyer.

Q. Well, you would certainly expect the defense team to provide you with all the records available to render an informed opinion, would you not?

A. Well, yes I would expect that.

Q. You have reviewed those medical records, haven't you.

A. Yes.

Q. You have charged for review of those medical records, have you not?

A. Yes.

Q. You understood it was necessary for you to understand those records for the purposes of rendering your opinions, is that correct?

A. Yes.

Q. From those medical records you learned that Mr. Jones was involved in a motor vehicle collision in January of 1982, isn't that true?

A. Yes.

Q. Those records indicated to you that he suffered a cervical sprain syndrome in 1982?

A. Yes.

Q. That is often referred to as a whiplash injury, isn't that true?

A. Yes.

Q. He treated for the symptoms for that whiplash injury for approximately six weeks, isn't that true.

A. Yes.

Q. At the conclusion of that treatment period of six weeks, his doctor indicated that he had no neurological findings, isn't that true?

A. That is correct.

Q. At that time, his doctor indicated his condition had resolved, isn't that true?

A. Yes.

Q. Isn't that exactly what Mr. Jones told you when you examined him?

A. Well, I can't remember exactly what he said, but he said the condition had resolved.

Q. Is that a yes or a no, Doctor?

A. That is a yes.

Q. For the balance of the year 1982 there is no indication that there was any additional medical treatment, is there?

A. Not that I am aware of.

Q. In the year 1983 there was no medical treatment for his condition, was there, Doctor?

A. No.

Q. In the year 1984 there was no indication of medical treatment for his medical condition, was there, Doctor?

A. No.

Q. In the year 1985 there was no indication of medical treatment for his medical condition, was there, Doctor?

A. No.

Q. In the year 1986 there was no indication of medical treatment for his medical condition, was there, Doctor?

A. No.

Q. In the year 1987 there was no indication of medical treatment for his medical condition, was there, Doctor?

A. No.

Q. In the year 1988 there was no indication of medical treatment for his medical condition, was there, Doctor?

A. No.

Q. In fact, Doctor, the very first time there was any evidence of any problems in that neck following the 1982 whiplash was on the day of the collision on December 5, 1989?

A. Well, that is all I am aware of.

Q. In fact, Doctor, the ambulance records prepared by the people who came to the scene of the collision indicated that there were immediate complaints of neck pain. Isn't that true?

A. Well, I haven't had the opportunity to see the ambulance record.

Q. Is it your testimony that the defense lawyer did not provide you the benefit of seeing the ambulance records relating to the collision we are talking about?

A. Not that I am aware of.

Q. Let me show you what has been previously marked for identification and introduced into evidence as the ambulance records relating to Mr. Jones. Have you had an opportunity to look at that, Doctor?

A. Yes.

Q. Does that record reveal complaints of neck pain immediately at the scene of the accident?

A. Yes.

Q. In fact that record reveals that Mr. Jones was taken from the scene on a back board.

A. Yes.

Q. That is a medical device used when there are concerns of neck injury. Isn't that true?

A. That is true.

Q. In the emergency room, isn't it true that Mr. Jones was complaining of left-sided neck pain emanating into his shoulder.

A. That is true.

Q. That would be consistent, would it not, Doctor, with a lesion of the disc, isn't that true?

A. It could be.

Q. Isn't it true for the next four weeks Mr. Jones treated with his family doctor for neck pain?

A. To the best of my understanding, that is true.

Q. During that time period, he underwent physical therapy for his neck, isn't that true?

A. Yes.

Q. In fact, he had seen a physical therapist 15 times during that first month period for neck pain?

A. True.

Q. He continued to treat for neck pain during the next four months?

A. That is true.

Q. When the neck pain did not resolve, Mr. Jones's family physician referred him to a specialist, correct?

A. Yes.

Q. That specialist ordered an MRI. Is that correct?

A. Yes, that is correct.

Q. That MRI revealed a herniated disc, did it not?

A. Yes.

Q. The first time the symptoms appeared for that herniated disc were on the day of the collision. Isn't that true?

A. Well, that is the first that I have ever been aware of.

§ 11.8 Abstract Medical Principles

In cases when the orthopedic injury is not objective or the impact on the client's life is not as clear, the cross-examination becomes more difficult inasmuch as the focus is shifted to a greater extent to abstract medical principles. The classic case would involve the hyperextension-hyperflexion injury often known as the myofascial strain, soft tissue injury, or whiplash. The patient has diffuse complaints of pain in the neck or low back that is not documented by any scientific diagnostic testing such as a myelogram, X ray, CAT scan, or MRI. Notwithstanding, the patient presents a constellation of symptoms that would be consistent with damage to the musculoskeletal system.

Plaintiffs present the case based on subjective symptoms and subjective findings from medical examinations. The defense almost universally argues that there is no objective proof of the injury, that the diagnosis is based on subjective complaints. As a result, they contend the plaintiffs have not sustained their burden of proof in the course of the litigation. The analysis of the case, therefore, must again focus on admissions that can be secured, deficiencies in the adversary's analysis based on the medical records, and impeachment focusing on why that witness's findings differ from every other physician on the case.

An inherent flaw in the argument that there is no injury because there is no objective finding is that it is contrary to basic principles involved in the practice of medicine. Medicine is not an exact science in which the physicians work from a constellation of symptoms to formulate a differential diagnosis and thereafter attempt to diagnostically establish a more precise diagnosis. Often there is no diagnostic testing to verify a condition, for example a headache. Accordingly, with this understanding, the plaintiff's attorney may cross-examine the doctor on the importance of subjective complaints:

Q. The difference between subjective complaints and objective findings boils down to what you can actually feel or see?

A. Yes.

Q. Your opinion indicating that my client was not injured is based on the fact that you personally have not found any objective findings that would lead you to believe that injury exists, correct?

A. Correct.

Q. You performed an orthopedic examination on my client, Mrs. Smith?

A. Yes.

Q. That examination contained a series of tests. Is that correct?

A. Yes.

Q. The tests you performed were legitimate and important medical tests?

A. Yes.

Q. Tests that you would perform on any patient who would come to you for treatment. Is that correct?

A. Yes.

Q. If the test wasn't an appropriate or legitimate test, you wouldn't perform it, would you, doctor?

A. No.

Q. You tested my client's range of motion for flexion, did you not?

A. Yes.

Q. And that calls for subjective response?

A. Yes.

Q. You tested the range of motion for extension, did you not?

A. Yes.

Q. And that calls for a subjective response, does it not?
A. Yes.
Q. You tested the rotation to the left, did you not?
A. Yes.
Q. And that calls for a subjective response?
A. Yes.
Q. You tested the range of motion to the right?
A. Yes.
Q. And that calls for a subjective response?
A. Yes.
Q. You performed the leg-raising test?
A. Yes.
Q. And that calls for indications of pain?
A. Yes.
Q. And that would be a subjective response?
A. Yes.
Q. You palpated for tenderness, did you not?
A. Yes.
Q. That is calling for subjective responses of pain, is that correct?
A. Yes.
Q. Notwithstanding the fact that all of these tests call for subjective responses, you nevertheless performed them, did you not?
A. Yes.
Q. In fact, the only test you performed that would call for an objective response were palpations for spasm and the reflexes?
A. Yes.
Q. And the reflexes only indicate damage to nerves, correct?
A. Yes.
Q. Even though a patient may have suffered an injury to the connective tissue of his spine, the nerve may nevertheless work, correct?
A. Correct.
Q. So that test wouldn't necessarily eliminate the existence of an injury, would it, Doctor?
A. Well, I guess it wouldn't.
Q. And you did palpate for spasm, did you not?
A. Yes.
Q. And a spasm is an objective finding?
A. Yes.
Q. You believe that is a test that cannot be faked by the patient, is that correct?
A. Yes.
Q. And you did not find spasm on the day you examined my client, correct?
A. Yes.
Q. But it is true, is it not, Doctor, that spasms are subject to periods of exacerbation and remission?
A. Yes.
Q. And that means that they can come and go, isn't that true?
A. Yes.

Q. And although you didn't find spasms on my client's spine on the day you were hired by the defense to exam her, the evidence is that she has had spasm since the time of this collision.

A. Well, I don't know if that's true or not, I wasn't there.

Once the attorney has established the importance of the subjective findings as well as the objective tests, the focus must then shift to show the adverse examiner's findings are at variance with all the other treating physicians. The inference the jury can make is that either everyone else in the world is a liar or the adverse examiner is being less than fair with them.

Q. The first time Mrs. Smith identified any medical record of problems in her neck was in the emergency room on the day of the collision.

A. I don't know if that is true or not.

Q. Showing you the emergency room record of September 19, 1991, there is an indication of symptoms in the neck, is there not?

A. Yes, there is.

Q. And from your vast review of all of the medical records for which you charge $750 over the cost of a regular exam, you did not find any indication of any other neck complaints did you?

A. No, I did not.

Q. Dr. Jones, Minneapolis Orthopedic Clinic, found spasm in the neck on October 1, 1992, isn't that true?

A. I'm not sure, I don't have the record in front of me.

Q. Well, I'm showing you the record, Doctor, and please review it. Isn't it true that the record indicates that Dr. Jones from Minneapolis Orthopedic Clinic identified muscle spasms in the neck?

A. I guess that's true.

Q. And on October 29, 1992, Dr. Jones identified muscle spasms in the neck, isn't that true?

A. Yes.

Q. And on November 15, 1992, Dr. Jones identified muscle spasms?

A. If you say so.

Q. Well, that's what the record says, isn't it, Doctor?

A. Well, I'll have to look. I guess that's true, yes.

Q. And on December 1, 1992, Dr. Jones found muscle spasm in the neck, isn't that true?

A. Yes.

Q. And Dr. Jones isn't the only person who found muscle spasms in the neck, that's true isn't it?

A. Well, I don't know if that's true or not.

Q. Well, let's look at the physical therapy records, Doctor. Lila Jones, the physical therapist on October 10, 1992, found spasms in the neck. Isn't that true?

A. Yes, I guess that is true.

Q. On October 17, 1992, Lila Jones found muscle spasms in the neck. Isn't that true?

A. Yes.

Q. On October 24, 1992, Lila Jones found muscle spasms in the neck. Isn't that true?

A. Yes.

Q. And on October 30, 1992, Lila Jones found muscle spasms. Isn't that true?

A. Yes.

Q. And on November 6, 1992, Lila Jones found muscle spasms. Isn't that true.

A. Yes.

Q. And on December 24th, on Christmas Eve, Mrs. Smith had to go to the emergency room for pain injections. Isn't that true?

A. Well, that's what the record says.

Q. And at that time they found muscle spasm. Isn't that true.

A. Yes.

§ 11.9 —Subjective Nature of Pain

Once the legitimacy of subjective complaints in the medical practice is established, it becomes possible to focus on the subjective nature of pain. Because pain is subjective and is impacted by bio-psycho-social issues, it is not readily quantifiable. As such, physicians, who are by nature scientific, shy away from any assessment of pain. Notwithstanding, the noxious stimulus of pain is precisely why people receive medical care.

The American Medical Association has developed a guide for permanent impairment evaluations that is used repeatedly by physicians for rating injuries for medical legal purposes. However, that impairment system is seldom, if ever, used in the medical profession outside of the medical legal context. Because of the need for objectivity in the medical community, pain had been expressly omitted from the rating system. Although the rating system may have some merit in the workers' compensation setting, it really has no legitimate function in the assessment of the impact on a person's life as a result of pain.

Appendix B in the AMA Guidelines specifically addresses the importance of pain in society, as well as to individuals. Often, health care providers are not knowledgeable on any section of the AMA Guidelines other than for their specific area of practice. However, the able trial attorney utilizing the learned treatise doctrine can effectively cross-examine any medical examiner as a result of Appendix B of the AMA Guidelines:

Q. Pain is a symptom of injury. Isn't that true?

A. Pain may or may not be a symptom of injuries. Certainly many people will complain of pain without necessarily having an injury.

Q. People with injuries complain of pain, that's true isn't it.

A. That is true.

Q. And if a person is suffering from symptoms of pain, you will not be able to predict with any certainty when that pain will resolve.

A. Not with any certainty.

Q. Pain by definition is subjective, isn't that true, Doctor?

A.   Yes, that's true.

Q.   That means you cannot feel, measure, or touch a patient's pain, correct?

A.   That is correct.

Q.   Even though you can't feel a person's pain, he nevertheless can have that pain, that's fair isn't it?

A.   Yes, it is.

Q.   You have indicated that according to the AMA Guidelines for evaluation of permanent impairment, my client does not have any permanent disability. Isn't that true, Doctor?

A.   That is true.

Q.   But in truth, Doctor, the AMA Guidelines evaluate impairment, not disability.

A.   I think that's a semantic distinction.

Q.   The AMA Guidelines for impairment don't even take pain into consideration, do they, Doctor?

A.   That is correct.

Q.   If a person is in pain but has full range of motion, under the impairment guidelines, they have no permanent impairment. Correct?

A.   Yes.

Q.   But they nevertheless continue to have pain.

A.   They may have pain.

Q.   And that pain may be a result of an injury to that person's body. Isn't that true?

A.   Yes.

Q.   And if the injury is permanent, the pain can be permanent.

A.   Yes.

Q.   And although the AMA does not utilize pain for their impairment ratings, they nevertheless address the seriousness of pain in the book.

A.   Well, I'm not sure that's true.

Q.   Calling your attention to the Guides to Evaluation of Permanent Impairment, Third Edition, Appendix B, page 239, I would request you read along with me, "The research briefing panel on pain and pain management of the National Academy of Science in 1985 reported that the discomfort and suffering associated with chronic pain disturb the quality of life and can produce complex and profound alterations in behavior. As a consequence, pain is a major health problem." Did I read that correctly, Doctor?

A.   Yes, you did.

Q.   Calling your attention to page 240, I'd again ask you to read along with me, "Pain, which is a purely subjective phenomenon, assessment of pain has been further complicated by its social and psychological ramifications. Pain cannot be observed; pain itself cannot be measured. The International Association for the Study of Pain (IASP) defines pain as an unpleasant sensory and emotional experience associated with actual or potential tissue damage and described it in terms of such damage." Did I read that correctly?

A.   Yes, you did.

Q.   Calling your attention to page 241 of the same book, Doctor, in the section entitled "Chronic Pain," the AMA again stated "It must be considered a pathological disorder in its own right. It is chronic, long lived, and progressive. Pain perception is markedly enhanced. Pain behavior becomes maladaptive and counter productive." Did I read that correctly, Doctor?

A. Yes.

Q. Going on, "Chronic pain improperly diagnosed and inadequately treated results in deteriorated coping mechanisms and pacing skills. Under such circumstances, persistent chronic pain results in progressive limitations and functional capacity which contribute to the evolution of chronic pain syndrome." Did I read that correctly?

A. Yes.

Q. The AMA clearly indicates that pain is a serious and debilitating disorder, isn't that true, Doctor?

A. Apparently, that is what they are saying.

Q. And my client, Marilyn Jones, is reporting that she is in pain.

A. That is correct.

Q. In fact, a person can have a legitimate medical basis for subjective complaints of pain without any objective findings to support that subjective complaint. Isn't that true?

A. Yes.

Q. And basically what that means is that you can have a legitimate basis for pain with a normal medical examination. Is that correct?

A. That is correct.

Q. And that is a well-known proposition in medicine. Isn't that true, Doctor?

A. Yes.

Q. As a result, you have provided medical treatment to patients even when there were no objective signs of the injury, isn't that true?

A. Yes.

Q. And that, of course, would be appropriate medical conduct, wouldn't it?

A. Yes.

Q. In fact, you have treated patients with normal orthopedic exams for myofascial pain, haven't you?

A. Yes.

Q. You have recommended physical therapy for them?

A. Yes.

Q. You have treated them with pain medication?

A. Yes.

Q. And you have even limited their employment in the past, haven't you?

A. Yes.

§ 11.10 Flexibility of Approach

Adequate preparation will help the trial attorney feel comfortable and confident in confronting an adverse doctor as an expert witness. A cross-examiner's most useful took is flexibility. The questioner must adapt the cross-examination to the attitude projected by the adverse witness. To the extent that valuable admissions are gained, a firm but gentle cross-examination can occur. To the extent that the expert reflects an attitude of the intractable hired gun, it may be more necessary to engage in the "rip and tear" of a confrontation, projecting righteous indignation and the use of questions that demonstrate bias and financial interest on the part of the witness. The use of a written outline of questions, while helpful, should be kept to a minimum. Flexibility must be preserved, or the battle can be lost.

Complete and thorough preparation is the best key to yield the most effective result for a cross-examiner. The most effective cross-examination produces admissions that reinforce aspects of the attorney's case. The next most effective cross-examination challenges the expert on the merits of his medical opinions. The least effective cross-examination succeeds only in challenging the expert personally, by impeachment or proof of bias. Often, it is tempting to approach an adverse witness in just the opposite order, but that yields less value to the overall task of informing and persuading a trier of facts.

ESTIMATES OF AVERAGE RANGES OF JOINT MOTION*

ESTIMATES OF

AVERAGE RANGES OF JOINT MOTION

The average ranges of joint motion cannot be accurately determined, due to the wide variation in the degrees of motion amongst individuals of varying physical build and age groups. The following estimates are to serve merely as a guide, and not as a standard. The patient's opposite extremity is perhaps the best "normal" standard. In those instances when the opposite extremity has been injured, or is not present, these figures may prove helpful. Four sources are used for references. An average of these estimates is given. The sources are as follows:

Column (1)

The Committee on Medical Rating of Physical Impairment, Journal American Medical Association.*

Column (2)

The Committee of the California Medical Association and Industrial Accident Commission of the State of California.**

Column (3)

A System of Joint Measurements, William A. Clarke, Mayo Clinic.***

Column (4)

The Committee on Joint Motion, American Academy of Orthopaedic Surgeons.

*Journal American Medical Association—"A Guide to the Evaluation of Permanent Impairment of the Extremities & Back." Special Edition, pg. 1-112, Feb. 15, 1958.

**Evaluation of Industrial Disability (Comm. of California Medical Asso. & The Industrial Acc. Comm. of the State of California) Oxford Univ. Press. 1960.

***Clark, William A., "A System of Joint Measurements." The J. Orthopaedic Surgery, Vol. 2: No. 12: Dec. 1920.

AVERAGE RANGES OF JOINT MOTION

JOINT	SOURCES				
	(1)	(2)	(3)	(4)	AVERAGES
ELBOW =					
FLEXION	150	135	150	150	146
HYPEREXTENSION	0	0	0	0	0
FOREARM =					
PRONATION	80	75	50	80	71
SUPINATION	80	85	90	80	84
WRIST =					
EXTENSION	60	65	90	70	71
FLEXION	70	70		80	73
ULNAR DEV.	30	40	30	30	33
RADIAL DEV.	20	20	15	20	19
THUMB =					
ABDUCTION		55	50	70	58
FLEXION					
I-P Jt.	80	75	90	80	81
M − P	60	50	50	50	53
M − C				15	15
EXTENSION					
Distal Jt.		20	10	20	17
M − P		5	10	0	8
M − C				20	20
FINGERS =					
FLEXION					
Distal Jt.	70	70	90	90	80
Middle Jt.	100	100		100	100
Proximal Jt.	90	90		90	90
FINGERS =					
EXTENSION					
Distal Jt.				0	0
Middle Jt.				0	0
Proximal Jt.			45	45	45
SHOULDER =					
FORWARD					
FLEXION	150	170	130	180	158
HORIZONTAL					
FLEXION				135	135
BACKWARD					
EXTENSION	40	30	80	60	53
ABDUCTION	150	170	180	180	170
ADDUCTION	30		45	75	50

AVERAGE RANGES OF JOINT MOTION

JOINT	(1)	(2)	(3)	(4)	AVERAGES
ROTATION					
Arm at Side					
Int. Rot.	40	60	90	80	68
Ext. Rot.	90	80	40	60	68
Arm in Abduction (90°)					
Int. Rot.				70	70
Ext. Rot.				90	90
HIP =					
FLEXION	100	110	120	120	113
EXTENSION	30	30	20	30	28
ABDUCTION	40	50	55	45	48
ADDUCTION	20	30	45	30	31
ROTATION					
In Flexion =					
Int. Rot.				45	45
Ext. Rot.				45	45
In Extension =					
Int. Rot.	40	35	20	45	35
Ext. Rot.	50	50	45	45	48
ABDUCTION					
In 90° of flexion			45 to 60		
			(depending on age)		
KNEE =					
FLEXION	120	135	145	135	134
HYPEREXTENSION			10	10	10
ANKLE =					
FLEXION	40	50	50	50	48
(plantar flexion)					
EXTENSION	20	15	15	20	18
(dorsiflexion)					
HIND FOOT (subtalar) =					
INVERSION				5	5
EVERSION				5	5
FORE FOOT =					
INVERSION	30	35		35	33
EVERSION	20	20		15	18

Heading row: SOURCES spans (1)(2)(3); (4) AVERAGES.

AVERAGE RANGES OF JOINT MOTION

JOINT	SOURCES (1)	(2)	(3)	(4) AVERAGES	
TOES =					
GREAT TOE					
I-P Jt.					
Flexion	30			90	60
Extension	0			0	0
Proximal Jt.					
Flexion	30	35		45	37
Extenstion	50	70		70	63
2nd TO 5th TOES =					
FLEXION					
Distal Jt.	50			60	55
Middle Jt.	40			35	38
Proximal Jt.	30			40	35
Extension	40			40	40
SPINE =					
CERVICAL					
FLEXION	30			45	38
EXTENSION	30			45	38
LAT. BENDING	40			45	43
ROTATION	30			60	45
THORACIC AND LUMBAR					
FLEXION	90			80	85
				4"	4"
EXTENSION	30			20-30	30
LAT. BENDING	20			35	28
ROTATION	30			45	38

GLOSSARY

abduction: The withdrawal of a part from the axis of the body. In reference to the vertebral column, it is synonymous with lateral flexion.

accommodation curve: *See* primary curve.

adduction: The act of drawing toward the axis of the body.

alar ligaments: The paired ligaments extending from the upper lateral aspect of the dens to the margins of the foramen magnum.

ankylosis: Abnormal immobility and consolidation of a joint.

anterior longitudinal ligament: One of the primary stabilizing ligaments of the vertebral column, extending down over the anterior surface of the vertebral bodies from the base of the skull to the sacrum.

annulus fibrosis: The outer fibrous component of the intervertebral disc. *See also* nucleus pulposus.

apical ligament: The small ligament extending from the apex of the dens to the anterior margin of the foramen magnum.

aplasia: Incomplete or defective development of tissue.

arachnoid: The middle of the three meningeal layers covering the brain and spinal cord.

arthrodesis: The surgical fixation of a joint by fusion of the joint surfaces.

arthroplasty: Plastic surgery of a joint or of joints; formation of movable joints.

arthrotomy: Surgical incision of a joint.

articular capsule: The connective tissue investment of a synovial joint. It extends between the participating bones and constitutes the peripheral limit of the space between the opposing joint elements.

articular facet: The smooth, cartilage-covered surface of a synovial joint element. The articular facets of the two or more bones contributing to a joint oppose one another.

articular process: A bony prominence participating in the formation of a joint. In the case of the vertebrae, the processes bear the articular facets.

articulation: A joint; the place of union or junction between two or more bones.

ataxia: Failure of muscular coordination; irregularity of muscular action.

athetosis: A derangement marked by a constant recurring series of slow vermicular movements of the hands and feet, occurring chiefly in children.

atlanto-axial joint: The articulation between the first and second cervical vertebrae. It is characterized by the presence of three separate synovial articulations, two lateral and one median.

atlanto-occipital joint: The articulation between the first cervical vertebra and the skull.

atlanto-occipital membrane: The connective tissue membrane extending from the arch of the atlas to the base of the skull. It has both an anterior and a posterior component.

atlas: The first cervical vertebra.

atrophy: A defect or failure of nutrition manifested as a wasting away or diminution in the size of cell, tissue, organ, or part.

axis: The second cervical vertebra, characterized by the dens, or odontoid, process.

calcaneus: (1) The heel bone, or os calcis; the irregular quadrangular bone at the back of the tarsus. (2) Clubfoot deformities in which the heel only touches the ground.

cauda equina: The leash of spinal nerves extending through the lumbar cistern below the termination of the spinal cord.

cavus: Exaggeration of the plantar arch of the foot, due to contraction of the plantar fascia or bony deformity of the arch.

cerebrospinal fluid: The specialized fluid bathing the central nervous system. It is located within the subarachnoid space.

cervical: Denoting a neck. With reference to the vertebral column, it is the region of the upper seven vertebrae.

chondromalacia: Softness of the articular cartilage, usually involving the patella.

choreiform: Resembling chorea, which is a convulsive nervous disease, with involuntary and irregular jerking movements; it is attended with irritability and depression, and with mental impairment.

circumduction: The active or passive circular movement of a limb.

clonus: Spasm in which rigidity and relaxation alternate in rapid succession. Ankle clonus and foot clonus, a series of convulsive movements of the ankle, induced by suddenly pushing up the foot while the leg is extended. Patellar clonus, produced by suddenly and forcibly pushing patella distalward with leg extended.

closed fracture: Loss of continuity of a bone; not in contact with outside environment. *See also* open fracture.

coccygeal: Referring to the coccyx.

coccyx: The caudal portion of the vertebral column. It consists of three to five rudimentary vertebrae which frequently fuse to form a single bony unit.

compensatory curve: In general terms, any curve of the vertebral column which develops in response to an unstable postural configuration. In more specific usage, it refers to the curves within the cervical and lumbar regions of the column.

compression fracture: Fracture of a vertebral body due to hyperflexion of the column.

congenital: Existing at or before birth.

conus medullaris: The tapered lower end of the spinal cord.

costal pit: The small articular facet(s) on the bodies of the thoracic vertebrae. The joint formed at this point is with the head of the rib.

coxa: The hip or hip joint.

crepitus: Bony crepitus, the crackling sound produced by the rubbing together of fragments of fractured bone. False crepitus, and joint crepitus, the grating sensation caused by the rubbing together of the dry synovial surfaces of joints. Silken crepitus, a sensation as of two pieces of silk rubbed between the fingers, felt on moving a joint affected with hydrarthrosis.

cruciform ligament: The cross-shaped ligament lying behind the dens of the axis. It contributes to the formation of the median atlanto-axial joint. *See also* transverse ligament of the atlas.

cubitus: The forearm.
1. *cubitus varus,* deformity of the forearm in which it deviates inwardly when extended ("gun-stock" deformity); diminution of carrying angle.
2. *cubitus valgus,* deformation in which the forearm when extended makes an increased angle with the arm; i.e., increased carrying angle.

cyanosis: Bluish coloring of the skin due to lack of oxygen in the blood.

dens: The bony prominence extending superiorly from the body of the axis. It is the axial component of the median atlanto-axial joint.

diaphysis: The shaft of a long bone.

diplegia: Paralysis affecting like parts on both sides of the body; bilateral paralysis.

dislocation: The displacement of any part, more especially of a bone.

dorsiflexion: Flexion or bending of the foot toward the leg.

dura mater: The outer and heaviest of the three meningeal layers.

dysplasia: Abnormality of development. Fibrous dysplasia, a disease of bone marked by thinning of the cortex and the replacement of the marrow by fibrous tissue containing bony spicules. The condition produces pain, disability, and gradually increasing deformity. Only one bone may be involved with the process later affecting several or many bones.

dystrophy: Defective or faulty nutrition.
1. *progressive muscular dystrophy,* progressive atrophy of the muscles with no discoverable lesion of the spinal cord.

2. *pseudohypertrophic muscular dystrophy,* a dystrophy of the muscles of the shoulder girdle and sometimes the pelvic girdle, commencing with hypertrophy and followed later by atrophy; it begins in childhood.

ecchymosis: A small spot or colored area appearing in large, irregularly formed hemorrhage-marked areas of skin. Changes from blue-black to greenish brown or yellow.

ectrodactylism: Congenital absence of a digit or of digits.

effusion: Intrusion of fluid into a body part.

epidural space: The space between the dura mater and the walls of the vertebral canal. It is filled with vascular elements and loose connective tissue. The site is used for administration of anesthetic agents.

epiphyseolysis: Separation of an epiphysis from its bone; especially "slipping" of the upper femoral epiphysis.

epiphysis: A piece of bone separated from a long bone in early life by cartilage, but later becoming part of the larger bone. It is in this cartilaginous center that growth in length of the bone occurs.

equinus: That in which the patient walks on the toes or the anterior part of one or both of his feet. It is due to elevation of the heel by contraction of the Achilles tendon.

eversion: A turning outward or inside out.

exostosis: Bony outgrowth arising from the surface of a bone, often involving conversion of muscular attachments into bone.

extension: A movement which brings the members of the limb into or toward a straight condition.

fasciotomy: Surgical incision and division of a fibrous membrane covering, supporting, and separating muscles or inner organs.

fibroblasts: Any cell or corpuscle forming supporting or connective tissue.

filum terminale: The thread-like extension of the pia mater from the end of the spinal cord to the sacrum.

flaccid: Weak, lax, and soft.

flexion: The act of bending or condition of being bent.

foramen: An opening or passageway (pl. *foramina*).

foramen magnum: The large opening at the base of the skull (within the occipital bone) through which the spinal cord passes.

fovea: Pit or shallow cuplike depression.

fracture: The breaking of a part, especially of a bone; loss of continuity of bone.

fusion: The operative formation of an ankylosis.

genu: The knee.
   1. *genu varus*, bow-leg deformity.
   2. *genu valgus*, knock-knee deformity.

gibbus: A hump or kyphos.

hallux: The great toe.
   1. *hallux varus*, great toe points toward midline of body.
   2. *hallux valgus*, great toe points away from the midline of the body.

heliotherapy: The treatment of disease by exposing the body to the sun's rays.

hemiplegia: Paralysis of one side of the body.

hemivertebra: An abnormal vertebra in which there is absence of a portion of the body, usually one lateral half.

heterotopic: Misplaced; pertaining to the development of normal tissue in an abnormal location.

hiatus: A gap or opening.

hyperemia: Excess of blood (circulation) in any part of the body.

hyperesthesia: Exaggerated sensation. A relatively common manifestation of spinal nerve involvement with IV disc herniations.

hyperextension: Extreme or excessive extension; extension beyond the axis of the body.

hypertrophy: The morbid enlargement or overgrowth of an organ or part due to an increase in size of its constituent cells.

implant: To insert or graft.

interspinous ligaments: Slight ligaments extending between adjacent vertebral spinous processes. They contribute to column stability.

intertransverse foramen: The aperture located within the transverse processes of every cervical vertebra. It transmits the vertebral artery as the latter ascends to gain the intracranial portion of the central nervous system.

intertransverse ligaments: Slight ligaments extending between adjacent transverse processes. They contribute in small part to column stability.

intervertebral disc: The connective tissue plate situated between two adjacent vertebrae. It constitutes the primary means of union between the movable vertebrae.

intervertebral foramen: Formed by the pedicles, articular processes, vertebral bodies, and discs of two adjacent vertebrae. It is the site of exit of the spinal nerves from the column.

inversion: A turning inward, inside out, upside down, or other reversal of the normal relation of a part.

involucrum: A covering or sheath, such as contains the sequestrum of a necrosed bone; localized overgrowth or hypertrophy of bone as response to infection.

ischemia: Local and temporary deficiency of blood, chiefly due to the contraction of a blood vessel.

kyphosis: Humpback; abnormal curvature and dorsal prominence of the vertebral column; curving posteriorward or backward. An exaggerated thoracic curvature.

laminae: The bony plates of the vertebral arch which extend from the posterior ends of the pedicles to the spinous process. They form the posterolateral wall of the vertebral canal.

ligamentum nuchae: The broad cervical enlargement of the supraspinous ligament of the column.

lordosis: Curvature of the spinal column with a forward convexity; curving anteriorward. An exaggerated lumbar curvature.

lumbar: Pertaining to the loins. That region making up the caudal end of the movable column.

lumbar cistern: The large subarachnoid space below the level of the spinal cord containing cerebrospinal fluid; a common site for spinal tap. *See* subarachnoid space.

lumbosacral joint: The articulation between the fifth lumbar vertebra and the sacrum.

lumbosacral angle: The angle formed at the junction of the fifth lumbar vertebra and the sacrum; frequently designated the sacrovertebral angle.

malunion: Union of the fragments of a fractured bone in faulty position.

manus: The hand.

meninges: The protective covering of the brain and spinal cord. *See also* dura mater, arachnoid, pia mater.

meningocele: Herniation of the meninges through an imperfection of one or more vertebral arches.

metaphysis: The line of junction of the epiphysis with the diaphysis of a long bone.

metaplasia: The change in the type of adult cells in a tissue to a form which is not normal for that tissue.

monoplegia: Paralysis of but a single part.

myelomeningocele (meningomyelocele):   Herniation of the meninges and nervous tissue through vertebral arch imperfections.

nonunion: Failure of the ends of a fractured bone to unite; false union, pseudoarthrosis.

nucleus pulposus: The gelatinous central mass of an intervertebral disc.

odontoid process: *See* dens.

open fracture: Loss of continuity of bone with exposure to the outside environment. (Old terminology: "Compound" fracture.)

ostectomy: The excision of a bone or a portion of a bone.

osteoclasis: The surgical or manual fracture or refracture of bones.

osteoma: A tumor composed of bone tissue and usually developing on a bone.

osteophyte: An abnormal bony spur or outgrowth.

osteotome: A knife for cutting bone; a chisel with both sides of cutting edge beveled.

osteotomy: The surgical cutting of a bone.

paraplegia: Paralysis of the legs and lower part of a body, both motion and sensation being affected.

paresthesia: Altered, abnormal sensation; sometimes present as a sign of spinal nerve compression.

pathognomonic: Characteristic symptoms indicative of a disease.

pedicle: The stout, bony rod projecting posteriorly from the posterolateral aspect of the vertebral body. It forms the lateral boundary of the vertebral canal.

periarticular: Surrounding a joint.

periosteum: The tough fibrous membrane surrounding a bone.

pia mater: The innermost of the three layers of the meninges. It is situated upon the surface of the spinal cord and the proximal portions of the spinal nerves.

plana: Flat surface.

plantar flexion: The sole of the foot in a condition of being bent; extension of the foot.

pollex: The thumb.

polydactylism: The occurrence of more than the usual number of fingers or toes.

posterior longitudinal ligament: One of the primary ligaments of the column. It is located within the vertebral column, upon the posterior surfaces of the vertebrae, and extends from the base of the skull to the sacrum.

primary curve: A curve which retains the initial, or fetal, configuration (i.e., an anterior concavity); the thoracic and sacral curves; also used to designate the initial curve in situations where the column may have two or more abnormal curvatures (for example, in scoliosis).

pronation: The act of turning the palm of the hand downward or toward posterior surface of body.

pseudoarthrosis: A false joint, as that sometimes seen following a fracture or in a failure of an arthrodesis or fusion.

quadriplegia: Paralysis of all four limbs.

rachischisis: *See* spina bifida.

reduction: The correction of a fracture, luxation.

recurvatum: A backward bending; a curvature backward.

resection: Excision of a considerable portion of an organ; especially, excision of the ends of bones and other structures forming a joint.

rotation: The process of turning around an axis.

sacral: Referring to the region of the sacrum.

sacroiliac (joint):   The synovial joint formed by the lateral extremities of the transverse processes of the upper sacral vertebrae with the iliac bone of the pelvis.

sacrovertebral angle: *See* lumbosacral angle.

sacrum: The triangular, curved plate of bone making up the major component of the fixed portion of the vertebral column. It contributes to the formation of the bony pelvis.

Schmorl's body: The hernial mass made up by nucleus pulposus when it extends into body of either of the adjacent vertebrae.

sclerosis: An induration, or hardening; especially hardening of a part from inflammation and in disease of the interstitial substance.

scoliosis: Abnormal curvature of the vertebral column, a lateral curvature. Typically has a rotatory movement associated with it.

secondary curve: *See* compensatory curve.

sequestrum: A piece of dead bone that has become separated during the process of necrosis from the sound bone.

spastic: Of the nature of or characterized by spasms or spasticity.

spina bifida: A defect of the vertebral arch in which the laminae fail to meet and fuse in the posterior midline.

spinal tap: The withdrawal of cerebrospinal fluid from the subarachnoid space; usually performed at the region of the lumbar cistern (i.e., the lower lumbar).

spinous process: The prominent midline bony process extending posteriorly from the vertebral arch.

spondylolisthesis: The forward movement of one vertebra upon another. It is found in association with some vertebral abnormalities or with some cases of vertebral dislocation.

spondylolysis: A defect in the vertebral arch which is situated so that the articular processes (superior and inferior) are separated.

spondylosis: Fusion of vertebrae or of vertebral processes. Some authorities classify spondylosis as a degenerative disease of the intervertebral disc.

subarachnoid space: The space between the arachnoid and pial layers of the meninges. It is filled by cerebrospinal fluid.

subdural space: The potential space between the dural and arachnoid layers of the meninges.

subluxation: An incomplete or partial dislocation.

supination: A turning of the hand so that the palm faces upward or toward anterior surface of the body.

sympathectomy: Removal of a portion of the sympathetic division of the part of the nervous system controlling involuntary bodily functions (autonomic nervous system).

sympathetic nervous system: The part of the autonomic nervous system that supplies the involuntary muscles.

synchondrosis: The union of bones by means of fibrous or elastic cartilage.

syndactylism: The condition in which two or more fingers or toes are more or less completely grown together or adherent.

syndesmosis: Artificial ankylosis by fibrous connection.

synostosis: The union of adjacent bones by means of osseous union of bones that are normally separate.

synovia: A viscid fluid containing synovin, or mucin, and a small proportion of mineral salts. It is transparent and alkaline, and resembles the white of an egg. Secreted by the synovial membrane, it is contained in joint cavities, bursae, and tendon sheaths.

synovial joint: A movable joint characterized by opposing articular facets and a surrounding connective tissue capsule which attaches to the margins of the facets. The space thus enclosed is filled with synovial fluid.

talipes: Clubfoot; a deformity of the foot in which it is twisted out of shape or position; literally, talus + pes or "ankle-foot."

tenodesis: Tendon fixation; suturing of the proximal end of a tendon to the bone.

tenorrhaphy: The union of a divided tendon by a suture.

thoracic: Referring to the chest; that portion of the vertebral column which articulates with the ribs.

tonus: The slight, continuous contraction of muscle, which in skeletal muscles aids in the maintenance of posture and in the return of blood to the heart.

torticollis: "Wryneck"; a contracted state of the cervical muscles producing twisting of the neck and an unnatural position of the head.

transplant: To transfer tissue from one part to another.

transverse ligament of the atlas: The horizontal component of the cruciform ligament and the stoutest of the ligaments of the median atlanto-axial joint.

transverse process: The bony process extending laterally from the arch of the vertebra.

valgus: Bent outward; away from the midline of body distal to joint described.

varus: Bent inward; toward the midline of body distal to joint described.

vertebral body: The primary weight-bearing component of the vertebra.

vertebral notch: Located just above and below the pedicles as they extend posteriorly from the body. These notches (superior and inferior) participated in the formation of the intervertebral foramina of the articulated column.

volar: Anterior or palmar surface.

whiplash: The sudden acute extension and flexion of the cervical column.

zygapophysis: An articular process of the vertebra, either inferior or superior.

INDEX